# Kuna Ways of Speaking

**Texas Linguistics Series**

Editorial Board

*Winfred P. Lehmann*, Chair
*Joel Sherzer*
*Carlota S. Smith*

# Kuna Ways of Speaking
## An Ethnographic Perspective

BY JOEL SHERZER

University of Texas Press, Austin

frontispiece: The 'gathering house.' Mola artist unknown. Photograph by David Stark.

First Edition, 1983

Requests for permission to reproduce material from this work should be sent to Permissions, University of Texas Press, Box 7819, Austin, Texas 78712.

Library of Congress Cataloging in Publication Data
Sherzer, Joel.
    Kuna ways of speaking.

    (Texas linguistics series)
    Bibliography: p.
    1. Cuna language—Social aspects. 2. Cuna language—Variation. 3. Anthropological linguistics. 4. Cuna Indians —Social life and customs. 5. Indians of Central America —Panama—Social life and customs. I. Title. II. Series.
PM3743.S53  1983    498'.2    83-1318
ISBN 0-292-74305-X

To Manuel Campos, Nipakkinya, Olowitinappi, Pinikti, Wipikinya, and all the Kuna women and men who in one way or another appear on these pages and make them possible.

# Contents

# Preface

In December of 1968 I made my first trip to San Blas. I began extended field research in 1970. I have returned to San Blas many times since then. During each period of research, I acquire a deeper understanding of Kuna verbal life and become even more aware of how rich and complex it is.

I am most grateful to the *saklakana* (chiefs) or Sasartii-Mulatuppu, who have always granted me permission to carry out research in their communities and who have been helpful to me in innumerable ways. The Kuna have been superbly hospitable hosts, sensitive to, interested in, and supportive of my research. I have never been treated as a stranger or an outsider. Rather, I have had the unique experience of being able and invited to participate in all Kuna activities, from the most ritual to the most everyday. On each visit to Sasartii-Mulatuppu, I have been treated as a member of the community. I have been provided with both a traditional Kuna name and a playful, humorous nickname. People have been warm and open with me, friendly, and understanding of my interests. Above all, everyone, men, women, and children, young and old, has been willing and anxious to talk with me, to explain at length the most complicated and esoteric of metaphors, or to joke with me and poke fun at me. In all this I consider myself most fortunate.

I would like to thank those individuals whose verbal performances are included here, as part of this study: Chief Armando González, Manuel Campos, Spokesman José Cristiano, Chief Dionisio, Benilda García, Donilda García, Kantule Ernesto Linares, Arango López, Chief Mantiwekinya, Chief Mastaletat, Chief Mastayans, Chief Nipakkinya, Spokesman Olowitinappi, Chief Muristo Pérez, Pranki Pilos, Chief Pinikti, Cecilia Quijano, Tilowilikinya, Tinilikinya, and Wipikinya. Jerónimo Cortez, Hortenciano Martínez, and Anselmo Urrutia aided me as assistants and consultants. Anselmo Urrutia especially has been a constant, sensitive, and interested collaborator in the analysis and translation of Kuna verbal performances.

I would also like to thank the government of Panama and in particular Patrimonio Histórico and its late director, Reina Torres de Araúz, for providing me the opportunity to carry out research in San Blas and inviting me to participate in Panamanian symposiums and congresses, where I was able to present the results of my research and discuss it with colleagues. The Smithsonian Tropical Research Institute, in particular Olga Linares and Martin Moynihan, provided me with assistance and resources.

My research among the Kuna was supported by National Science Foundation grant GU-1598 to the University of Texas, a National Institute of Mental Health small grant, summer grants from the University of Texas Institute of Latin American Studies, and a John Simon Guggenheim Memorial Foundation fellowship.

I have greatly benefited from the valuable and insightful comments of the following persons on earlier versions of this manuscript: Keith Basso, Richard Bauman, Mac Chapin, Erving Goffman, James Howe, Dell Hymes, Judith Irvine, Scott Rushforth, Henry Selby, Dina Sherzer, and Dennis Tedlock. Dell Hymes has been a constant inspiration to me in all my research and writing. He first introduced me to the ethnography of speaking in a class at the University of Pennsylvania in 1965. Since that moment he has encouraged, constructively criticized, and always supported my individual contribution to the ethnography of speaking. This book would not have been possible without his teaching, writing, critical commentary, and encouragement. The title derives from one of his many significant publications.[1] Dina Sherzer has accompanied me on most of my research trips to San Blas and has been an active collaborator in investigations dealing with Kuna language, culture, and society.

Finally, I would like to thank Holly Carver, University of Texas Press manuscript editor, for her excellent editorial assistance in the last stages of the preparation of the manuscript.

Men and a woman in a boat. Mola artist unknown. Photograph by David Stark.

Women preparing to attend an evening 'gathering.'

Chief Mastayans making a basket in the 'gathering house.'

Mulatuppu Chief Mantiwekinya responding as a visiting 'chief' chants.

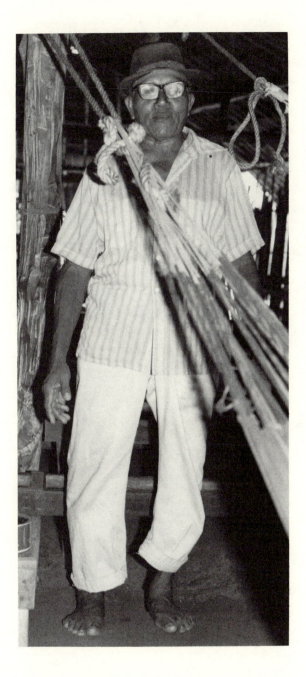

Spokesman Pedro Arias speaking in the 'gathering house.'

'Medicinal specialist' Olowitinappi working in the mainland jungle.

'Medicinal specialist' carrying hot peppers. Mola artist unknown.
Photograph by David Stark.

'Medicinal specialist' Manuel Campos counseling medicine.

'Medicinal specialist' Wipikinya looking at just gathered medicine with his wife and son.

Preparation of *inna*. Mola artist unknown. Photograph by David Stark.

Inebriated individuals at the puberty rites festivities. Mola artist unknown.
Photograph by David Stark.

Kantule Ernesto Linares and his assistant performing in the 'inna house.'

*Kanturkana* performing. Mola artist unknown. Photograph by David Stark.

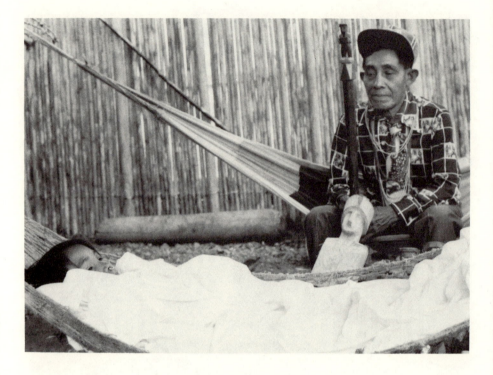

'*Ikar* knower' Lanni with child in hammock and wooden 'stick doll.'

Box of wooden 'stick dolls.'

Curing ritual. Mola artist unknown. Photograph by David Stark.

# Kuna Ways of Speaking

# 1. For a Kuna Ethnography of Speaking

On arriving in San Blas, visitors feel at once that they have entered another world, perhaps an idyllic one. There is the tropical lushness of the Darién jungle. There is the beauty of the coral islands, with their thatch-roofed, bamboo-walled, oblong houses and the surrounding cool blue water. There is the striking color of the women's clothing, especially the magnificent molas, the appliqué and reverse-appliqué blouses. There live the Kuna, less than one hour away from modern Panama City. It is no wonder that San Blas has attracted so many visitors—from adventurers to tourists, from missionaries to anthropologists. The Kuna can be and have been studied from the perspective of their economic, political, or social structure, their religion, or their ecology.[1] It is my aim to enter their world through speaking, not just because the Kuna dedicate a vast amount of time to talk, which they do, but because their world is perceived, conceived, and especially organized and controlled by means of language and speech. An investigation focused on language and speech is thus a very productive way into an understanding of Kuna culture and society, perhaps the most productive way. First an overview, a glimpse of who, where, when, and why the Kuna.

## The Kuna

There are Kuna Indians in both Panama and Colombia; the overwhelming majority live in Panama. Most of the Panamanian Kuna live in the Comarca de San Blas, a string of island and mainland villages along the Caribbean coast, from east of the Canal Zone almost to the Colombian border. According to the 1970 census, there were 23,945 Indians in San Blas. These Kuna are frequently referred to as the San Blas Kuna or the San Blas Indians.[2] The Comarca de San Blas is a reserve, belonging to the Kuna according to legislation of the Panamanian government; this reserve includes the islands and the nearby mainland jungle. The contiguous area across the mountain

range known as the Cordillera de San Blas along the Río Bayano constitutes a separate Kuna reserve. Along the Río Bayano there are
small Kuna villages. Another group of Kuna live along the Río Chucunaque in the Darién jungle, within an area east of the Bayano reserve and also contiguous to the San Blas reserve. The population of
these interior Kuna areas, along the Bayano and the Chucunaque, is
between 1,200 and 1,500.

There is continual contact between the interior and the San Blas
Kuna, there being a distance of one or two days' walk between most
interior villages and the nearest island village. Interior Kuna walk to
the coast to buy cloth, cooking utensils, and other goods and to
study ritual tradition. They bring for sale or gifts smoked game, such
as iguana, and certain plants which are used cosmetically. San Blas
Kuna travel less frequently to the interior, but individuals do go
there for medicinal purposes, and specialists and aspiring specialists
visit for the study and performance of ritual. Visiting other villages,
especially for traditional and ritual purposes, is important for the
Kuna; such visiting explains in part the closeness felt between the
two regions and their linguistic and cultural similarities. It is also
important to point out, with regard to the population of San Blas,
that large numbers of individuals, especially men, leave San Blas, for
periods ranging from a few months to several years, to work in the
Canal Zone, Panama City, or other areas such as the banana planta-
tions of Changuinola in Bocas del Toro. Such individuals tradition-
ally return to their San Blas village.

It is interesting to speculate about the original homeland of the
Kuna. The Kuna moved to the San Blas islands from the coastal
mainland in the early part of this century. The founding of the more
recently settled island villages occurred within the memory of the
oldest living inhabitants. This means that certain aspects of Kuna
culture, especially those dependent on a sharp distinction between
island-village and mainland-workplace, are relatively recent. The existence of tightly organized, nuclear villages, however, is characteristic of all Panamanian Kuna.[3] The Kuna villages of the interior
Darién jungle are probably close to the original homeland of the
Kuna. Groups migrated across the mountains, first to the coast and
ultimately to the islands. Kuna mythology talks of a Colombian origin. However, at the time of Kuna ethnic-geographic unity, there was
no Panama-Colombia distinction. On the basis of current geo-
graphic distribution, linguistic differentiation, known migrations,
and mythic tradition, we can posit the probable homeland of the
Kuna in the Darién jungle, somewhere near the present Panamanian-
Colombian border.

This study is based mainly on fieldwork in San Blas and, more particularly, on extended research on a single large island, Sasartii-
Mulatuppu. I will refer to the island as the Kuna do, as Mulatuppu.
Mulatuppu, located in the eastern portion of San Blas, is a large island in terms of population. According to the 1970 census, there
were 1,626 inhabitants. These individuals are not all in the village at
any given moment, since there are always people working outside of
San Blas. In addition Mulatuppu owns land further east along the
coast, where at all times of the year families spend time farming.
They live there for periods ranging from several days to several
months, in a work colony called Sukkunya or Puerto Escocés.

Mulatuppu is an active, exciting place in terms of both ritual and
everyday life. At ten o'clock in the morning, it seems a sleepy, tran-
quil village. But at five in the afternoon, when all men and women
have returned from working in the jungle and when small children
are out of school, there is the hustle and bustle of a city. Kuna villages are densely organized: Mulatuppu is almost entirely covered
with houses, and the relatively shallow sea around is being filled in
in order to build still more houses. Houses are close to one another,
their roofs often touching over narrow, sandy paths. Every inch of
space, both inside and outside houses, is used to the utmost capacity. Mulatuppu does not offer the sloppy overcrowdedness of urban
slums, however. Rather, there is a tight, well-ordered, dense use of
space. Houses are impeccably neat; streets are swept clean; boats are
carefully lined up along the shore; dogs are kept inside houses and
taken to the sea to urinate and defecate, thus paralleling human behavior; pigs, the only other domesticated animals, are kept in spe-
cially built pens and bathed every afternoon. The dense organization
of these villages is a manifestation of the Kuna aesthetics of space,
according to which space should be used to the utmost and filled in
with a tight, repetitive, well-ordered pattern. This organization is
also found in social structure, visual art (the women's molas), and
verbal discourse.

Because of the size and density of its population, Mulatuppu has
certain features characteristic of cities, unlike the smaller, more isolated communities more typically studied by anthropologists and
the smaller Kuna villages. There is impersonality; there is fear of
robbery and other intrusions into property; there is the possibility
that significant events occurring in one place within the village are
not known about in another part of the village; and there is a complex overlapping of factions. But social, political, and ritual activity
is alive and dynamic. Such recent developments as the spread of Panamanian schools, the building of a hospital, and increasing migra-

tion to the Canal Zone and Panama City have not diminished this activity. Every evening meetings are held in the large *onmakket neka* (gathering house) at which *saklakana* (chiefs) chant in their ritual language, long speeches are made, legal disputes are resolved, or village affairs are publicly discussed. During the day specialists gather medicinal plants in the mainland jungle and render the medicine effective by performing incantations to it. Chants are performed regularly as part of the curing process and for a variety of magical purposes. Puberty rites for young girls are held at various times within the year.

The Kuna are agriculturalists who farm the nearby mainland jungle, using the slash-and-burn technique. Bananas of various types are the staple food, the base of most meals; coconuts, which function as money, are sold to Colombian traders and are used in grated form in many dishes. Root crops, peach palms, corn, sugarcane, avocados, mangoes, lemons, and hot peppers are the other principal crops. Farming is both an individual and a collective enterprise. Collective groups range in size, sometimes including the entire village; bananas and coconuts are the crops most frequently farmed collectively. Food is also acquired through fishing in the sea near the island and through hunting, although game is becoming relatively scarce in San Blas, especially near the more populous islands.

A striking feature of the Kuna economic system, especially of agriculture, is that the Kuna do not live on or adjacent to the land which they farm. Rather, the island-village is the place of family life, leisure, politics, and ritual, and the mainland is the place of work. For ecological and especially for social and political reasons, the Kuna have chosen to live in tight, nuclear villages rather than to spread out and use the land maximally. The land they farm may be quite far from the village, but they return home every day. The Kuna believe that they should live in such villages in order to carry out their political and ritual business as a group.[4] This sharp division between workplace and village, between mainland and island, stresses the island-village as the place of leisure and of ritual and political activity.

The San Blas Kuna carry on a lively commerce with Colombians from the port cities of Barranquilla and Cartagena. The Colombians dock their colorful boats in a different village each night, purchasing coconuts in large quantities from the Indians and selling such Colombian merchandise as rice, sugar, and hammocks. Despite the length and frequency of contact with these sailors, Kuna culture has been influenced by them only marginally—strict ethnic boundaries are maintained. The Kuna refer to the Colombians as *sichikana* (blacks) and consider them to be inferior. Some villages do not allow them to spend the night. Where they do spend the night, they sleep on the decks of their boats or on the nearby docks. There are some mitigating factors in this Kuna-Colombian relationship. Kuna men often hang out on the boats while they are docked, chatting with the sailors and among themselves. And a number of long-term friendships exist between Colombian sailors and Kuna individuals or families. The presence of the black sailors is very much a part of life in San Blas.

Temporary migration to the Canal Zone, to Panama City, and to other parts of Panama is another source of income for the Kuna; most send money or goods back to their families in San Blas. A third major source of income, in addition to farming and work outside of San Blas, is the women's mola. Outside of San Blas, the Kuna are probably best known for these colorful products of an appliqué and reverse-appliqué sewing technique. Most molas are first worn as blouses and then, when used, sold as single panels. (A mola blouse is formed by two panels sewn together.) The women sell the molas either directly to outsiders or, increasingly rarely, to Kuna middlemen.

With regard to political organization, there is considerable structure at the ethnic or tribal level, especially in San Blas. Three caciques for San Blas, each from a separate region, are ranked in order of authority. These caciques represent the Kuna in dealings with the Panamanian national government. Twice a year a general congress is held in one of the villages of San Blas. This general congress is attended by representatives from all San Blas villages as well as by non-Kuna Panamanian officials. Problems are discussed and decisions are made which affect all of San Blas. There is a great deal of ritual activity as well which involves relations among different villages. A general congress for traditional chanting by 'chiefs' is held every three months, with representatives from all San Blas. In addition San Blas is divided into three regional sectors (east, central, and west) for traditional chanting onmakket (gatherings). Representatives of each village within each sector gather periodically in one of the villages of the sector for several days of chanting. This provides an opportunity for ritual leaders to listen to and evaluate each other's performances and to otherwise communicate with one another.

It is common practice for 'chiefs,' especially prestigious ones or those who aspire to prestige, to travel frequently to other villages, where they spend several days talking and chanting. 'Chiefs' and other ritual leaders and specialists also travel within San Blas and to the interior in order to study with well-known experts or to teach and visit with their students. All this travel means that there is much intervillage communication, from the most formal and ritual to the most informal and everyday.

While there are structure and unity, both official and unofficial, at the level of the Kuna as an ethnic group, the most intense, active, day-to-day organization is at the level of the village. Politically, each village has its own organization consisting of 'chiefs' and other officials. In addition, each village has other ritual leaders—specialists in medicine, curing, magic, and puberty rites. Ideally each village is politically and ritually complete, each possible Kuna role being filled. But, while this ideal is met and by necessity must be met in the political organization (see chapters 2 and 3), this is not so with regard to other ritual roles. Some roles have more than one occupant in a particular village; others have none at all. Once again, village size is an important factor. The larger a village is, the more specialists one is likely to find living in it. This means that inhabitants of smaller villages might find it necessary to go outside the village for the curing of particular diseases or the performance of particular rituals—expensive and time-consuming operations. There are thus certain advantages to living in larger, more densely populated villages, in which there is a greater frequency and intensity of political, ritual, and, ultimately, speaking life.[5]

## Language and Speech in Cross-Cultural Perspective

The nature and the role of speaking are not universal, not everywhere the same. So the particular Kuna organization of and use of language and speech must be seen in contrast with other possibilities: the Apache of the North American Southwest, who are spare, laconic, careful, but highly witty in their speech; the Abipones of the South American Gran Chaco, whose life was organized around hunting and warfare and for whom success in these endeavors, not speaking ability, was a source of prestige and leadership; the Wolofs of Senegal, among whom there is a disdain for verbal expression by the higher caste and a concomitant monopoly on certain forms of verbal and especially verbally artistic activities by the lower caste; North American blacks, among whom complicated verbal forms, playful and poetic, related to group leadership patterns emerge in the vernacular language; the Vakinankaratra of Madagascar, for whom indirectness is a primary and organizing principle for many forms of discourse and distinguishes men's and women's speech patterns; the Mayan Chamulas of Chiapas, Mexico, for whom the metaphor of heat is a dominant cultural theme which can be used to classify the structure of all genres of speaking; and the Balinese of Indonesia, for whom constant attention to deference and demeanor is intimately bound to speech levels, indirectness in speech, and symbolism, all related to a complex of communicative forms from drama to the gestures of face, hands, and feet.[6]

It is obvious to any outsider after the shortest of visits that the Kuna love to talk, that there is plenty of talk in Kuna life, and that language and speech play a significant, indeed central, role in Kuna culture and society. But it is especially a complex of characteristics that uniquely distinguishes Kuna language and speech from the speaking patterns of other societies. There is the use of a set of sharply distinct yet related linguistic varieties and styles, with subvarieties and substyles within them, marked by grammatical and lexical differences, the latter intertwining with metaphor and other forms of symbolism.

The linguistic varieties and styles clearly differentiate three distinct ritual traditions—political, curing and magic, and puberty and the roles associated with them—from each other and from everyday verbal interaction. There is the extensive and incredibly varied set of forms and genres of speaking and chanting, from everyday greetings and reports to the public and ritualized performance of myths, stories, tribal history, and personal experiences and dreams. This performance, part of a rich and dynamic oral tradition, is both the essence of the definition, practice, and acquisition of all Kuna leadership roles and the central, defining, and organizing feature of all rituals as well as many everyday events. There is the set of patterns and configurations which both distinguish and relate the various Kuna ways of speaking, from ritual to everyday. Probably the most striking of these is the centrality of the role of speech play and verbal art, especially their intersection, in all Kuna verbal life.

Other significant and organizing patterns are the interplay of talk and silence; the structuring of both talk and chants in the form of ritualized dialogue; the frequent use of verbal advice as both counsel before an action and punishment after one; the multiple reporting and retelling of the same information, especially reporting and retelling within reporting and retelling; the focus on and elaboration of reflexive and metacommunicative language; the creative use of both fixed, memorized verbal forms and flexibly manipulated speech; and the interesting relationship between intelligibility and reportability. There is the relative lack of development of other communicative and artistic modes (with the striking and important exception of the women's molas) in comparison with speaking.[7] This set of characteristics forms a dynamic whole, involving a constant di-

alectic interplay between harmony and conflict, tradition and innovative adaptation, and ritual and everyday life, with speaking at
the center.

All observers of the Kuna have been struck by the significance of
language and speech in Kuna life and have drawn on aspects of language and speech in their analysis of Kuna politics, religion, medicine, philosophy, or history. The Swedish ethnographer Erland Nordenskiöld and his colleagues at the Göteborgs Etnografiska Museum
collected and published extensive Kuna textual material. Nils Holmer, in his Kuna dictionary and his grammatical studies, makes
constant reference to forms and genres of speaking, so that it becomes obvious, while not explicitly stated, that every aspect of the
Kuna language, from sound patterns to vocabulary, is intimately
linked to styles of and social contexts for speaking. David Stout, in
his discussion of Kuna culture and society, focuses on certain lexical
items whose meanings demonstrate the relationship between language and speech and Kuna world view on the one hand and Kuna
social organization on the other.[8]

In my study, language and speech are examined in and for themselves, as the central and organizing focus. Analysis is based on naturally occurring speech, observed and recorded in actual contexts
and studied in terms of its relationship to these contexts. In spite of
a growing interest in oral discourse and oral literature within several
disciplines, this is the first book-length treatment of the complete
range of forms of discourse in a nonliterate society, based entirely on
naturally occurring and recorded speech. Franz Boas, Edward Sapir,
and other North American linguists and anthropologists who carried out research in the pre–tape recorder era often produced excellent collections of North American Indian texts, but these texts
are not natural, since they were dictated by informants to field-
workers.[9] Linguists and anthropologists working today have typically
continued the tradition of collecting texts dictated by single informants to field-workers, now using tape recorders. Scholars studying
oral literature, such as Ruth Finnegan, Albert Lord, Harold Scheub,
and Dennis Tedlock, have all tended to limit themselves to a single
genre within a community's verbal repertoire and to work with in-
formant-specialists in this genre.[10] William Labov's studies of personal narrative, again a single genre within a community's verbal
repertoire, are based for the most part on taped interview sessions,
not naturally occurring events.[11] While Gary Gossen's *Chamulas in
the World of the Sun* purports to present the full range of Chamula
oral tradition and is exemplary in this respect, it is heavily dependent on idealized recording sessions and reconstructed discourse.[12]

In contrast, all the forms of discourse on which this study is based and which are analyzed within it were recorded in actual, natural Kuna contexts. These include everyday informal conversations, learning and teaching sessions, public political meetings, and curing and puberty rituals. In addition, an important aspect of my approach is the extended characterization and discussion of specific examples of language use, situated in terms of Kuna grammatical, discourse, and poetic structures and social and cultural contexts.

The subject matter of this book is thus speaking; by men, women, and children from early morning to late at night—spoken, chanted, shouted, or weeped, serious or comical, ritual or banal. The ultimate goal is the description of the overall Kuna theory and practice of speaking. Because of the central and organizing role of language and speech in Kuna life, I am able as well to present new and different insights into the nature of Kuna social and political organization, religion, economics, medicine, world view, and aesthetics.[13]

## The Ethnography of Speaking

The ethnography of speaking is an approach to and perspective on the relationship between language and culture and language and society. It is a description in cultural terms of the patterned uses of language and speech in a particular group, institution, community, or society. Thus the ethnography of speaking of the Kuna is a description of language and speech in Kuna life and a presentation of Kuna theories and practices of speaking, both as overtly articulated by members of the community and as practiced by them in many activities, from ritual to everyday.

In a series of papers in the 1960s, Dell Hymes called for an approach which deals with aspects of language and speech that fall between or otherwise escape such established disciplines as anthropology, linguistics, and sociology.[14] Essentially, his argument was that language and speech have a patterning of their own, as do social organization, politics, religion, economics, and law, and that therefore they merit attention by anthropologists—they cannot be taken for granted as somehow given or everywhere the same. This patterning is not identical to the grammar of a language in the traditional sense and yet is linguistic as well as cultural in organization.

Hymes introduced the notion of speech events as central to the ethnography of speaking; he argued that analysis of speech events requires study of the interrelationships among a number of factors—basically settings (times and places for events), participants (possible and actual addressers, addressees, and audience), purposes (functions and goals of events), linguistic varieties and styles, verbal organization in terms of constituent speech acts, modes and manners of delivery or performance, norms of interaction, and speech genres. He also stressed the importance of paying serious attention to the various functions of speech (not only the referential but also the socioexpressive, the metacommunicative, and the poetic). The careful study of components of speaking with regard to both terminology and patterned organization, as well as of the relationship between these components and the functions of speech, leads to a description that captures each society's unique cultural organization of language and speech.

Collections of papers published in the 1960s and 1970s have helped to further and develop the ethnography of speaking.[15] The papers describe aspects of language and speech previously overlooked or else treated as secondary or marginal by anthropologists, sociologists, and linguists. Research to date has focused on particular topics—the description of a community's linguistic resources, organized as styles of speaking (for example, men's and women's speech or baby talk), the analysis of particular speech events (drinking encounters or greetings), and the role of speech in a specific area of social and cultural life (politics or religion).[16] Here I propose a study which brings together and integrates all aspects of language and speech in a social and cultural context for a single society, that is, a comprehensive Kuna ethnography of speaking.[17]

I begin (see chapter 2) by describing the complex set of Kuna sociolinguistic resources. These resources include not only grammar in the traditional sense but also a complex of linguistic potentials for social use and social meaning—grammatical variables, styles, terms of reference and address, lexical relationships, the musical patterns and shapes of chanted speech, and the gestures accompanying speech. Attention is paid to attitudes toward the various linguistic varieties and styles. Analysis of these sociolinguistic resources requires a description of everyday, colloquial Kuna, the various ritual varieties of Kuna, and the patterned interrelationships among them. An adequate Kuna grammar must be both sociolinguistic and ethnographic; in particular, it must describe the systematic relationships that exist among the varieties and styles of Kuna. Because of the importance of chanting in the verbal repertoire, my analysis also includes the musical structure of chants, especially the relationship between this musical structure and Kuna discourse structure more generally. Kuna gestures, in particular the very significant deictic facial gesture, the pointed lip, are shown to be intimately related to both grammatical and discourse structure (see chapter 6).

Chapters 3 to 5 are devoted to an extensive and intensive exploration of the forms of discourse central to the three pervading areas of Kuna ritual life—politics, curing and magic, and puberty rites. Associated with each of these areas are a unique set of speech acts and events as well as a unique patterning and organization of the components of speaking.

Chapter 6 focuses on the discourse of everyday life—greeting and leave-taking, conversation, commanding and requesting, narration, gossip, and humor. Everyday discourse and verbal interaction are both related to and contrasted with ritual speech. In particular I demonstrate that, in addition to the clear constellations and focuses distinguishing everyday and ritual speech, there are also aspects of the relationship between the ritual and the everyday which must be dealt with in terms of continua, intersections, and overlaps of various kinds—grammatical, social organizational, poetical, musical, and contextual. My analysis of Kuna discourse, both ritual and everyday, is informed by and rooted in Kuna conceptions of language and speech but is not restricted to or limited by overtly expressed, especially lexical, manifestations of these conceptions.

I bring together and integrate the totality of Kuna speaking practices in two concluding chapters. Chapter 7 presents a set of patterned interrelationships linking in various interesting ways the many types of Kuna discourse and verbal interaction. Some patterns seem to contradict each other. Thus an important set of Kuna discourse forms is characterized by creative, strategic, and adaptive manipulation of language and speech, while another set is characterized by the repetition of fixed, memorized texts. Both of these themes or patterns make good sense in the context of a nonliterate society in which so much of the world is perceived, conceived, and created through talk. At a more abstract level, all Kuna speaking can be viewed as highly adaptive and strategic, finely attuned to contexts of usage and able to change in order to meet challenges from both within and without Kuna society. Another important Kuna pattern of speaking is a focus on speech play and verbal art, on playful and aesthetic aspects of language and speech; this feature of speaking maintains a semiindependence from other functions and uses of language and speech—referential, political, and curative and magical. Some patterns of speaking, like particular speech acts and events, are labeled in the Kuna lexicon and the names for them are in common use. They constitute an important aspect of the Kuna theory of language and speech. Other patterns are not named but can be seen to emerge in the process of speaking. Still other patterns can be related to cross-cultural, comparative, and perhaps universal dimensions of speaking. All Kuna patterns of speaking will be analyzed in terms of their role and contextualization in Kuna social and cultural life.

Chapter 8, which concludes the book, describes the processes involved in the transmission and acquisition of speaking ability; it ends with a focus on the interplay of continuity and change, tradition and adaptation, and harmony and conflict.

In this study I will show that language and speech are indeed central to Kuna life—crucial in the definition and exercise of most social roles, major and minor; significant in most social and cultural activities, again in both their definition and practice; primary in determining, defining, and transmitting social and cultural meanings and structures; and in general something individuals are always interested in and concerned with. All this will be demonstrated through a close analysis of Kuna discourse. It is by means of producing, structuring, performing, listening to, teaching, and learning oral discourse that the Kuna perceive their own culture; and it is through the precise, fine-grained approach to this same rich and diverse verbal material that I offer here that we as outsiders and analysts can come to appreciate, understand, and explicate the Kuna theory and practice of speaking and the role of speaking in Kuna life.

At the same time, this close analysis of Kuna verbal life extends to broader areal, typological, and theoretical issues, such as the role of language and speech among American Indians, the relationship between ritual and everyday speech, the nature of verbal art and verbal performance in nonliterate societies, and the search for universal dimensions of language use. Every element of data presented in this book, every description, every analysis can be viewed as a potential question to be asked most immediately of other South American tropical forest groups, more generally of all American Indian societies, and ultimately of any community or society.[18]

## Related Perspectives

In recent years there has been a converging interest in various disciplines in the study of forms of discourse. Serious attention to the structure of both spoken and written discourse has been paid by linguists, philosophers, anthropologists, sociologists, folklorists, and literary critics. While some of this research has looked to discourse as the place most likely to find expression of other concerns, whether these be grammatical, philosophical, sociological, or literary, there is increasing focus on the study of the structure and structuring of discourse in, for, and of itself.

This ethnography of speaking shares interests and concerns with other approaches to discourse, while at the same time contributing to issues that have been raised by them. Recent linguistic research in the analysis of discourse has focused on a variety of topics— textual structures beyond the sentence, the various forms and processes of cohesion linking utterances to one another, the structure of speech acts, the structure of narrative, the relationship between what is actually said and assumptions and presuppositions that are not said, the organization of conversation, the linguistic description of style, including personal and social variation, the linguistic manifestation of politeness and deference, and the formalization of discourse structure.[19] Contributing to the growing interest in the linguistic analysis of discourse, *Kuna Ways of Speaking* examines the language and speech of a nonliterate American Indian community, involving in particular close attention to a range of forms of discourse from the most everyday and informal to the most ritual and formal, all based on the observation of, participation in, and recording of actual and naturally occurring events.

This study shares with symbolic anthropology an interest in symbolic aspects of culture, especially when these are manifested verbally. Of the themes that have emerged within approaches to cultural symbolism in recent years, two are most relevant to the ethnography of speaking. One is the notion of thick description made explicit by Clifford Geertz, which involves an interpretive method, akin to literary criticism, and aims at peeling away bit by bit, layer by layer, the complex overlapping meanings expressed in culturally symbolic behavior. This means paying attention to circumstantial aspects of social and cultural life and focusing on small, specific matters, which often seem unimportant to anthropologists used to studying more traditional, broader areas.

A second theme stressed by Geertz, Victor Turner, and others concerns the social use of symbols in actual contexts and how symbols are developed and even emerge creatively in the course of social action and interaction.[20] There are Kuna symbols and symbolic organizations which are esoteric, known to a few ritual specialists, and there are others which are known to all members of the community, constantly reiterated in many contexts. There are symbols which are secret, not to be divulged or explained to the noninitiated, and there are others which are publicly interpreted. There are symbols which are conventional and traditional, repeated over and over, and there are others which are creatively invented by a single individual for a unique purpose, usually on the model of conventional Kuna symbolism. In this ethnography of speaking, symbols and symbolisms per se are not the primary focus. Rather, they are viewed as sociolinguistic resources, part of the complex of resources which includes as well phonological, morphological, syntactic, and semantic patterns and terms of reference and address, such as names. All these resources are drawn on in various but related ways as part of the structure, process, and strategy of speaking. Kuna symbols are thus both rooted in and created through speaking.

Like ethnoscience and cognitive anthropology as well as symbolic anthropology, the ethnography of speaking is concerned with community members' conceptions and representations of their own culture and with their formalized frames for communicative action and interpretation.[21] Attention will be paid to the rich Kuna terminology for forms of discourse as well as for components of speaking, as one analytical tool in the analysis of Kuna language and speech which is most relevant for an understanding of their own theory of speaking. While terminology is an important source of Kuna conceptions concerning language and speech, the analysis of terms for talk, like the analysis of symbols, is not an end in itself—for terms for talk, like symbols, are communicative resources which vary from person to person and from context to context and are used strategically in the course of speaking. In addition, there are significant features of Kuna language and speech that are not labeled, and there are labels that are ambiguous without reference to and contextualization in concrete instances of usage.

This study contributes to our understanding of the nature and structure of oral literature in nonliterate societies, in particular to crucial issues concerning the production, performance, retention, and transmission of oral literature.[22] Like Roman Jakobson and scholars influenced by him, I am concerned with the types of coherence and cohesion characteristic of verbal art, especially the use of syntactic and semantic parallelism.[23] In addition to such general and probably universal features of verbal art as parallelism and metaphor, I will discuss the Kuna conceptions and definitions of verbal art in terms of what individuals enjoy hearing and seeing performed and how they talk about and otherwise evaluate performances. Recent discussion of American Indian literature has focused on both grammatical and discourse organization and features of performance.[24] Both will be of great importance here in the analysis of Kuna verbal art. Some of the verbal forms I analyze are learned by memory and are expected to be reproduced identically each time they are performed. Others are creatively and strategically composed during their performance. My study permits comparison of the structure of these two basic types of discourse. I also analyze forms of discourse which cannot be considered literary in the strict sense—

arguments, reports, conversations, greetings, and other instances of everyday verbal interaction. A complete ethnography of speaking must come to terms with the full range of discourse forms—from poetic to banal, from ritual to everyday.

The writings of Claude Lévi-Strauss have focused attention on American Indian discourse as crucial to an understanding of their culture, society, and thought.[25] But while Lévi-Strauss' primary concern is myths, their abstract, logical structure, regardless of where, how, or in what language they are found, my interest involves concrete forms of discourse and their use in actual Kuna social and cultural contexts. At the same time, I agree with Lévi-Strauss' view that beneath the surface of overt verbal forms and practices are often lurking more abstract patterns, especially oppositions and conflicts. A primary Kuna sociocultural opposition which will be of concern in this study is that between the ideal of idyllic harmony and the everyday actuality of conflict. This opposition is in turn related to other Kuna sociocultural oppositions, such as that between tradition and change, older men and younger men, and women and men.

The ethnography of speaking shares with recent research in the sociology of knowledge and everyday life a concern with how reality, knowledge, and sociocultural experience are constructed, perceived, transmitted, and actually performed through the filter of everyday discourse. Sociologists of language and communication have shown how language is used to signify and achieve such social meanings as deference, respect, insult, allegiance, and distance. They have contributed to an understanding of the structure of such basic forms of discourse as everyday conversation.[26] They have drawn on examples from modern urban society for most of their insights; I offer here the contribution of a nonliterate, tropical forest society, in which everything is learned, reported, argued about, and remembered through talk and where politeness, respect, deference, silence, and turn taking are organized quite differently and have meanings very different from those in middle-class urban society. The Kuna are particularly interesting in this regard in that a striking feature of all their discourse is its self-conscious and reflexive character. Speakers quite often comment on what they are doing and saying as they do it and say it, and such commentaries form an integral, structured part of the discourse in which they are embedded.

Finally, this study is related to a long line of scholarship demonstrating an interest in and indeed a fascination with the powerful place of the word, of language and speech, in American Indian life.[27] But, as important as language and speech may be in American Indian societies, their role, function, and patterning are by no means everywhere the same. In fact, the available data point to striking and significant differences.

## Theoretical Issues

In this study I address a set of issues concerning the study of language and speech in a social and cultural context. There is first a need for the development of precise, cross-culturally and empirically valid terms and definitions for features, dimensions, and patterns of speaking. The cross-cultural, comparative approach will provide a meaningful typology, theoretical generalization, and formalization as well as a perspective from which to distinguish the universal from the particular and the surprising and special from the ordinary and expected and in which to place areal and historical developments. Sociolinguists and ethnographers of speaking have continually insisted on the complexity of the relationship between language and speech on the one hand and sociocultural assumptions, presuppositions, and concerns on the other. Existing frameworks, which make use of such dimensions as formal-informal, elaborated-restricted, direct-indirect, and polite-nonpolite, have not been sufficiently explored with regard to their ability to account for this complexity in its full cross-cultural depth. The development and elaboration of theoretical frameworks for the analysis of speech must proceed hand in hand with a detailed ethnographic investigation of particular communities, situations, and events.

Second, there is the relationship between speaking patterns and the other sociocultural patterns found in a society—social organizational, political, ecological, economic, or religious. There are anthropological theorists who would always see one of these aspects of a society as basic. Such a view would always have speech patterns be secondary, superficial reflections of the more basic structure. But in many situations in many societies speaking has a structure of its own which can play a major role in defining, determining, and organizing sociological structures.[28] Most roles in Kuna social life are defined in terms of speaking. And all roles are constantly redefined and played out through the use of language and speech (see chapter 2). Since Kuna political organization, curing, religion, and much of economic life are organized in terms of and by means of language and speech, these cannot be understood without paying close attention to their intimate relationship to the structure of speaking.

Another issue concerns the relationship between ritual speech and more everyday speech. Ethnographers of speaking have paid considerable attention to ritual speech. It is often the case that such speech is highly marked as special in several ways—it is tightly organized and codified and overtly labeled, its rules are consciously followed, and it is verbally artistic. While some attention has been paid to such colloquial and seemingly more spontaneous forms as greetings and ordinary conversation, the ethnography of speaking, like ethnography more generally, has been attracted by events which are most striking to outsiders and probably most special to insiders of a community as well. And there is evidence that, in relatively small, nonindustrial, and homogeneous societies, ritual events can offer, in a highly structured, microcosmic form, a replica of what the society and culture are all about. At the same time, the ethnography of speaking must be able to account for everyday and seemingly banal uses of speech as well. The challenge is to analyze the subtleties of everyday communicative behavior, of the structure of hints, suggestions, and avoidances occurring not as public, formal events but as part of daily face-to-face interaction in societies around the world. I consider a major contribution of this study to be my focus on both ritual speech and everyday speech, especially on the many multifaceted, intersecting, and dynamic links between them.

Finally, since one of the goals of this book is to present the Kuna point of view, their own conceptions and practices of speaking, the use of Kuna terms and the presentation of actual instances of verbal discourse are crucial to this goal. But the representation and translation of Kuna words, concepts, and forms of discourse on the printed page present problems for both the author and the reader. I cannot require readers to memorize long lists of Kuna words in order to understand a book written essentially in English. I have thus opted for the following solution. The first time a Kuna word is used in the first five chapters, it will be followed by an English translation in parentheses—thus *sakla* (chief). Most subsequent references in each chapter will be in quotes—thus 'chief.' In this way the reader is reminded that 'chief' stands for *sakla* and that the connotations of the English word do not operate for the Kuna. While this method of reminding the reader of the use of Kuna terms and concepts has the disadvantage of slowing the eye, it has the advantage, crucial to my ethnographic approach, of remaining as faithful as possible to the native point of view. (There are certain words in Kuna for which no satisfactory translation exists. For this reason I have left a few words in Kuna throughout—for example, *kantule, ikar,* and *inna.*)

The presentation of Kuna forms of discourse, the texts, as they appear on the printed page raises other problems. In chapter 2, exemplary texts are presented in Kuna together with English translations.

In subsequent chapters, illustrative textual material is generally presented in English only. The translations are intended to be readable and understandable to readers who do not know the Kuna language, presumably the majority. At the same time, these translations are relatively literal, in order to preserve for the reader the distinctive characteristics of Kuna style. In particular, the rich and diverse set of Kuna line-framing words and phrases ('well,' 'then,' 'thus,' 'indeed,' 'say,' 'see,' 'hear,' and so on) is rendered literally. (See discussions in chapters 2 and 7.) The problem of the adequate rendering of Kuna oral terms, concepts, and forms of discourse in printed English is ultimately one of frame.[29]

There are thus three compelling reasons why Kuna language and speech merit this extensive discussion and analysis from the perspective of the ethnography of speaking. First, in and for themselves. The study of Kuna ways of speaking is fascinating because of the dynamic diversity of Kuna verbal life, which maintains tradition and at the same time adapts to a constantly changing world. In particular, the Kuna present a striking case of the organizing and central role of language and speech in all of social and cultural life. Second, as a contribution to Kuna studies. This ethnography of speaking builds on the fairly extensive published literature dealing with the Kuna but highlights their culture and society in a new, unique, and significant way from the perspective of language and speech. Third, as relevant to theoretical questions concerning the study of language and speech in social and cultural context, especially as an argument for the significance of the ethnographic approach to the cross-cultural study of speaking. While maintaining a focus on the details of Kuna language and speech, I will open a dialogue with concerns and issues within sociolinguistics and the ethnography of speaking in particular and within anthropology, folklore, and linguistics more generally.

# 2. Language and Speech in Kuna Society

This chapter provides a general overview of Kuna language and speech from two perspectives. First, I present the sociolinguistic resources available to Kuna speakers, the various languages, dialects, and styles in use in their society. There are systematic relationships among the different Kuna linguistic varieties and styles which are rooted in the sociocultural contexts of their use. Grammatical patterns and rules are intimately and inextricably linked with sociocultural meaning and function. Second, I examine Kuna social organization from the point of view of speaking. Most Kuna roles, from the most ritual to the most everyday, are so tightly bound up with language and speech that it is impossible to analyze Kuna social structure and social organization without becoming involved in the details of the practices, processes, and structure of speaking. From the point of view of the community as a whole, there are three independent sets of roles—those involved in politics, in magic and curing, and in girls' puberty rites. With each are associated distinct types of speaking abilities, and each constitutes a separate source of authority and prestige, rights and duties. While Kuna society from one perspective seems idyllically harmonious, there are also significant tensions and conflicts. Speaking plays a central role in the dialectic interplay between the harmonious and the conflictual.

## Kuna Linguistic Varieties and Other Languages

Language use among the Kuna is recognized and labeled in various ways. One is in terms of names for speech events and the *ikarkana* (ways, texts) associated with them.[1] Another is in terms of roles in Kuna society, often determined by and named for a way of speaking. Still another way is in terms of the various linguistic varieties or languages in use. I will examine these now in some detail. There are four named Kuna linguistic varieties which have formal characteristics clearly distinguishing each from the others, while at the same time relating them in interesting ways.

*Tule kaya* (the *tule*, person, or Kuna language), the language of all Kuna, encompasses a range of styles from informal to formal. This language is contrasted with, on the one hand, the languages of other people—*waka kaya* (Spanish language), *merki kaya* (English language), *sokko kaya* (Choco language), and so forth—and, on the other hand, Kuna ritual languages—*sakla kaya* (chief language), *suar nuchu kaya* (stick doll language), and *kantule kaya* (*kantule* language). From a linguistic point of view, there is a single Kuna language, shared by all Kuna, wherever they live. Geographical differences are slight and few in number. They are noted by the linguistically acute Kuna and commented on; they offer no impediment whatsoever, however, to communication. In practical terms, and these are very practical given the intense communication among all Kuna, there is one Kuna language. It is not closely related, genetically, to any other language, one of the factors which marks Kuna ethnic distinctiveness.[2]

'Chief language,' also called 'gathering house language' or 'God's language,' is named for the principal individuals who know and use it, the primary setting in which it is used, or the primary topic dealt with in it. 'Stick doll language' is named for the overt addressees of the chants performed in curing rituals. These anthropomorphic figures, with hats and long noses, are made from various jungle trees; they represent the spirits of these trees. This linguistic variety is understood and used by the 'stick dolls'; by the spirits of animals, plants, and objects; and by the *ponikana*, the evil spirits, which cause disease. It is used by *ikar wismalat* (*ikar* knowers), who address the spirits directly in the chants they perform. '*Kantule* language,' named for the *kantule* (the director of girls' puberty rites), is understood by the spirit of the flute to whom the *kantule* chants during the ritual.

This discussion so far deals with the four major named *kaya* or linguistic varieties. But *kaya* also has a looser, less official meaning, not unlike that of "talk" in English (as in teacher talk, student talk, or kid talk): it is often used to stand for the linguistic characteristics associated with particular social groups or verbal genres. Thus there are *arkar kaya* (the language of the chief's spokesman), *ome kaya* (the language of women), and *kwento kaya* (the language of storytelling), different styles of *tule kaya* which will be discussed and illustrated in this chapter. Used in this way, *kaya* has a rather narrow range of productivity, essentially limited to those social roles or verbal genres which the Kuna perceive as being associated with distinct ways of speaking.[3]

In addition to the varieties of Kuna, Spanish and English are frequently found in Kuna villages, especially in San Blas. As is to be expected, given the increasing contact with and integration into the Panamanian system, more and more Kuna speak Spanish, the national language of Panama. It is primarily those individuals who have worked in the Canal Zone, Panama City, or other parts of Panama such as Changuinola who know Spanish. Their degree of proficiency depends on the amount of time spent away from San Blas. In addition, Kuna men and sometimes women who have been sent by their families to Panama City for part of their education speak Spanish. There are also Kuna men who, through frequent commercial contact with both urban Panamanians and Colombians, have learned to speak Spanish. In recent years, the spread of schools, first by missions and now by the Panamanian government, has of course increased the potential for the learning of Spanish by young people. The success of the educational program cannot yet be determined. At first it was officially monolingual in Spanish but bilingual in practice since the teachers, who are for the most part Kuna themselves, found it necessary to speak Kuna as well as Spanish in classes. Then an official bilingual program was introduced, with materials prepared and written in Kuna as well as in Spanish. Given the predominantly positive attitude felt by most Kuna toward their language and its traditions as well as toward the Spanish language, this bilingual education program should be successful.

The attitude toward knowledge of Spanish, as toward language and languages in general, is positive—the more one knows, the better. In fact, knowledge of Spanish, in addition to Kuna, is a definite asset. Of course there are contexts where Spanish should not be used, just as there are contexts in which the use of ritual varieties of Kuna, rather than colloquial Kuna, is expected. Thus Kuna is the language of the 'gathering house,' the political meeting place. Highly acculturated Kuna, especially those who live more in Panama City than they do in San Blas, tend to intersperse a considerable amount of Spanish into their discourse when making speeches. The resulting grammatical pattern is definitely Kuna, albeit almost a pidginized form when the Spanish intrusions become excessive. Some examples are *dipórsio ekichis* (he asked for a divorce) from the Spanish *divorcio*, *inpéstigar sae* (to investigate) from *investigar*, *súsio kuali* (it became dirty) from *sucio*, *respetar sae* (to respect) from *respetar*, and *molestar sae* (to bother) from *molestar*. Such use of Spanish is at times criticized by other Kuna, in more or less playful terms.

A considerable number of Kuna know English, again with varying degrees of proficiency. There are a few older men who in their youth were sailors on North American ships and still remember some of the words and phrases they heard and used, in English or even sometimes in other languages, such as French. They usually know the colorful, popular, and obscene language of sailors—as a result, they are most humorous interlocutors. Younger men who work or have worked in the Canal Zone also pick up some English. English is valued and appreciated perhaps even more than Spanish. People like to hear it spoken, even if they do not understand it, and those who know a little will often try it out on a visiting native speaker of English. This gives them pleasure and pride and provides amusement for themselves as well as others. For ritual and traditional leaders, especially political leaders such as 'chiefs,' knowledge of English, like that of Spanish, is quite positively valued by others. It is one more bit of linguistic ability at their disposal, linguistic ability being one of the primary criteria for selection as a 'chief.'

There are also Kuna individuals who know some Choco, the language of the Choco Indians who inhabit the Darién jungle and who, while traditional enemies of the Kuna, are respected for their formidable medicinal and magical tradition. Certain Kuna curing specialists have studied with the Choco to learn their medicinal practices and perhaps secret verbal charms or chants as well; these are the men who know a little Choco. I have never encountered a Kuna who had anything even approaching conversational knowledge of Choco.

In general the Kuna take great pleasure in learning languages and words from languages. This is so even if there is no obvious immediate practical use. There is always a potential use—that of showing off one's knowledge in matters linguistic. Thus the Kuna will ask

**Figure 1.** Linguistic Varieties and Languages among the Kuna

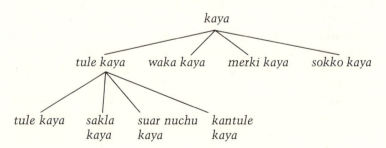

visitors, both publicly and privately, to tell them words in their language. And, even if the source of this knowledge is not all that proficient, there is always interest. If someone knows a little English or Choco, for example, others will ask, 'And how do they say such and such?' and then repeat the word and practice it themselves. Pleasure is also derived from observing others learn a language. The different linguistic varieties and languages in use among the Kuna and their relationships are shown in figure 1.

## From Vocabulary to Metaphor

With the perspective of this general overview of the sociolinguistic resources in use among the Kuna, we can now proceed to a discussion and description of the linguistic varieties. Corresponding to the named differences among Kuna linguistic varieties are actual linguistic differences. The varieties are so different from one another that each requires separate learning, and for the most part a variety is not comprehensible without such learning. The differences among the linguistic varieties involve aspects of phonetics-phonology, morphology, syntax, semantics, and discourse structure. But no doubt the most striking feature distinguishing these varieties and the one that is most diagnostic for the Kuna themselves is vocabulary. Another way to conceive of this situation—one that is clearly in keeping with Kuna social and cultural conceptions and considerations— is that many objects and activities, especially basic features of the Kuna ecology and important aspects of society and culture, have associated with them not one but a complex of names, each of which is appropriate for use in a different, well-defined situation. This lexical differentiation is used to distinguish the four major Kuna linguistic varieties as well as to make subcategorizations within them. There are several ways in which this works.

First, discrete, categorical cases occur in which the same meaning or concept is translated by a distinct lexical item in each or some of the different varieties. Table 1 provides examples of this kind of lexical differentiation. In some cases the difference between varieties involves the use of distinct prefixes and/or suffixes with the same lexical stem, as in table 2.

Such prefixes as *olo-* and *ipe-* and such suffixes as *-pilli* can also be used along with lexical differentiation, as in some of the examples in table 2. The prefixes *olo- mani-*, *ina-*, and *ikwa-* and the suffixes *-kinya*, *-appi*, *-lele*, *-tilli*, and *-liler* are used with nouns in both 'chief language' and 'stick doll language.' They are involved in the formation of the *nuka sunnat* (true name) of the objects labeled by the nouns. According to the Kuna world view, all plants, animals,

**Table 1.** Lexical Differentiation in the Four Kuna Linguistic Varieties

| English | 'Everyday Kuna' | 'Chief Language' |
| --- | --- | --- |
| foreigner | *waka* | *tulepiitti* |
| white-lipped peccary | *yannu* | *oloweliplele** |
| curassow | *sikli* | *olokupyakkilele** |

| English | 'Everyday Kuna' | 'Stick Doll Language' |
| --- | --- | --- |
| woman | *ome* | *walepunkwa* |
| water | *tii* | *wiasali* |
| specialist | *wisit* | *kana, apisua* |
| eye | *ipya* | *tala* |
| house | *neka* | *posumpa* |
| knife | *esa* | *ipetintuli** |
| to wash | *enukke* | *yatwe* |
| small | *pippikwa* | *totokkwa* |

| English | 'Everyday Kuna' | '*Kantule* Language' |
| --- | --- | --- |
| woman | *ome* | *yai* |
| water | *tii* | *nukku kia* |
| cup | *noka* | *kila* |
| bead necklace | *winkwa* | *kala purwa* |
| chicha | *inna* | *waalina* |
| slowly | *pinna* | *yulullu* |
| to feel happy | *yer ittoe* | *ana pina kine* |
| broken | *pichisa* | *tupya* |

*See the following discussion of prefixes and suffixes.

and objects have souls, as do humans; some plants, animals, and objects were once human. The 'true name' is their human name. Humans, especially women, also have 'true names.' These are also called *kammu nuka* (flute name), after the flute central to girls' puberty rites, at which these names are given. Human 'true names' also make use of these same prefixes and suffixes. Now it is mainly older men who are publicly called by their traditional 'true names,' such as Nipakkinya, Mantiwekinya, and Olowitinappi.[4] Since Spanish and North American names are now much more common, at least in everyday usage, the more traditional names for both humans and animals are felt to be quite humorous out of their serious contexts of usage.[5] In fact, some of the animal 'true names,' such as *olopiskaliler* for *tulup* (lobster), are used playfully and jokingly, like the *totoet nuka* (play names) and riddle names of animals (see chapter 6).

**Table 2.** Use of Prefixes and Suffixes to Distinguish Linguistic Varieties

| English | 'Everyday Kuna' | 'Chief Language' |
| --- | --- | --- |
| bench | *kana* | *olo-kana* |
| hammock | *kachi* | *po-kachi* |
| necktie | *korpatta, morsuit* | *olo-korpatta* |

| English | 'Everyday Kuna' | 'Stick Doll Language' |
| --- | --- | --- |
| hammock | *kachi* | *ipepo-kachi-pilli* |
| blouse, shirt | *mola* | *uu-mola* |
| blowgun | *puti* | *olo-puti* |
| to change | *kwake* | *ulu-kwake* |
| to palpitate | *tutumakke* | *ak-tutumakke* |

| English | 'Everyday Kuna' | '*Kantule* Language' |
| --- | --- | --- |
| blouse, shirt | *mola* | *ilukka-mola* |
| beads | *wini* | *esa-wini-kachi* |
| to enter | *toke* | *ulu-toke* |

Note: Hyphens are used to indicate the affixes.

In addition to distinguishing the four major linguistic varieties, lexical differentiation also marks subvarieties and subgenres which are due to regional differences or to differences in subtradition, that is, different sets of teachers and students. Such lexical elaboration and specialization are most characteristic of certain areas of the Kuna vocabulary—ecology (especially animals and plants), celestial bodies, sociopolitical organization, and curing. Table 3 gives examples of the lexical elaboration and differentiation of animal names. The alternate words for curassow, tapir, agouti, and collared peccary in 'stick doll language' are from two versions of *pisep ikar* (the way of the basil), a chant used for effective hunting, both of which are used in Mulatuppu. Notice the use of the prefixes *olo-*, *ina-*, and *mani-* and the suffixes *-lele*, *-liler*, and *-appi*, which indicate that these are not merely different words for the animals but actually different names for them.

Within the colloquial language as well, there are many instances of the proliferation of lexical expressions for a single meaning. In the everyday verbal play and joking of which the Kuna are extremely fond, many animals are labeled with a set of humorous 'play names' or nicknames, a selection of which is presented in table 4. The names are created by means of a play on a physical characteristic of the animal (see also chapter 6).

**Table 3.** Lexical Elaboration and Differentiation of Animal Names

| English | 'Everyday Kuna' | 'Chief Language' | 'Stick Doll Language' |
|---------|-----------------|------------------|----------------------|
| curassow | sikli | olokupyakkilele<br>olomiikinyaliler | sitoni<br>mii |
| tapir | moli | oloalikinyalilele<br>olohalikinyappi<br>oloswikinyaliler | ekwilamakkatola<br>ekwirmakka |
| agouti | usu | olokwirkwikkalilele<br>oloyayakkinyaliler<br>olousluliler | yaya<br>yayamakka |
| collared peccary | wettar | olomurkikkaliler<br>olomurkippilele<br>inamuikkaliler<br>olomoikinyappi | manikwillosakpia<br>murkimanikwillosakpia |

**Table 4.** Animal 'Play Names'

| English | 'Everyday Kuna' | 'Play Names' |
| --- | --- | --- |
| deer | *koe* | *upsan saya* (cotton ass) |
| | | *ipya kwiintakleke* (eyes open) |
| crab | *suka* | *pormo yarkan* (tin can back) |
| | | *kapur ipya* (hot pepper eyes) |
| | | *kampulet mali* (chair feet) |
| rabbit | *sule* | *nappa nono* (head on ground) |
| lobster | *tuluppa* | *ipya kallakallat* (eyes moving back and forth) |
| | | *napkiar pepe* (thorny forehead) |
| agouti | *usu* | *muttu saya* (black tar ass) |
| | | *korta mali* (tar feet) |
| octopus | *kikkir* | *morpattun mali* (button feet) |
| land turtle | *yarmoro* | *ipya muru satue* (defecates eyes open) |

Euphemisms are another example of lexical proliferation in everyday speech. As in many other societies, the Kuna use euphemisms in the areas of bodily functions, body parts, childbirth, and sex. A common euphemism for defecate is *akkue* (to empty). Euphemisms for urination, such as *tise nae* (to go to the water), relate to the fact that such bodily functions are performed in the sea. The area of conception and childbirth is a particularly sensitive and taboo subject, intimately related to curing and magical control. The usual euphemism for the act of conception is *mimmi pakke* (to buy a child). Some euphemisms for pregnancy are *nus yoles* (a worm entered), *ipya kummas* (the eye got burned), and *sakkan pichisa* (the wing is broken). The infant itself is euphemistically called *sikkwi* (bird). It is interesting to note here the use of the animal world in these euphemisms—worm, wing, and bird. The current word for baby, *koe*, also means deer and may have been euphemistic in origin. The conventional euphemism for snake is *tupa* (vine); snakebite is *tupa warmakke* (to meet a rope).

Related to euphemisms are day and night names for various animals and plants. While few in number today, there might have been more of them at one time. The day names are taboo at night and should be replaced with the night names; if not, there will be certain malevolent consequences which themselves are sometimes an aspect of the night name, such as *kaya piri* in table 5. Table 5 provides examples of day and night names in current usage. Related both to euphemisms and to the distinction between day and night names is

**Table 5.** Day Names and Night Names in 'Everyday Kuna'

| English | Day Name | Night Name |
| --- | --- | --- |
| guava | *marya* | *kaya piri* (curved |
| snail | *salu* | mouth) |
| peach palm | *nalup* | *tios uwaya* (God's ears) |
| | | *ikko turpa* (spine fruit) |

the taboo on uttering animal names while hunting. Since animals have souls, they, like humans, can hear their own name pronounced, which accounts for this taboo.

Next, there is the case of words which exist in the colloquial language but are somewhat esoteric in the sense that not everyone knows or uses them; they are typically more commonly known by older men, especially those acquainted with ritual matters. Members of the community who do not know such words use other, more ordinary words in their place. These esoteric words are more likely to occur in ritual language than in everyday, colloquial speech. They are also part of the vocabulary that 'chiefs' and other ritual leaders brag about when talking about their knowledge of tradition. The common word for to bathe is *ope*. Another word meaning to bathe, *appallukke*, is considered esoteric and is rarely heard in everyday speech. It is used with this meaning in both curing and puberty rites chants. Similarly, the word *sikwa* (rapidly) is esoteric in colloquial speech compared with the much more common *kwaekwaekwa*. But *sikwa* occurs with greater frequency in ritual varieties.

Many examples of esoteric vocabulary involve Kuna words for objects or concepts for which there are also Kuna words of Spanish origin (now integrated into the Kuna lexicon but clearly loanwords in origin). The most common way to say to walk about (especially within a village) is today *pasearsae*, from the Spanish *pasear*. But the more purely Kuna way of expressing this is *pippirmakke*, literally 'to turn about.' The Kuna 'gathering house' is often called the *konkreso*, after the Spanish *congreso*. But the truly Kuna way of referring to the 'gathering house' is *onmakket neka*. In ritual contexts within the 'gathering house,' it is referred to by a variety of labels, for example, *ittoet neka* (listening house).

The words for numbers provide another example. It is quite possible to count as high using the Kuna numeral system as using borrowed Spanish words. But in ordinary, colloquial interaction, speakers typically use Spanish loans for higher numbers. Thus, 234 according to the Kuna system is *tulattar irpo kakka turkwen kakk ampe kakka pakke* (100 twice plus 20 plus 10 plus 4), while the Spanish way is *dos cientos treinta y cuatro*. In 'gatherings,' where traditional language is expected and valued, speakers are under greater public pressure to use the more esoteric and somewhat cumbersome Kuna numerals. Thus I once observed, in an evening 'gathering,' Kuna men discussing village economic matters and counting in rather high numbers. On this occasion, someone called out *tule kaya* (Kuna language), and the men switched to Kuna, speaking much more slowly in order to pronounce the somewhat unwieldy numbers.

Matters can be even more complicated. The colloquial word for necktie in Kuna is *korpatta* (a loan from the Spanish *corbata*) or *morsuit* (long cloth). A common way of saying or chanting necktie in the 'gathering house' is *olokorpatta*, making use of the prefix *olo-*, typical of the ritual language of the 'gathering house.' But still another word, *morkechu*, is known to some Kuna traditionalists and used in the 'gathering house.'

The coining of Kuna words out of the native vocabulary for new objects is active, creative process that is not limited to traditional and ritual contexts. Such words demonstrate the inventiveness and playfulness of the Kuna in language use and their cleverness at using native vocabulary when desired in order to avoid loans. Kuna men who have worked in the Canal Zone have invented terms for the different kinds of eggs that they served U.S. soldiers. Eggs sunny-side up are *tuttukwa* (soft); eggs over easy are *pinnakwa* (slow, easy); scrambled eggs are *ichi ichi* (all bumpy). Catsup is called *san okinnoeketi* (meat reddener). A napkin is called *kaya elieti* (mouth wiper). Carpenters have Kuna names for tools: sandpaper is called *karta muru muru* (paper full of points); a screwdriver is called *kinki unket* (nail undoer). While words for North American—style eggs and tools are in fairly common usage, the Kuna also take pleasure in coining new words on the spot for immediate and personal use, even though these may often go no further than a single verbal interaction. Thus one afternoon I came upon two very elderly men who were making small purses that they would either use as gifts or sell. They conversed a bit about what to call them and then came up with *mani osopet* (that which causes money to be saved).[6]

Certain lexical taxonomies or semantic fields are more developed or elaborated in ritual varieties of Kuna than in colloquial Kuna. Specialists in ritual who are intimately familiar with the natural, cosmological, and spirit worlds and their interrelationships are most

**Table 6.** Selection of Members of the Hot Pepper Semantic Field

| English | 'Everyday Kuna' | 'Stick Doll Language' |
| --- | --- | --- |
| hot pepper | *kapur* | *nele pinaisepa nele* |
| red hot pepper | *kapur kinnit* | *nele yolina nele* |
| *sankwa* (type) pepper | *kaa sankwa* | *ulu sankwali nele* |
| red *sankwa* pepper | *kaa sankwa kinnit* | *sankwali nele yolina nele* |
| blue-green *sankwa* pepper | *kaa sankwa aratti* | *sankwali nele ulurapaneleye* |
| white *sankwa* pepper | *kaa sankwa sippukwa* | *sankwali nele waka sipu nele* |
| *upina* (type) pepper | *kaa upina* | *nele kaa upina nele* |
| multicolored *upina* pepper | | *nele kaa upina nele ulu kokomakka nele* |
| misty pepper | | *nele pookwar nele* |
| transformed like the sea | | *muupakka opinaleye* |

knowledgeable with regard to associated semantic fields in their full lexical complexity. The actual words involved might have distinct means of expression in the different linguistic varieties, or they might be esoteric and not known to most people. A good example is the taxonomy of *kaa* and *kapur*, hot peppers (*Capsicum* species) which are used in curing rituals. As will be shown in chapter 4, the elaborate taxonomy of hot peppers forms the basis of a major portion of *kapur ikar* (the way of the hot pepper), a chant addressed to the spirits of hot pepper which is used in calming high fever. Table 6 presents a small selection of members of this taxonomy, in both 'everyday Kuna' and 'stick doll language.' The list includes naturally occurring forms, such as *sankwa* pepper, as well as forms which, while not existing in nature, are part of the pepper spirit world and therefore the pepper spirit semantic field, such as misty pepper. Figure 2 presents the hot pepper taxonomy. In one version of 'the way of the hot pepper' which I have recorded and analyzed, fifty-three types and subtypes of hot pepper are listed.[7] Analogous ritual taxonomies exist for many other animal and plant species. Knowledge of and especially utterance of long and complex lexical taxonomies are important aspects of magical power and control (see chapter 4).

Finally, words from colloquial Kuna may take on a different meaning in ritual contexts. The effect is allusive and often poetic in a fig-

**Figure 2.** Hot Pepper Taxonomy

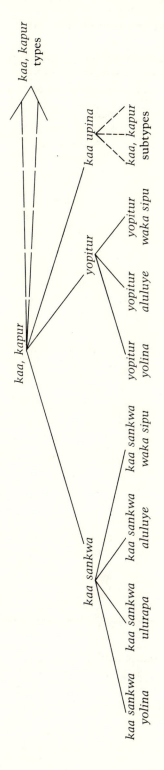

**Table 7.** Figurative Vocabulary in the Three Ritual Varieties of Kuna

| English | 'Everyday Kuna' | 'Chief Language' |
|---|---|---|
| woman | *ome* | *tuttu* (flower) |
| village | *kwepur, nek-kwepur, tup-pu* (island) | *kalu* (stronghold of animals, spirits), *tiwar* (river) |
| thunder | *mala* | *pap kinki sakla* (God's rifle) |
| to become a 'chief' | *saklase kue* | *urse onakkwe* (to be placed in a boat), *kaski mese* (to be placed in a hammock) |
| 'policeman' | *suaripet* (owner of the stick), *polisía* | *tule olowaripet* (the man who owns the golden pole) |
| to come | *tanikki* | *wimakke* (to sweat) |

| English | 'Everyday Kuna' | 'Stick Doll Language' |
|---|---|---|
| to be born | *kwalluleke* | *akteke* (to land) |
| Kuna person | *tule* | *inna ipet* (owner of the *inna*) |
| evil spirit, sickness | *poni* | *urwetule* (angry person) |
| to walk | *nae* | *aypanne* (to swing back and forth like a hammock, used to describe ritual specialists walking to the '*inna* house') |

| English | 'Everyday Kuna' | '*Kantule* Language' |
|---|---|---|
| pieces of meat | *kallis* | *ipya suli* (no eyes) |
| to drink | *kope* | *puklu sae* (to do like a drinking gourd) |

urative, usually metaphorical sense. Examples of single items from the three Kuna ritual varieties are listed in table 7. The figurative language of these varieties is often organized according to entire sets of words and semantic fields. Thus in 'stick doll language' elements

**Table 8.** Clothing Used to Represent Parts of Plants and Trees

| English | 'Everyday Kuna' | 'Stick Doll Language' |
|---------|-----------------|-----------------------|
| seeds   | *kwakwa*        | *wini* (bracelet, anklet beads) |
| flowers | *tuttu*         | *kurkin* (hat) |
| leaves  | *kakan*         | *mola* (blouse, shirt) |

of clothing are used to represent the parts of plants and trees, as shown in table 8.

It is especially in the 'chief language' of 'gathering house' chanting and speaking that figurative and metaphorical speech abounds—this is the most characteristic marker of a good speaker. In 'gathering house' discourse, metaphorical sets and semantic fields are open to individual development and creative adaptation. Thus not only do flowers represent women, but the size, color, and type of flower or its place and way of growing can be described in order to symbolize women and children of various types or the raising of children by women. The different poles utilized in the construction of a Kuna house, their size and location, are used to represent the different roles in village political organization; the central pole represents the 'chief,' secondary poles represent the *arkarkana* (chief's spokesmen), and other poles represent other officials. This symbolism can be further developed, creatively and individually, so that a central pole which is rotten represents a bad 'chief' who must be removed from office or a pole which had its rotten part cut away represents a 'chief' who has been reinstated.[8] (See the further discussion in chapter 3.)

Kuna figurative, symbolic vocabulary is not, then, a static set of lexical replacements—rather, there is an active system of relationships. When a 'chief' chants or speaks about the physical structure of a Kuna house, he is commenting both on the house itself and on Kuna political organization. And, as he develops the metaphor in personal ways, he throws a new and often poetic light on his audience's understanding of house construction, political organization, and their interrelationship.

This discussion of Kuna vocabulary has gone beyond lexical differentiation and specialization per se into the realm of allusive, figurative, and poetic language. It is necessary to do so because for the Kuna the two constitute part of a single complex, namely, that which distinguishes ritual language and speech from colloquial. What's in a name for the Kuna? Plenty. As has been shown here, many objects and activities, including plants, animals, political roles, and ordinary actions, have not one or even several but many names, ranging from humorous 'play names' and nicknames through secret and magical names which are used in ritual. Attention to these different names, to their structure, meaning, and usage, takes us into the heart of Kuna politics, medicine and curing, magic, rhetoric, poetry, and humor.

## Grammatical Structure

Lexical differences are the most diagnostic, distinguishing features of Kuna linguistic varieties from the native point of view. At the same time, these vocabulary differences are integrated with the phonological, morphological, syntactic, and stylistic properties which characterize each linguistic variety.

### *Phonology*

Kuna has a relatively simple phonetic inventory. There are five vowels: *i, e, a, u,* and *o*. These can occur long or short. The consonants are *p, t, k, kw, s, m, n, l, r, w,* and *y*. All consonants, except *w*, can occur either long or short, actually double or single. The long *s* is pronounced *ch*. Short *p, t, k,* and *kw* are pronounced as the corresponding voiced sounds; long *p, t, k,* and *kw* are pronounced voiceless. (See the guide to pronunciation.) Syllables are of the form (C)V(C). Thus no more than a single consonant can occur at the beginning or end of a word. The maximum word internal consonant cluster is two.

Many Kuna forms (nouns, verbs, affixes) occur in both a long form and a short form, the long form consisting of a final vowel which is deleted in the short form. Examples (with the deletable vowel in parentheses) are *nek(a)* (house), *takk(e)* (to see), *an(i)-* (I, me), and *-s(a)* (past). The selection of a short or a long form depends on an interaction of linguistic and social contexts and rules.

The four linguistic varieties are identical with regard to the phonetic inventory. The only exception is the sound *h*, which occurs, extremely rarely, in word initial position in 'stick doll language.' The important phonological difference between 'everyday Kuna' on the one hand and the ritual varieties on the other is the use of long and short forms. Shorter forms (in which final vowels and, in a few cases, the entire final syllable are deleted) are most characteristic of informal, rapid speech. Longer forms occur in slower, more emphatic, more formal, and more ritual speech. The fullest forms occur in chanted speech, especially in the most conservative (from the Kuna point of view) of the varieties, 'stick doll language' and '*kantule* language.' The deletion of the final vowel often results in the coming together of more than two consonants, which is impossible according to Kuna syllable structure. The consonants are then simplified to two by rules of consonantal assimilation. As a result, words in ritual varieties of Kuna typically are fuller and longer than the same words in colloquial Kuna. At times, due to the interplay of vowel deletion and consonantal assimilation, the relationship between the long and the short forms of the same word is not obvious. Table 9 provides examples.

The short forms typical of Kuna colloquial speech can be described in terms of a series of ordered rules. According to this analysis, the longer forms more characteristic of ritual varieties and styles are steps in the derivation of the colloquial forms; that is, they derive from the same abstract, underlying forms but do not carry the derivation as far. The rules, in order of their application, are as follows.

1. Vowel deletion: the deletion of the final vowel of stems and affixes. Examples are:

   *neka* (house), *nekurpa* (under the house)
   *mae* (he sucks), *masa* (he sucked), *masmoka* (he sucked also)

2. Consonant deletion rules: when more than two consonants cluster intervocalically, the cluster is reduced to two.

   a. When a double-stop consonant clusters with another consonant, the double-stop consonant is reduced to a single-stop consonant. Examples are:

   *tuppu* (island), *tuptakke* (he sees the island), where *ppt* > *pt*

**Table 9.** Kuna Words in Long and Short Forms

| English | Long Form | Short Form |
|---|---|---|
| he did not see either | *taysasulimoka* | *tachurmo* |
| he did not speak | *sunmaysasuli* | *sunmachuli* |
| in the hammock | *kachikine* | *kaski* |
| they enter | *upoekwichiye* | *upokwisye* |
| in the middle | *apalakine* | *aparki* |
| he is mentioning me | *aninukapipiemaiye* | *annuypimai* |
| to go to help | *penetakkenae* | *pentaynae* |
| when it gave fruit | *turpamakketakokua* | *turpamaytakoku* |
| I left you also | *pankusamalamokaye* | *pankusmarmoye* |

   b. When more than two consonants cluster intervocalically, all but the last two in the cluster are deleted. (Rule 2b operates after rule 2a.) Examples are:
   *takke* (he sees), *taysa* (he saw), *tasmoka* (he saw also), where *kss > ks > ys* and *ysm > sm*
3. Consonantal assimilation rules.
   a. *l > r* / -C, -#. Examples are:
   *mila* (tarpon), *mirwarpo* (two tarpons), *anmir* (my tarpon)
   b. *k > y* / -C other than *k*. Examples are:
   *takke* (he sees), *taysa* (he saw)
   c. *p > m* / -m. Examples are:
   *kape* (he sleeps), *kammai* (he is sleeping in a lying position)
   d. *t > n* / -n. Examples are:
   *ittoet* (listening), *ittoenneka* (listening house)
4. Single and double consonant readjustment rules.
   a. *p, t, k, kw* > voiced (pronounced *b, d, g, gw*)
   *pp, tt, kk, kkw* > voiceless (pronounced *p, t, k, kw*)
   b. *ss > ch* (palatal affricate). An example of 4b, as well as of some of the other rules discussed above, follows (written here, as distinct from all other examples in this book, in phonetic rather than phonemic transcription):
   *dake* (he sees), *daysa* (he saw), *daysuli* (he doesn't see), *da-chuli* (he did not see)

The operation of these phonological rules can be demonstrated in the derivation of 'he did not speak' (phonetically, in colloquial Kuna, *sunmachuli*):

| 1. * *sunmakke* | - | *sa* | - | *suli* | (underlying form) |
|---|---|---|---|---|---|
|    speak |   | past |   | negative |   |
| 2. * *sunmakk* | - | *sa* | - | *suli* | (rule 1) |
| 3. * *sunmak* | - | *sa* | - | *suli* | (rule 2a) |
| 4.   *sunmay* | - | *sa* | - | *suli* | (rule 3b) |
| 5. * *sunmay* | - | *s* | - | *suli* | (rule 1) |
| 6. * *sunma* | - | *s* | - | *suli* | (rule 2b) |
| 7.   *sunmachuli* |   |   |   |   | (rule 4b) |

This derivation involves the operation of the sequence of ordered rules twice, once to arrive at form 4 and again to arrive at form 7. Form 7, *sunmachuli*, occurs in colloquial speech. None of the other steps in the derivation of this form occurs in any Kuna linguistic variety or style, except 4, *sunmaysasuli*. For this reason, forms 1, 2, 3, 5, and 6 are written with a preceding asterisk. Form 4 occurs in colloquial speech as an emphatic or stressed form. It also occurs in formal speechmaking, historical-political-religious chanting in 'chief language,' medicinal and magical chants in 'stick doll language,' and magical chants in *'kantule* language,' to a greater extent in each.

This phonological analysis reflects the relationship between Kuna ritual and everyday speech, in that the forms more characteristic of ritual, traditional speech, like form 4 above, are more abstract and underlying versions of the colloquial forms. These phonological rules, then, are not merely mechanisms for generating linguistic forms; they have sociolinguistic reality and validity in that they capture the relationship among the various Kuna varieties and styles of speaking. This analysis of the operation of Kuna phonological processes furthermore reflects the Kuna conception of the relationship between colloquial and ritual speech, according to which the latter should be longer and fuller, more basic and more conservative.[9] From the Kuna point of view, the fuller, longer forms are clearer, more easily understood, and thus appropriate for such uses as talking to foreigners and children as well as addressing representatives of the spirit world, who play a major role in the prevention and curing of disease.[10]

### Morphology, Syntax, and Style

The most characteristic feature of Kuna morphology is affixation, especially suffixation. Most words, most notably verbs, which are the semantic core of Kuna sentences, are formed by adding several suffixes to the stem. The nominal structure is relatively simple. Prefixes indicating person (possession) precede the stem; suffixes indicating number and location follow the stem—for example, *ipe-pir* (on the hill, literally hill-on), *suar-ki* (with a stick, literally stick-with), *an-neka* (my house), and *ome-kan* (the women, woman-plural).

The Kuna verbal structure consists of a few prefixes and many suffixes. The grammatical description of the verb thus involves a statement of each of these prefixes and suffixes, their meanings, their grouping into classes, their possibilities of order, and their possible cooccurrences. As in the noun, person is prefixed; the subject pronoun precedes the object pronoun: *an-takke* (I see), *pe-takke* (you see), and *an-pe-takke* (I see you). Certain verbal modifiers are also prefixed and can occur either before or after the person markers: *an-wis-kunne* (I eat a little bit) and *yappa-an-kunne* (I don't feel like eating). The causative prefix *o-* immediately precedes the verb stem: *kunne* (to eat) and *o-kunne* (to feed).

There is an extremely large number of verbal suffixes. A description of their meanings and rules of cooccurrence is central to Kuna grammar, including the differentiation of styles. Some of the many

Kuna verbal suffixes follow. Suffixes indicating tense are *sa* (past) and *oe* (future); those indicating aspect are *natappi* (walking, going, on the way), *tappi* (arrived there and completed action), *nonikki* (came), and *sokkali* (about to); and those indicating position are *sii* (sitting), *nai* (hanging), *kwichi* (standing), and *mai* (lying). Other suffixes are *mala* (plural), *suli* (negative), *moka* (also), *pali* (again), *pie* (want to), *ye* (optative, emphatic), *kala* (in order to), *te* (then, in past), *ku* (when, in past), *le* (when, if, in future), and *nae* (go to a location).

Examples of complete verbs, which indicate the way in which suffixes are strung together and the way in which this stringing of suffixes interacts with the phonological rules, are as follows: *an-tay-sa-sur-moka* (I didn't see either, literally I-see-past-negative-also), *pe-masku-cha-r* (when you have finished eating: you-eat-past-when in future), *pe-kap-o-ye* (you'll probably sleep: you-sleep-future-probably), *sunmak-kwichi* (he is speaking: speak-standing), *tani-pal-oe* (he will come again: come-again-future), *purkwe-pi-suli* (he does not want to die: die-want-negative), *an-kap-sokkali* (I'm about to go to sleep: I-sleep-about to), and *palima-t-ku* (then, when he pursued him: pursue-then-when).

All the nominal and verbal affixes which occur in colloquial Kuna are found in the ritual varieties as well. Some of these have a greater frequency and an apparently greater range of meaning in particular varieties or styles. Thus -*ye*, which in colloquial Kuna is a verbal or nominal suffix indicating an optativelike feeling and a vocative on nouns, especially in repetition and insistence, occurs with great frequency in 'stick doll language,' the language of magic and curing—perhaps as an emphasis on the optative mood of the magical chants which are performed in this variety but also as a poetic line marker and a place filler, giving the performer time to remember the next line of these memorized chants. The suffix -*ye* can be viewed as a verbally artistic embellisher as well; it is sometimes repeated two or three times. There are also prefixes and suffixes which, along with words and phrases, serve as markers of the linguistic varieties and the styles within them, although some of them have explicit referential meanings as well.

Typical Kuna word order parallels the order of morphemes within the verb in that the subject precedes the object which precedes the verb: *tule ome taysa* (the man saw the woman, literally man-woman-saw). With regard to syntactic patterning, ritual speech tends to occur in full, complete sentences rather than in the more abbreviated sentences characteristic of colloquial speech. This is true of formal speech in many societies. But in Kuna there is furthermore the fact that ritual speech is characterized by a striking morphological, syntactic, and semantic parallelism, with the result that referential, informational, and narrative content moves along at a very slow pace. What is expected in ritual speech—and part of what makes such speech longer and fuller and thus appreciated as verbally artistic—is the repetition associated with this parallelism.

A striking feature of Kuna speaking and chanting, in each of the varieties and styles, is the existence of a line structure related to but independent of sentence structures. Lines are marked by a set of distinct devices, not all of which operate in every case. These devices have other functions besides marking lines; as a result, there is not always congruence among them. First, lines are marked grammatically by means of an elaborate set of line initial and line final affixes, words, and phrases.[11] Among the various other functions of these elements is metacommunication; they signify such notions as 'say,' 'see,' 'hear,' and 'in truth.' They are furthermore simultaneously sociolinguistic markers in that the different linguistic varieties as well as the different verbal styles and genres within them have distinct sets of line markers. Second, especially in more formal and ritual styles, lines are marked by extensive syntactic and semantic parallelism. This parallelism is organized in terms of line structure and in turn contributes to this structure. Third, lines are marked by intonational patterns, in particular in spoken speech by the structure of pauses and in chanting by a melodic shape.[12] Fourth, lines are marked according to a coparticipant interactional structure in which an addressee responds with one of a set of ratifiers after each line. This pattern is common in many styles of speaking; it is formalized in certain types of ritual chanting.[13] In the more formal, literary styles of Kuna used in ritual contexts, lines are grouped into larger structural units—verses, stanzas, and episodes.

The four major Kuna linguistic varieties have now been described and differentiated in terms of an interplay of lexical, phonological, morphological, syntactic, and stylistic patterning. The overall result of this interplay is best appreciated through illustration and example. In the examples presented in this study, I have used intonation patterns, pauses, and chanted melodic shapes as the basis for my transcription of lineal and verse organization. Each new line begins at the left margin and ends with a period. Short, nonterminal pauses within lines are indicated by commas in the Kuna transcription. The first letter of each line in the English translation is capitalized. Verses are set apart by means of an extra space between lines. Other markers of line and verse organization, such as grammatical elements, words and phrases, syntactic and semantic parallelism, and coparticipant ratification, are also represented. In this way, the poetic organization of Kuna oral discourse is visually depicted on the printed page, and the interaction, sometimes reinforcing, sometimes contrasting, of different organizing principles and structures can be appreciated.

### 'Everyday Kuna'

While 'everyday Kuna' is distinct from the three ritual varieties, there are significant linguistic differences among its various styles, ranging from more informal, casual, and spontaneous verbal interactions to more formal speech. The examples offered here are intended to demonstrate this range of styles. They are presented in order of increasing formality, which is marked by a greater use of long forms, involving both the inclusion of potentially deletable vowels and more morphemes per word; more complete sentences; more parallelism; and a more overtly marked line structure.

First, a portion of a discussion among a group of men one evening in the Mulatuppu 'gathering house' concerning getting an outboard motor for a trip the following day. Since several village leaders would be making the trip and representing the village, the village would pay the owner of the motor for its use. The participants are labeled by letters.

A:  *emite, mottor satten an amisi.*
    Now, I see there's no motor.
    *takkarku, Tensikat, mottor 'namo' soye 'aineypa.'*
    Thus, Dempsey's motor 'will be gone,' he says, 'away.'
    *pia nao?*
    Where to go?
    *pait anai Sirilokat 'Sukkunyap namo' soye.*
    Cirilo's 'will be at Sukkunya,' he says.
    *toakat mottor wis mai?*
    Whose motor is available?
B:  *José kachuli?*
    José's is not here?
C:  *nate Ustup, Ustupse nate.*
    He went to Ustuppu, to Ustuppu he went.
A:  *toakat mai pinsa?*
    Whose do you think is available?
D:  *mottor niymalat kormalale, pinsa naosulit.*
    Tell those who have motors, they're not going for nothing.
E:  *mani apesursi?*
    They don't want money?
F:  *nekkwepur peysoysit 'pe penukkoet.'*
    The town is telling you, 'it will pay you.'

G: *mottor amis we, anpa yoe?*
  Did you get the motor yet?
H: *satte.*
  There are none.
G: *iy saosunna?*
  What to do?
  *mottor ipmalat iy soylesisunna, ateka 'pinsa nao' sokeye.*
  The owners of the motors are saying 'they want to go for nothing,' they say.[14]

This conversation is characterized by the extreme use of short forms, that is, almost all potentially deletable vowels have been deleted. For example, *peysoysit* (is telling you) derives from *pek(a)-sok(e)-si(i)t*. Sentences are relatively short, and there are relatively few suffixes attached to each verb. Most of the elements characteristic of more formal styles of 'everyday Kuna' are absent. An exception is the verb suffix *-sunna* (in truth), which is used twice. Apart from *emite* (now), *takkarku* (thus), *soke* (say), and *-sunna* (in truth), none of the large set of affixes, words, and phrases that can be used to mark line structure is found here.

Second, a portion of a conversation between two elderly Mulatuppu men, T and O, who have been friends for years and who pass many hours of every day sitting and chatting with one another. This conversation contains the narration of an incident in which a boat turned over on the sea and one person was killed.

T: *ur emis noniypi ur emis nonikipi.*
  Today a boat came, today a boat came.
  *tak wa.*
  A Colombian one.
  *waka.*
  Colombian.
O: *wiste an peyso kanoa.*
  I don't know, I tell you a boat.
  *a esela.*
  There's a sailor.
T: *kanoa naisi?*
  There's a boat?
O: *tekitte.*
  Hello [to an entering person].
T: *pinse we a an Oloaknaikinya an pok sunmaysi we anki toynonito.*
  I was talking with Oloaknaikinya and he [another person] came in.

O: *aa. aa.*
Ah. Ah.

T: *tek an ai sunmaarparsunna, a peka an soyparkorsunno.*
Well I'll retell to you what I was talking about with our friend.

O: *eye.*
Yes.

T: *ai sunmarto.*
Our friend said.
*'al an pey soket tule naypikusatye.'*
'I tell you someone got hurt.'

O: *mm.*
Mm.

T: *tule naypikusatki sokkarku, an yosku immar ekiset aa.*
While he was talking about the person who got hurt, I asked him
    questions about it, ah.

O: *eye.*
Yes.

T: *eti sursok, aa.*
Only that, ah.
*kep anka sokkarsunto.*
He told me.
*napir sok aa.*
It's true, ah.
*Ukkupsenikine, wak.*
In Ukkupseni, a foreigner.
*purkwisat, pe wis soketa merki.*
He died, I tell you an American.

O: *aa.*
Ah.
*merki purkwisa.*
An American died.

T: *merki purkwisa.*
An American died.
*apa anka naisunto.*
He was speaking to me about this.
*wete ittosit.*
He [another person] was listening.
*'walapakke' soke.*
'There were four,' he says.

O: *merki.*
An American.

T: *'mottorki tani' soket.*
'They were coming in a motorboat,' he says.

O:  *aa.*
Ah.

T:  *urmorpalit, an epinsaparto, pinse an ittoet.*
Probably with a sail, I think, that's my opinion.

O:  *aa.*
Ah.

T:  *'mottorkin kwenti' anka soket.*
'They had a motor,' he says to me.

O:  *aa.*
Ah.

T:  *'purwa noar' soysunto.*
'The wind came up,' he said.

O:  *mm.*
Mm.

T:  *tanikki.*
As they came.
*kolompiapa tani ittole.*
It seems they were coming from Colombia.
*pia tanikki, kolompian par anso.*
Where were they coming from, Colombia, I think.

O:  *mm.*
Mm.

T:  *kep ur aypittesunto.*
Then the boat turned over.
*na parittochurmala.*
They didn't feel anything anymore.
*oete.*
Lost.

O:  *mm.*
Mm.

T:  *warkwenti amilesto, purkwemai.*
One was found, dying.

O:  *mm.*
Mm.

T:  *nek tinase, naynoni surpa, eti per yokkus.*
He came up on the beach, the others were lost.

O:  *Ukkupsenikine, piali Ukkuppakine?*
At Ukkupseni, or at Ukkuppa?
*amilenonikki?*
They found one?
*ee Kwepti, suli napiri.*
At Kweptii, no.

T:  *Ukkupseni.*

At Ukkupseni.
o: *Ukkupseni.*
At Ukkupseni.[15]

As in the previous example, the forms used here are mainly short. Thus *parittochurmala* (they didn't feel anything anymore) derives from *pal(i)-itto(e)-s(a)-sul(i)-mala*, in which all potentially deletable vowels are deleted. The line structure of the narration is marked by both o's ratifying utterances (*aa, eye,* or *mm*) and a few line-marking devices used by T, such as the line initial word *kep* (then), the verbal suffix *-sunna* (in truth), and the line final verb *soke* (say, he says).

Next, the opening portion of *kaa kwento* (the story of the hot pepper). This was narrated one morning in the Mulatuppu 'gathering house' by a Mulatuppu 'chief' to a group of men, in particular, to a visiting 'chief' from another village.

*teee, takkarkute mu warkwen mai soysunto.*
Well, there was once a grandmother it is said.
*muu.*
A grandmother.
*mute takkarku sirwer ipet mu ma takken soke.*
And this grandmother was the owner of a plum tree see say.
*mu sirwer ipet.*
The grandmother was the owner of a plum tree.
*mu sirwer ipette mai takkarku ipakwena.*
The grandmother was the owner of the plum tree then one day.
*sirwer turpamaytakokua.*
When the plum tree gave fruit.
*yer kepeunti sirwer turpamaytakoku kwane.*
In the past when the plum tree gave fruit one could gather a lot.
*silekwa pakkekwatse kwantii.*
One could gather up to four basketsful.
*teki silekwa pakke kwantii ipakwenki sirwer iskuarto ipe.*
Well one day this plum tree that gave up to four baskets went bad.
*sirwer takkarku, e turpa patterpakuar takken soke.*
The plum tree's fruit fell to the ground see say.
*sirwer turpa taynae eipet taynaoku, sirwer turpa pattemai, per-kwaple.*
When the owner of the plum tree went to see it, the fruit had fallen, all of it.[16]

While the language here, as in the other examples of 'everyday Kuna,' is characterized by the use of short forms, there are also features characteristic of the more formal 'gathering house' speech-making style. Verbs are followed by more suffixes than in more informal, colloquial speech. For example, *turpamaytakokua* (when it gave fruit) is derived from *turpamakk(e)-tak(e)-o(e)-ku(a)*. Lines are more clearly marked by initial words, such as *takkarku* (thus) and *teki* (well, then); final words, such as *soke* (say); final phrases, such as *takken soke* (see say); and verb suffixes, such as *-sunna* (in truth). There are also some of the repetition and parallelism highly characteristic of more formal, especially ritual, varieties and styles of speaking and chanting.

Next, the opening of a report, delivered in the Mulatuppu 'gathering house' to a group of men one evening by a renowned *inatulet* (medicinal specialist) just returned from a period of study in a distant village.

*teki emite wey peki pankusmarmoye.*
Well now I left you here.
*takkaliku, Tikirse ante kapitap.*
Thus, I slept there in Tikre.
*aimal ikal ittoeti antaile.*
The friends were listening to each other I saw.
*emi, pemar konkreso imaysat ikarsunto.*
About the general congress that you attended.
*tek aimar per sunmaysaku, kakkwen an kar soymosunto.*
Well when the friends had finished talking, I also said a few words to them.
*'we Inapakinya soysa takken' an kar soke.*
'Inapakinya [a well-known deceased Mulatuppu 'chief'] said this,' I said to them.
*'"emi ome seret an kwen iptaypisurye.*
'"I do not want to leave this old woman.
*we ome nuchukkwa anka uylenaitti tayleku an wiokoye."*
I will be too poor for this young woman that you are giving me."
*soysa takken' an kar soke.*
He said see,' I said to them.[17]

Like the previous example, this report, while in 'everyday Kuna,' including its short forms, illustrates features of the 'gathering house' speechmaking style. Verbs often have three or more suffixes. Lines are marked by initial and final affixes, words, and phrases. In addition, this example contains quoted reports of speech and quotes within quotes, a frequent means of Kuna narration, especially in more formal styles of speaking and chanting.

Next, a portion of a speech in the 'gathering house' by a woman during a meeting of the Mulatuppu women's cooperative. This recently constituted cooperative has a variety of functions, from making and selling molas to sweeping the streets of the village. This particular meeting deals with getting everyone to share in the work of sweeping the streets. The speaker is a leader of the group. Linguistic differences between Kuna men's and women's speech are relatively slight; they involve the tendency for women to use underlying potentially deletable vowels more than men, to use a small set of words more than men, to use a slightly different range of intonational patterns, and to laugh in a very marked conventional and stylized way. In addition, women's speechmaking style tends to make use of a unique set of line-ending suffixes.

*kwenna kwenna napir panka pinsaet taytitimarparye.*
There are some people who are always advising you.
*kwenna kwenna napir panka ipmar soynonimaloet.*
There are some people who are always saying things to you.
*napir anittotimo takkenye.*
I always listened well, see.
*kin estutio imaytipinmoye.*
I studied this.
*a sortakanye pekasoytakkenye, taysa.*
Followers, I tell you this, saw.
*anmar emi nopsulin takkenye.*
There is no jealousy among us, see.
*ai tekirtina neyturwisunnoye.*
Friend, that is how street sweeping should be.[18]

In this speech, verbs often have three or more suffixes. Line structure is marked by initial and final words, phrases, and verb suffixes. *Takkenye* (see), which can occur as either a verb suffix or an independent word, is used by both men and women, but it is particularly characteristic of women's speechmaking style as a line final marker. There are also some repetition and parallelism here.

The most formal of the 'everyday Kuna' styles is that used by 'chief's spokesmen' when interpreting the chanting of 'chiefs' in the 'gathering house.' Here is an example.

*teki saklati setokwenpa anmarka ikar uytemalatti emina palitotmala.*
Then starting early this evening the chief began to chant for us.
*ittonanasun ittolemarsun pittosursokene.*
We were hearing it we were listening to it don't you hear say.

*inso tayle tayleku saklati anmarka soke.*
Thus the chief says to us.
*'sikwa tayle pekina wekina pankutmala.*
'I left you here for a while.
*inso tayleku niwarkwen na petu pankuchun' takken soke.*
Thus I left you for one month,' see say.

*'emit tayleku na pemarse nonimarpali, per nuekanpi ittoleke, wes nonipar' takken soke.*
'Now thus I returned to you, everything is well, I returned here,' see say.[19]

The 'chief's spokesman' style is characterized by a clearly marked line structure. Unique markers of this style are a characteristic slowing of tempo at the ends of lines and verses, the line initial phrases *inso tayleku* (thus) and *emite tayleku* (now thus), and the line final phrases *pittosursokene* (don't you hear say) and *takken soke* (see say). *Pittosursoke(ne)* and *takken soke* often come at the end of several consecutive lines, marking and constituting them as a unit, which can be labeled a verse.[20] There are relatively short pauses after lines, longer pauses after verses.

The examples I have presented here illustrate the diversity of styles possible within the most colloquial variety of Kuna. They demonstrate the range of speaking styles, from informal to formal. While these styles differ from one another in a number of ways, they share the basic grammatical structure and vocabulary of 'everyday Kuna,' which distinguishes them from the three ritual varieties, to which I now turn.

### *'Chief Language'*

In addition to the grammatical features described above, 'chief language,' especially when chanted, is characterized by a set of linking and framing morphemes, words, and phrases, which formally mark line and verse openings and closings. Verses typically consist of two lines; there are also one-line and three-line verses. Verses often begin with *sunna* (in truth) or *al inso* (thus) and end with *soke* (say), *oparye* or *oparwe* (say, utter),[21] or *takleye* (see). The first line of a verse often ends with the phrases, sometimes combined into single words, *sokelittole* (say hear), *takle soke* (see say), or *takle sokelittole* (see say hear). This poetic discourse structure is furthermore marked by a melodic shape and a ratification, *teki* (indeed), chanted by an *apinsuet* (responding chief) after each verse. The chanting 'chief' begins each verse as the long final vowel of the *teki* of the 'responding chief' is still fading. Similarly, the 'responding chief' begins his *teki* during the lengthened final vowel of the verse of the chanting 'chief.'

The chant presented here deals with ancestors of the present inhabitants of the village of Mulatuppu; this particular section describes the plants and animals provided by God for these people. In this representation, vowels which are deleted in colloquial speech are placed in parentheses, affixes which are used especially in 'gathering house' chanting are placed in brackets, and linking words and morphemes are underlined. The verse of the chanting 'chief' is labeled cc; the line of the 'responding chief,' RC.

CC: *we yal(a)se pap(a)[l] anparmial(i)mar[ye]* <u>*soke[l]*</u> <u>*ittole.*</u>
God sent us to this mountain world say hear.
*eka masmu[l] akkwekar[ye]* <u>*opar[we]*</u>.
In order to care for banana roots for him utter.

RC: *teki.*
Indeed.

CC: *eka[l] inso tarkwamu[l] akkwekar[ye]* <u>*soke[l]*</u> <u>*ittolete.*</u>
In order thus to care for taro roots for him say hear.
<u>*sunna*</u> <u>*ipiti*</u> <u>*opar[we]*</u>.
In truth utter.

RC: *teki.*
Indeed.

CC: <u>*al*</u> <u>*inso*</u> *eka[l] wakup tul(a)[l] akkwekar* <u>*soke[l]*</u> <u>*ittole.*</u>
Thus in order to care for living yams for him say hear.
<u>*al*</u> <u>*ipiti*</u> <u>*opar[we]*</u>.
Utter.

RC: *teki.*
Indeed.

CC: <u>*al*</u> <u>*inso[l]*</u> *eka moe tul(a)[l] akkwekar* <u>*soke[l]*</u> <u>*ittole.*</u>
Thus in order to care for living squash for him say hear.
<u>*al*</u> <u>*ipiti*</u> <u>*opar[we]*</u>.
Utter.

RC: *teki.*
Indeed.

CC: <u>*al*</u> <u>*inso[l]*</u> *eka[l] osimu[l] akkwekar* <u>*soke[l]*</u> <u>*ittole.*</u>
Thus in order to care for pineapple roots for him say hear.
*pap(a)[l] anka[l] yal(a)[l] uksamar[ye]*.
God gave us this world.

RC: *teki.*
Indeed.

CC: '*wek(i) pulakwal(e) pan(i) nanamalo' <u>sokete.</u>*
'Here together you will be,' say.

*pap(a) soys(a) ku[ye] opar[we].*
God said, utter.
RC: *teki.*
Indeed.
CC: *pap(a) yannu kalukan(a) urpis(a)[ye] soke.*
God left white-lipped peccary strongholds say.
*aa[l] akkwekan nonimar soke.*
We came in order to care for them say.
RC: *teki.*
Indeed.
CC: *pap(a) moli kalukan(a)[l] urpis(a) takle soke.*
God left tapir strongholds see say.
*ka[l] akkwekan nonimar[ye] soke.*
We came in order to care for them for him say.
RC: *teki.*
Indeed.
CC: *pap(a) wetar tul(a) urpis(a) takle[ye] soke.*
God left living collared peccary see say.
*a[l] akkweka nonimar[ye] soke.*
We came in order to care for them say.
RC: *teki.*
Indeed.
CC: *pap(a)[l] us(u) tul(a)[kwa] urpis(a) takle soke.*
God left living agouti see say.
*a[l] akkweka nonimar[ye] soke.*
We came in order to care for them say.
RC: *teki.*
Indeed.[22]

The extensive syntactic and semantic parallelism of this example
is typical of the parallelistic organization of the chanting of 'chiefs.'
The melodic shape of the first lines is diagramed in figure 3 in terms
of the interplay of pitch and duration.[23] The first few lines begin
high, using microtones; they descend gradually to a semitonal arrangement of pitches 3, 2, and 1. The higher pitches are more guttural and harsh. All beats fall at regular intervals. The next lines begin slightly higher; they descend gradually to the same semitonal
pitches. Final vowels are lengthened. There is also a decrease in vol-
ume and a slowing of tempo at the end of lines and verses.

### 'Stick Doll Language'

A portion of *kurkin ikar* (the way of the hat), used in curing severe
headaches and improving brainpower, illustrates the characteristics

**Figure 3.** Melodic Shape of the Chanting of a 'Chief'

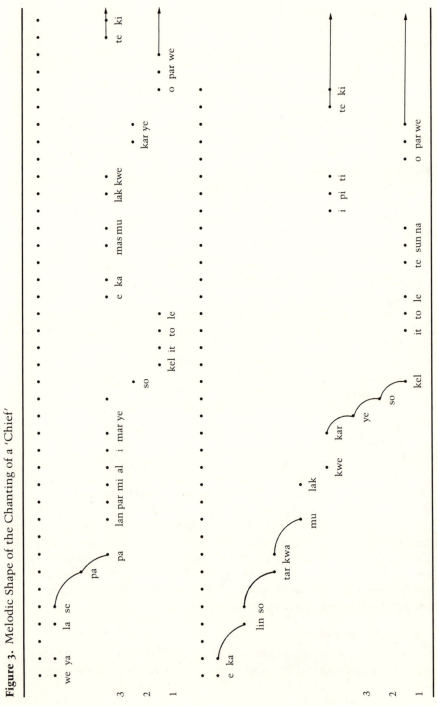

Note: Dots indicate beats; numbers indicate pitch levels.

**Figure 4.** Melodic Shape of 'The Way of the Hat'

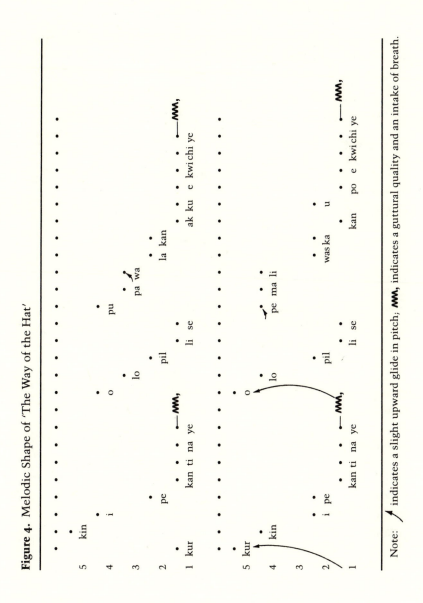

Note: ↗ indicates a slight upward glide in pitch; ∿, indicates a guttural quality and an intake of breath.

of this variety. This chant calls on particular trees (by addressing itself to their spirits) to use their strength in order to aid the ailing individual. Vowels which are deleted in colloquial speech are placed in parentheses, affixes which are used especially in 'stick doll language' are placed in brackets, and words particular to 'the way of the hat' are underlined.

*kurkin ipekan[ti][na][ye].*
Owners of *kurkin.*
*[olo]pillise pupawal(a)kan akku(e)kwich(i)[ye].*
To the level of gold your roots reach.

*kurkin ipekan[ti][na][ye].*
Owners of *kurkin.*
*[olo]pillise pe maliwaskakan upo(e)kwich(i)[ye].*
Into the level of gold your small roots are placed.

*kurkin ipekan[ti][na][ye].*
Owners of *kurkin.*
*[olo]pillise pe maliwaskakan(a) piokle[ke]kwich(i)[ye].*
Into the level of gold your small roots are nailed.

*kurkin ipekan[ti][na][ye].*
Owners of *kurkin.*
*[olo]pillipi[ye] ap(i)ka(e)kwich(i)[ye] kurkin ipekan[ti][na][ye].*
Within the very level of gold you are resisting, owners of *kurkin.*

*[olo]pilli aktikkimakk(e)kwich(i) kurkin ipekan[ti][na][ye].*
In the level of gold you weigh a great deal, owners of *kurkin.*

*[olo]pilli kwamakk(e)kwich(i) kurkin ipekan[ti][na][ye].*
In the level of gold you are firmly placed, owners of *kurkin.*

*[olo]pilli aktitimakk(e)[kwa] kwich(i)[ye] kurkin ipekan[ti]*
    *[na][ye].*
In the level of the gold you are moving, owners of *kurkin.*

*[olo]pillipi[ye].*
Within the very level of gold.
*kin(a)ka(e)kwich(i)[ye].*
You are accumulating.[24]

This example opens with a clearly structured line and verse pattern, marked by the combined, reinforcing use of syntactic and semantic parallelism, grammatical elements and vocabulary, and melodic shape. Each verse begins with the vocative line *kurkin ipekantinaye* (owners of *kurkin*). This line ends with the suffix *-ye* (optative). The second line of each verse begins with the word *olopillise* (to/into the level of gold) and ends with the verbal suffix sequence

-*kwichi* (are standing) plus -*ye*. Line final vowels are lengthened. Then in verse four a new pattern is introduced, providing a non-parallelistic contrastive interlude: *kurkin ipekantinaye*, which was previously line initial, becomes line final. This new parallel pattern, in which each verse consists of a single line and in which there is no explicit subject, is followed for three more verses. The example ends with two short, nonparallel lines, providing another moment of contrast. Figure 4 illustrates the melodic shape of the first two verses. Note the drop in pitch at the end of lines and verses.

## 'Kantule *Language*'

The most striking distinguishing characteristic of '*kantule* language' is its lexical differentiation from the other varieties of Kuna. The chant drawn on here for illustration, *iet ikar* (the way of the haircutter), is performed during girls' puberty rites; this portion of the chant describes a young girl's preparation for these rites. Lexical items particular to this variety are underlined.

*yainua* sunna *yakkiriteye.*
The girl goes very quietly.
*sakli ulakine.*
Because of her hair.
*saklikia ulakine.*
Because of her many hairs.
*sakli* tukku *ulakine.*
Because of the end of her hair.
*yainua uparpa* imakte.
The girl's underwear makes noise.
*yainua uparpa pukki nite.*
The girl's underwear can be heard far away.
*yainua kala tere* imakte.
The girl's coin necklace makes noise.
*yainua kala tere pukki nite.*
The girl's coin necklace can be heard far away.
*yainua kala purwa* imakte.
The girl's bead necklace makes noise.
*yainua kala purwa pukki nite.*
The girl's bead necklace can be heard far away.
*yainua* sunna yakkiri nae.
The girl goes very quietly.[25]

Once again, lines in this example of ritual language are marked by a parallelistic structure, and line final vowels are lengthened. Figure

**Figure 5.** Melodic Shape of 'The Way of the Haircutter'

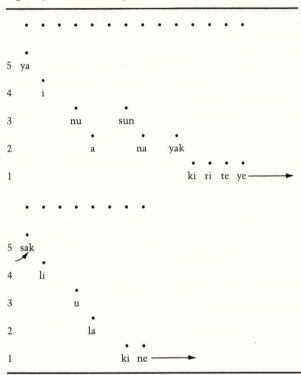

5 illustrates the melodic shape of the first two lines. Again, there is a drop in pitch at the end of lines.

I have explored Kuna sociolinguistics from the perspective of the sounds, words, grammatical patterns, spoken styles, chanted melodic shapes, and languages in use. But this perspective is incomplete without relating it to Kuna social organization and social life, the necessary contexts for a complete understanding of language and speech among the Kuna.

## Language and Society

Kuna social organization can be fruitfully viewed in terms of sets or systems of roles—in politics, curing and magic, puberty ritual, and everyday affairs. Consideration of language and speech is essential to an understanding of the definition, determination, and practice of these roles. At the literal center of Kuna life is the *sakla* (chief). (Although I translate *sakla* as 'chief,' this should not suggest the connotation of chief as a powerful authoritarian figure. The Kuna 'chief' is, rather, a specialist in tribal tradition who, by means of verbal artistry and rhetoric, convinces, advises, and offers guidance.) Ideally the 'chief' is the best speaker in the community. In practice this means that he has an extensive knowledge of tribal history and tradition and can apply this knowledge creatively to practical, everyday problems in the place where he displays his abilities and exercises his authority—the 'gathering house.' Strength of character and personality are essential qualities of a 'chief,' and his speaking ability is the primary reflection of these qualities. Speaking ability and, especially, knowledge of traditions are crucial in the selection of a 'chief.' A 'chief' displays his knowledge in the form of long chants and speeches in the 'gathering house,' using the ritual 'chief language.' He should also be willing and able to speak often and at length in 'gathering house' meetings on any and all topics that arise, not necessarily in the 'chief language' variety per se, although older and especially extremely traditional 'chiefs' will sprinkle just about any discourse with some 'chief language' vocabulary.

In recent years some villages have split the role of 'chief' into two parts, having one 'chief' for political matters who leads meetings dealing with day-to-day issues and represents the village in contacts with the Panamanian government and other 'chiefs' for tradition who chant legends, myths, and tribal history. Both types must be good speakers, each in his own way. This role splitting encourages and enables younger men, good speakers and dynamic leaders, to rise to leadership positions. At the same time it permits older leaders, knowledgeable in tradition, to retire gradually and gracefully, retaining an important role in society and maintaining their prestige. Ultimately, practical political knowledge and traditional knowledge are linked together. If a 'chief' is good at both, he can be both, thus acquiring even more prestige.

Each village, even small ones, has several 'chiefs.' Larger villages have as many as twelve, sometimes more. Several islands in San Blas are divided into two villages, each with its several 'chiefs.' Other islands have recently fused two villages into one, combining all the 'chiefs,' with the result that there are many. There are various reasons for the larger number of 'chiefs' per village. At least two per village are required by the structure of Kuna traditional chanting. According to this structure, one 'chief' chants to another, who ratifies by responding after each line (see chapter 3). Since chanting and responding are tiring—chants usually last from one to two hours—this is not something to burden a single individual with night after night. It is thus a good idea to have more than two 'chiefs.' Furthermore each 'chief' has a different repertoire, a different style, and a different voice, and the variety and novelty provided by a large rotation of chanters are much appreciated by audiences. Add to this sickness, fatigue, and the travel to neighboring villages that is expected of 'chiefs,' and it becomes quite logical to have many. Finally, the existence of many 'chiefs,' and of many of the other 'gathering house' officials as well, allows for the sharing of political power and of the prestige associated with public performance of tradition.

The other Kuna political leaders are the various officials of the 'gathering house'—the *arkar* (chief's spokesman) and the *suaripet* (policeman, literally owner of the stick), also called by the term *polisía*, borrowed from the Spanish. The 'chief's spokesmen,' like the 'chiefs,' must be well versed in Kuna tradition and be good speakers. They are in line to be 'chiefs,' and they publicly demonstrate their speaking ability by interpreting the chants and speeches of 'chiefs' and by generally being willing to stand up and speak in the 'gathering house.' The 'spokesmen' are also students of tradition, traveling with 'chiefs' in order to learn and improving their speaking ability by interpreting 'chiefs' visiting from other villages or those of villages they themselves visit. There are many 'spokesmen' in each village.

Villages typically have many 'policemen,' more than they have 'chiefs' or 'spokesmen.' (Although I translate *suaripet* as 'policeman,' this is by no means the uniformed, authoritarian figure characteristic of most countries.) The 'policemen' are often younger men, though some, especially the leaders, are older. Each carrying a stick, the official badge of their office, the 'policemen,' like medieval criers, wander through the village in a long single file in the late afternoon of days in which evening 'gatherings' for men and women are to be held. They urge attendance at these 'gatherings' by calling out fixed cries, such as *mormaynamaloe* (go and sew your molas)[26] and *onmakket neyse namaloe* (go to the gathering house). They also announce other village meetings and communal duties to be performed, such as the preparation of food and beverages for political leaders visiting from other villages. During 'gatherings' the 'policemen' keep people from falling asleep by touching them and screaming in loud, booming voices *kapitamarye, nue ittomarye* (don't sleep, listen well). At 'gatherings' in which one or more visiting 'chiefs' perform, the 'policemen' serve beverages to all those present. They perform various duties for 'chiefs,' such as bringing individuals who have been accused of wrongdoing to the 'gathering house.' They also accompany 'chiefs' and 'spokesmen' on trips to other villages. While knowledge of traditions and good speaking ability per se are not requisites for 'policemen,' the role draws men into Kuna ritual tradition, especially the system of the 'gathering house.' As 'policemen,' they must attend 'gatherings' and they must stay awake and listen; in general they must be positively and actively involved in 'gathering house' activities. Respected 'chiefs' often begin their careers as 'policemen,' then become 'spokesmen' and, finally, 'chiefs.' With regard to language and speech, they thus move from watchful listeners and observers, to interpreters of others, to primary performers of Kuna verbal traditions.

'Chiefs,' 'chief's spokesmen,' and 'policemen' are the primary official roles of the Kuna 'gathering.' There are also other named roles. The 'chiefs' of every village have secretaries, whose task it is to write their letters, accompany them on trips to Panama City, read correspondence to the village, take and keep the roll of attendance at 'gatherings,' and perform other tasks. Knowledge of Spanish being essential, the secretary is thus selected from among the usually younger and relatively more acculturated men.

Of the men who attend Kuna 'gatherings,' some are active talkers, even though they might not fill one of the major 'gathering house' roles. They become unofficial political leaders because of their willingness and ability to stand up and speak in the 'gathering house.' Their point of view is taken seriously; they are listened to and argued with. This unofficial role is sometimes called by the Spanish-derived name *posero*;[27] the Kuna term sometimes used for such individuals is *tikkarpalit* (those against the wall), referring to the place on the outer rim of the 'gathering house' where they sit, as distinct from the 'chiefs' and the 'spokesmen' in the very center. These individuals are viewed as being potential 'spokesmen' and 'chiefs.' They either become 'gathering house' officials or else are considered to be too talkative without really having anything to say, a mockery of the model of a good Kuna speaker.

Thus 'gathering house' roles, official and unofficial, are ultimately and often intimately connected with talk. Knowledge of tradition and of 'chief language' and ability to talk at length, creatively, and effectively are highly valued and play a primary part in the selection of individuals for these roles. The focus on speaking ability goes beyond recognized 'gathering house' roles to include all participants in 'gathering' activities. Anyone who speaks, whether to accuse, defend, report, ask for permission, or comment, is expected to speak at length, cleverly, and creatively. The more he or she does so, the more it is appreciated.

A second domain of Kuna ritual life, distinct from that of the 'gathering,' is that of medicinal curing and magic. Curing as a process begins when the family of the sick individual calls a *nele* (seer) in order to diagnose the disease. This is an ascribed role, 'seers,' (men or women) being born with the ability to communicate with spirits. On the basis of this ability, 'seers' diagnose diseases and determine the causes of other evils, such as thefts. But they must actively practice their given ability or they will lose it. Thus while one is born a 'seer,'[28] the role is intimately involved with speaking and communicative abilities, since the task of 'seers' is to communicate actively with the spirit world and to relate and interpret spirits' messages to living Kuna. There are special medicines and chants whose purpose is to improve these abilities. *Nele kurkin ikar* (the way of the seer's hat) is a chant used to cure the headaches that 'seers' get from having to store so much knowledge in their heads; it enables them to expand their brain size and learn still more. Thus Kuna 'seers,' although born with a potential ability which is the official defining characteristic of their role, achieve prestige, as do other Kuna leaders and officials, by means of active and practiced abilities in language use.

After a disease has been diagnosed by a 'seer,' the cure is achieved by means of medicine gathered and prepared by an *inatulet* (medicinal specialist) and the performance of the appropriate curing *ikar* (way, text) by an *ikar wisit* (*ikar* knower). The 'medicinal specialist' is an expert in the pharmaceutical properties of local plants and animals. At the behest of clients—patients or patients' families—he searches for and prepares medicine. But this is not sufficient in itself. For the medicine to be potent and effective, it must be advised and given life. This is achieved by means of chants called *ina uanaet* (medicine counsel) which are directed to the medicine and the spirits of the medicine by the 'medicinal specialist.' Thus the task of the 'medicinal specialist' is twofold: in part to be knowledgeable about local medicine, in part to know the chant appropriate to each type of medicine.

The '*ikar* knowers' achieve their positions by means of the memorization and performance of long curing and magical *ikarkana*. The word *ikar* has several meanings and it is worth dwelling on them for a moment, since they are central to an understanding of Kuna speaking practices. *Ikar* signifies a path or way in a concrete sense and as such refers to cleared paths in the mainland jungle where the Kuna farm, hunt, and gather medicinal plants. In addition, quite like English and other Indo-European languages, *ikar* signifies a way of life or a manner of behavior, good or bad, or a tradition. *Ikar* also refers to a personal experience or adventure or, more generally, a historical event or set of events. Finally, *ikar* signifies a text or a portion of a text (with the understanding that Kuna texts are oral, not written), usually a chant, as well as a subtext or unit within a text. I will continue to use the Kuna word *ikar* throughout this study, with the combined and intersecting meanings of way, text, and chant.

Each curing *ikar* defines a role in Kuna society, namely, that of the 'knower' of that *ikar*. And, since there are many *ikarkana*, there are many different possible roles in this domain. A man can be a *kapur ikar wisit* (knower of the way of the hot pepper), used in curing high fever; a *kurkin ikar wisit* (knower of the way of the hat), used in curing headaches and improving brainpower; or an *apsoket* (mass curer and exorcist), 'knower' and performer of a long *ikar* against epidemics and the abundance of evil spirits. To be recognized officially as a 'knower' of a particular *ikar* is to be a representative of the role defined by that *ikar*. *Ikarkana* also go beyond the realm of curing per se, in that there are *ikarkana* for effective hunting and fishing, for warding off or grabbing snakes, for attracting swarms of bees and wasps, and for being able to touch a hot harpoon.

The third major ritual tradition among the Kuna is that associated with girls' puberty rites. This tradition too defines a ritual role according to speaking ability—the *kantule*, the leader and director of the puberty ritual, performs long *ikarkana* which he must know from memory. His assistants in this demanding performance are also his students, learning from him the *ikarkana* which will permit them to be *kanturkana* as well.

Speaking ability thus defines an extensive and varied complex of leadership and ritual roles in Kuna society. These are summarized in table 10.

The investigation of Kuna ritual and leadership roles highlights the salience of speaking in Kuna social life. Since most, and on close analysis probably all, Kuna ritual and leadership roles are defined in terms of speaking, they require a lifelong focus on the acquisition and practice of verbal abilities. In worldwide, cross-cultural perspective, there are several Kuna roles in which verbal ability is spectacularly impressive—outstanding 'chiefs' who perform several different three-hour chants over a period of two days, creatively developing personal but culturally meaningful metaphors during this perfor-

**Table 10.** Kuna Leadership and Ritual Roles

---

Political Organization
  Official
    *sakla* [*saklakana*], chief
    *arkar* [*arkarkana*], chief's spokesman
    *suaripet* [*suaripkana*], policeman
  Unofficial
    *tikkarpalit* [*tikkarpalitmala*], active gathering house talker

Medicinal Curing and Magic
  *nele* [*nelekana*], seer
  *inatulet* [*inaturkana*], medicinal specialist
  *ikar wisit* [*ikar wismalat*], *ikar* knower
    *kapur ikar wisit*, knower of the way of the hot pepper
    *kurkin ikar wisit*, knower of the way of the hat
    *masar ikar wisit*, knower of the way of the bamboo cane
    *apsoket*, mass curer and exorcist
    etc.

Girls' Puberty Rites
  *kantule* [*kanturkana*], director of the puberty ritual
  assistants to the *kantule*

---

Note: The plural form is given in brackets.

mance; the 'mass curer' who performs a memorized chant which lasts eight consecutive evenings; the *kantule* who, in a state of extreme inebriation, performs a memorized chant lasting three or more days. Every Kuna village has several and most have many individuals possessing verbal abilities comparable to the phenomenal virtuosity displayed by the Slavic *guslar* (singer of tales), the Javanese-Balinese *dalang* (puppet performance narrator), and the African epic poet.

More than one 'gathering house' role cannot be held at the same time. This follows logically from the structure of 'gathering house' chanting and speaking and from the fact that individuals often progress from 'policemen' to 'spokesmen' to 'chiefs.' On the other hand, all other ritual and leadership roles can be held simultaneously with one another and with one of the 'gathering house' roles as well. Given the large number of possible roles, each individual has a unique constellation. One might be a 'chief' and a *kantule*; or a 'chief's spokesman,' a 'medicinal specialist,' a 'knower of the way of the hot pepper,' and a 'knower of the way of the hat'; or a 'medicinal specialist' and a 'knower of the way of the bamboo cane.'

These different roles highlight different conceptions and types of speaking ability, favoring specialization and allowing for personal preference. The 'gathering house' is ideal for persons who like and who are good at being individually creative, adaptive, and flexible with language. It is the place for the good talker, where good talkers are defined as people who are good on their feet, ready and willing to develop verbal strategies appropriate to new situations. It is the realm of politics par excellence. On the other hand, curing and puberty rituals are arenas of tradition which appeal to the word-for-word, line-by-line memorizer. In these domains, good speaking ability means the ability to reproduce the same long text, from memory, when it is called for. While individuals may cut across these different traditions, they tend to be good at and hence become known for one or another role. An examination of particular cases nicely illustrates this situation.

Muristo Pérez is an ideal 'gathering house' leader. For several years he was first or head 'chief' of Mulatuppu, and he continues to be one of the village's outstanding political leaders. He is extremely intelligent, verbally quick and witty, and has a fine sense of humor. He loves to talk and is respected for his willingness to give long speeches in the 'gathering house' on a wide variety of issues. He intersperses the most serious of discourse with clever, quite funny commentary. Olowitinappi (who died in 1975) was a respected 'chief's spokesman' who knew Kuna tradition well. He always attended 'gatherings' and spoke occasionally, in a quiet, almost shy manner not typical of 'gathering house' speakers. But Olowitinappi's great love and the realm of his greatest success was medicine and curing. He would often go to the mainland jungle twice a day in order to gather medicinal plants. And he knew a large number of very long curing chants. His knowledge of 'the way of the basil,' used for hunting effectiveness, was one of the reasons he was such an excellent hunter. It is not surprising that his reputation was above all that of a 'medicinal specialist' and '*ikar* knower.' In 1970, Olowitinappi was sent at community expense to an interior jungle village in order to study snakebite medicine and curing. Manuel Campos (who died in 1974) was a typical curing specialist. He rarely attended 'gatherings' and spoke there even more rarely. He much preferred to spend his evenings practicing one of the many chants he knew from memory or one he was still in the process of learning. He would boom these out into the night for family and neighbors all to hear, in addition of course to whatever spirits might be listening.

The Kuna concept of *kurkin* nicely captures the notion of discrete, accumulative roles. *Kurkin* literally means hat or headdress, but one of its several related senses (including brain, brainpower, and ability) is the Kuna concept of role. Thus, one individual can ask another *kurkin kwapikwa pe nikka*? (how many *kurkin* do you have?), that is, how many unique abilities or roles do you possess? The system permits a finely tuned balance between competition and cooperation. The more *kurkin* one has the more prestige one has, and there is incentive to keep acquiring new *kurkin*. While individuals are compared and ranked in the public eye, the roles themselves are also ranked within each of the Kuna role systems. Thus, in the 'gathering house,' the 'chief' is the most highly ranked role; then come 'chief's spokesman' and 'policeman.' 'Seer' and 'mass curer' are the most highly ranked roles within the curing and magical system. The latter typically learns his long *ikar* after first mastering other *ikarkana*, having thus acquired the roles associated with them as well. The *kantule* is the most highly ranked of the various puberty rites specialists. It is interesting that, of the many named roles in Kuna society, only a few are used as terms of reference and address. These are precisely the highly ranked and prestigious 'chief,' 'seer,' and *kantule*, terms which are used especially when the individuals in question are exercising these roles.

There is also a notion of the best or most knowledgeable performer in each role within a community, and individuals become known throughout San Blas and sometimes the entire Kuna world because of their ability in a particular role, thus attracting students who come to study with them. 'Chiefs' in particular are supposed to travel in order to show off their abilities. Interisland ritual 'gatherings' place a large number of 'chiefs' and 'spokesmen' from various villages on public display—they chant and speak one after the other in what is obviously a competitive event, in addition to its other ends. At the same time, since each individual has a unique constellation of roles and specialized abilities within these, unlimited competition between representatives of the same or different roles is controlled. And there is a need for cooperation as well. There might always be a disease for which there is only one specialist in a community. Or one of the specialists might be away in another community and a second will have to be called on. 'Chiefs' within a village rotate so that each one gets an opportunity to chant. Thus everyone who has *kurkin* gets a chance to use and display their abilities. There is a place for everyone.

In addition to the roles in Kuna society associated with the political and ritual traditions, there are those involved in day-to-day activities. There are the leaders of such activities as house building, boat repairing, planting, and harvesting. The groups involved in these activities range in size from a few associates who have formed a cooperative to an entire village. Although such people are chosen in part for their ability to perform the tasks in question—house building, canoe building, and so forth—they are selected primarily for their leadership ability, which signifies the ability to lead with language and speech, to speak loudly, fluently, often, creatively, and effectively. It is significant that these task leaders are called 'chiefs,' for example, *nek sopet sakla* (house-building chief) or *okop sakla* (coconut chief). Similarly, in any organization that arises among the Kuna, and many do—cooperative enterprises and associations for a great range of purposes—leaders are chosen for their ability to talk effectively.

While there is some intersection in the activities associated with each of the independent sets of roles in Kuna society, there is none in the performance of the roles themselves. A 'chief' is the village leader within the 'gathering house,' but he has no authority outside of it. He must follow the directions and leadership of other individuals when operating within other social organizations—curing, puberty rites, house building, or agricultural work. In fact, it is very difficult to recognize or distinguish a Kuna 'chief' from other members of a community outside of the 'gathering house.' The existence of independent sets of roles and of many discrete roles within each set encourages the participation of all members of the community in social life, offers many opportunities to achieve positions of prestige and authority, and prevents the accumulation of too much power in the hands of too few people. The overall organization includes both a generalized notion of prestige and authority based on the accumulation of roles and a segmented notion of prestige and authority based on particular roles.[29]

Finally, there are the roles involved in everyday family and friendship links—father, mother, son, daughter, wife, husband, in-law, and friend. In all these relationships, language and speech are centrally involved in the constant processes and patterns of conversing, counseling, reformulating, interpreting, reporting, teaching, and learning.

### The Idyllic and the Conflictual

I have described Kuna social life—especially the relationship between language and speech and social organization—as harmonious, almost idyllic. In the ideal, and often in practice, this is the way things are. But, at the same time, the Kuna sociolinguistic system involves and gives rise to a series of conflicts, with the result that there is a delicate dialectic interplay between the idyllic and the conflictual. This interplay can be viewed in terms of a set of related oppositions. It is part of a larger, complex dynamic involving tradition, adaptation, and change and will be discussed in this context in the following chapters.

### Speaking Ability Ideally and Actually

While there are a remarkable number of good speakers among the Kuna and these persons tend to be drawn into leadership roles, there are also leaders who are not effective verbally. Often such ineffective speakers are individuals who have learned to go through the motions of Kuna verbal performances, who have made the effort to acquire the form necessary for the position they hold, but who are more mechanical than creative in their exercise of it. A good example is provided by certain 'chief's spokesmen' who can interpret a chant only in the most general terms, either because they cannot remember what the 'chief' chanted or because they do not understand his metaphors. I have heard members of the audience, after an evening 'gathering,' criticize such individuals who, they said, kept repeating 'the chief counseled us' and 'told us to behave properly' but never explained what it was that the chant contained.

Ideally, village leaders are persons of high moral standing and character. Their speaking ability is viewed as both a reflection of and an aspect of their personality. But there are times when an individual's moral character is at odds with the role he holds in the community. He might have been caught stealing. Or he might publicly display greed or anger. Such individuals, especially if they are 'gathering house' leaders, are removed from office. Yet they continue to be known and respected for their speaking abilities. As a result they are often selected again for positions of leadership. There are thus individuals who have passed in and out of leadership roles, and there is sometimes an uneasy relationship between the idealized speaking ability which defines a role and the actions and personality of the actual representatives of that role.

Again ideally, members of the Kuna community appreciate the verbal abilities of their leaders and respect, support, and follow these leaders because of these abilities. But there is great variation in the degree to which and the way in which this verbal ability is appreciated. Since the 'gathering house' is the political, ritual, and ceremonial center of Kuna villages, all members of the community are encouraged, expected, and in some cases required to attend the evening chanting and speaking meetings there. Yet attendance is sometimes quite low. In Mulatuppu, men frequently check the 'gathering house' in the evening to see what is happening there. They spend a while there listening to leaders chant or speak, perhaps converse quietly with friends, or doze off for a moment. Attendance is high only when matters of excitement or import are being discussed or when well-known leaders from other villages are performing. Women attend 'gatherings' at which 'chiefs' chant in greater numbers and with greater frequency than men. They are not permitted to attend men's talking meetings unless they are specifically invited to talk about a particular matter. As a result, it is mainly male political leaders and potential political leaders who spend all their evenings in the 'gathering house,' and they thus tend to form a relatively close knit and insular communicative group.

Similarly, with regard to the efficacy of language and speech, in ideal terms it is through and because of language and speech that many things, social, political, medicinal, and magical, are believed to occur. It is by counseling the village that 'chiefs' convince people to behave properly; it is by communicating with spirits that *'ikar knowers'* combat evil and sickness. And yet, in spite of the nightly chanted and spoken admonishments by village leaders, there is improper behavior. It is frequently said and many Kuna seem to believe that thefts are common; that people do not work as hard as they should, either at such economic endeavors as farming or at the learning of ritual tradition; and that there is much jealousy and bickering. And, in spite of the efforts of the 'medicinal specialists' and the *'ikar knowers,'* there are evil and sickness.

Thus the ideal function of speaking and speaking ability, which the Kuna frequently verbalize and seem to believe in quite strongly, does not always conform to actualities. Rather, a delicate balance between ideal and actual practice is maintained and paralleled by a balance between belief in and support for the system and questioning of it.

### Competition and Cooperation

The relationship between language and speech and social organization that I have described here implies harmonious cooperation and integration among the various political and ritual leaders and the various types and levels of Kuna social organization. In practice there is much competition, intervillage, intravillage, and personal.

The competition among villages is sometimes manifested in regional terms. There are differences and disagreements between the eastern and western portions of San Blas with regard to the appropriate topics for chants. 'Chiefs' from the western portion prefer chants about Kuna myths and legends and criticize 'chiefs' from the eastern portion who chant about their personal experiences and dreams, as well as biblical themes. There are also competition and friction within regions. Ritual leaders from one village sometimes criticize those of a nearby village, attacking not only their speaking ability but their overall leadership and moral character as well. Two competitive villages may coexist on a single small island. Many San Blas islands, including Mulatuppu, have had a history of splitting into two villages, fusing into one, and splitting again. During moments of division, two separate, independent, and competing political organizations exist, each with its own 'gathering house' and meetings.

The three Kuna ritual traditions, while independent of one another, can also be in conflict. There are 'medicinal specialists' who do not attend meetings in the 'gathering house' and who publicly affirm their disinterest in its tradition. Their prestige and influence emerge from their own domain. On the other hand, 'chiefs' and other political leaders are critical of individuals who do not participate in 'gatherings' and sometimes try to force their participation. A concrete example of the competition between the 'gathering' and curing traditions is the habit of certain '*ikar* knowers' to practice, booming out their texts for all to hear, in a house near the 'gathering house' on evenings when men's talking meetings are held there.

There can also be conflict between various individuals who hold the same role within the same village. For example, 'chiefs' jockey for position in their communities and have personal followings. It sometimes happens that the first, head 'chief' of a village is good verbally but weak politically. In such cases, men's talking meetings are taken up with much bickering and with repetitions of the same arguments. In both talking and chanting meetings there are repeated speeches and chants by village leaders counseling people to behave properly, which means not to be jealous of one another but to cooperate. Yet simple projects, like fixing a wooden bridge between the island and the mainland, do not get done.

Each curing and magical *ikar* exists in different versions. Ideally all are equally effective. But in practice some '*ikar* knowers' have reputations for knowing an *ikar* better or for knowing more effective versions. When a teacher and students of the same *ikar* live in the same village, they are ranked, with the teacher being ranked highest. Teachers and students often criticize each other. Students claim that their teacher will not let them finish learning an *ikar* or that he will not admit that they have learned it. Teachers argue that their students have not completely mastered the *ikar*. This is no doubt one of the major reasons why it is common practice to learn an *ikar* from a renowned teacher from a distant village. In this way both teacher and student gain prestige and at the same time avoid subsequent conflict. Also, certain 'knowers' learn their *ikarkana* in dreams from spirits or deceased specialists. While these 'knowers' have patients and students, there is antagonism toward them on the part of those 'knowers' who have learned in the more ordinary way, with a live, human teacher, especially if they claim to be specialists in the same *ikar*.

It is important to stress that the competition which emerges from the Kuna sociolinguistic system occurs against the backdrop of and in dialectic interplay with the ideal of harmonious cooperation among individuals and social organizations. The competition is typically not open, overtly hostile, or constant. At the same time, it exists as part of the dynamic of Kuna language and society.

### Older Men and Younger Men

Since Kuna ritual roles involve the learning of long and often difficult verbal traditions, it is relatively older men who achieve positions of leadership. Furthermore, certain verbal traditions, especially the most prestigious, are in practice restricted to older men. Younger men must apprentice themselves to older leaders, specialists, and teachers and wait their turn—this causes considerable frustration on the part of the younger men. Because of this social and political situation, coupled with economic pressures, Kuna men are leaving their villages in increasing numbers and staying away longer than in the past. The unfortunate result is that San Blas villages are losing some of their most intelligent young men, who prefer cooking and washing dishes in Panama City to the economic and social frustrations of San Blas.

At the same time, young Kuna do not reject their culture. They are proud of and steadfastly maintain its primary outward symbols, especially the Kuna language and the women's clothing. An organized group of youths, the Juventud Kuna, is very vocal in its stressing of the maintenance of Kuna language and culture, both within and outside of San Blas. But the Juventud Kuna's approach, while politically militant, is culturally symbolic in its rejection of the depth, breadth, and detail of older traditionalists, from whom they meet opposition—the latter claim that the former talk about Kuna tradition but refuse to make the effort to learn it; the former claim that they are progressive and that the older traditionalists are too conservative.

## Men and Women

Linguistic differences between Kuna men's and women's speech are relatively slight. The main difference concerns the speech acts and events that are used by men and women. Two speech events, *koe pippi* (lullaby) and *poe* (tuneful weeping), both in 'everyday Kuna,' are unique to women (see chapter 6). But the large set of ritual and traditional forms of discourse (see chapters 3 to 5) which are the essence of the definition and practice of Kuna leadership roles, while ideally available to both men and women, is in practice restricted to men. While the Kuna can point to instances of a woman who once held a leadership role or a woman who knows and performs a curing *ikar*, this is in fact extremely rare. The distinction between men's and women's 'gatherings' is a sharp one, and it is at men's 'gatherings' that most important political matters are discussed and re- solved. At women's 'gatherings' women are supposed to make molas and listen to the chanting of the 'chief.'

No one denies the significant roles that women do hold, however. All women make molas, the symbolic markers par excellence of Kuna culture, traditional and modern, as well as an important source of prestige and income.[30] A set of women, the *iet* (haircutter) and her assistants, play a basic and central role in one of the most traditional of all Kuna ritual events, girls' puberty rites (see chapter 5). Another set of women, the *muu* (midwife) and her assistants, are involved in a crucial, extremely secretive, and highly respected activity—the de- livery of babies. But both roles are defined and practiced according to nonverbal abilities and tasks. Essentially all public, political, and rit- ual speaking roles are held by men. In this matrilocal society in which both women and men are extremely talkative, it is possible for women to exert considerable influence within the confines of their homes, an influence that carries well beyond the home into po- litical and ritual domains. But women's primary medium of aes- thetic expression is the visual mola, which they often make, signifi- cantly, in the 'gathering house' while listening to the chanting of the 'chiefs.'

While most official and unofficial public roles in Kuna society are held by men, no one questions that women are good speakers, and they are recognized as such by men and women alike. In Mulatuppu in recent years, women hold 'gatherings' with their own leaders and discuss such matters as their mola cooperative and women's tasks in the village. Organized and run entirely by women, these 'gatherings' are dynamic, vibrant verbal events. They are strikingly parallel to the men's 'gatherings,' down to the finest detail. Leaders make long

speeches, advising and encouraging the audience to carry out assigned tasks properly. Any woman can and often does stand up and,
either agreeing or disagreeing with the leaders, speak as eloquently
as they do. When women are called upon to speak at men's 'gatherings,' they are as fluent, eloquent, and sure of themselves as male
speakers. Also, since women 'seers' communicate with the spirit
world, they are called on to help solve crimes and other matters for
which spirit assistance is required. And they relate their supernatural communications to their communities in the form of public
speeches in the 'gathering house.'

Women's limited access to public speaking roles and to associated
positions of authority and prestige within the Kuna social organization has not seemed to result in the frustration and conflict characteristic of other societies.[31] This is perhaps because of the carefully
worked out division of labor, the economic independence of women
(they inherit their own land), the matrilocal rule and the influence
women can exert within the home, and the at least ideal potential
for women to participate in village politics and ritual. But, while
there is no women's liberation movement in San Blas, women have
increasingly formed their own political and economic organizations,
such as the Mulatuppu mola cooperative. Given the Kuna tendency
to adapt flexibly to new situations and needs, I expect that both
women and younger men will be increasingly involved in significant
roles in Kuna verbal life.

# 3. The 'Gathering House':
# Public and Political 'Gatherings'

My analysis of Kuna discourse begins in the *onmakket neka* (gathering house), the vital center of Kuna political, social, and verbal life. The 'gathering house' is a talking place, a chanting place, an arguing place, an agreeing place, a serious place, and a joking place. There *saklakana* (chiefs) and other village leaders display their knowledge and verbal ability and exercise their political authority. Kuna tradition, mythical, historical, and religious, is publicly performed. Village problems are discussed and decisions are made. Wrongdoers are publicly tried and punished. Individuals who have spent time away from the village and have just returned report on their trips and activities. Anyone who has had an extraordinary experience relates it to everyone else. Men gather to learn news, gossip, tell stories, and joke. Women wear their newest, finest molas while cutting and sewing new ones. And anyone and everyone goes to talk and be talked to, see and be seen. It is town hall, courtroom, church, and social hall, all in one.

The 'gathering house' is located in or near the center of every Kuna village. With its bamboo walls and thatched roof, it has the same structure as all traditional Kuna houses except that it is much larger than family dwellings. It stands out because of its size, especially in the largest villages, in which it has the capacity for more than one thousand persons. In the center are strung hammocks in which 'chiefs' sit or lie. At both ends of these hammocks are long benches with backs, for the *arkarkana* (chief's spokesmen). Long backless benches throughout the 'gathering house' are used by both men and women. In Mulatuppu, in the corners of the 'gathering house' near each entrance, are one or two wooden armchairs. A long table on one side is used by the village secretaries. On one or several of the towering poles in the center of the 'gathering house' hang large photographs, in black and white or in color. The photographs are of the best-known deceased 'chiefs' of a village, current political leaders or candidates, and well-known figures who appeal to the Kuna, such as John Kennedy. The 'gathering house' is always impeccably neat and clean, kept so by women who are assigned to regularly sweep the earth floor and generally tidy up. Everything is in excellent working order, thanks to the vigilance of the *suaripkana* (policemen).

## Men's and Women's 'Gatherings': Chanting

The 'gathering house' is the setting for various events. I begin with the one which occurs every other evening and is attended by both men and women; it is characterized by the *namakke* (chanting) of 'chiefs' to the assemblage. On days when these 'gatherings' will occur, in the late afternoon, the 'policemen' walk in single file through the streets of the village and announce the evening's event repeatedly, urging people to attend. The most common of their cries focuses on women: *mormaynamaloe* (go and sew your molas). For the entire duration of this evening 'gathering,' most women constantly cut and sew their attractive blouses—they do not come just to listen, as do the men.

About 7:00 P.M., as it begins to get dark, the women start filing toward the 'gathering house.' They go in groups, usually from the same household and usually taking young children with them. The women are dressed in their finest clothes, including a personally made mola and a store-bought *muswe* (headkerchief), as well as gold jewelry, with large plate necklaces and earrings so enormous that they must be held on with string. They use a great deal of perfume and red makeup. They carry with them their evening's work—a small basket containing a mola that they are currently working on, needles, thread, scissors, and cloth—and a small homemade kerosene lamp. Each woman always sits in the same place in the 'gathering house,' as does each man. She puts her kerosene lamp on a small table in front of her, the table being intended especially for this purpose, places her young children on the ground in front of her on blankets or large pieces of plastic, and talks with other women while beginning to work on her mola. The men are freshly bathed and wear their best clothes—western-style slacks, shirt, and hat; they, like the women, are barefoot or wear rubber sandals. They also often use perfume. The men sit on benches around the outside of the women.

The total configuration is as follows. In the center of the 'gathering house,' sitting or lying in hammocks, are the 'chiefs' of the village and any visiting 'chiefs.' The 'chiefs' wear hats and often ties;

they are practically always barefoot. Around them sit the 'chief's spokesmen' on their long benches. Some 'chiefs' may sit on these benches as well, as do certain other respected ritual specialists, such as *inaturkana* (medicinal specialists), *ikar wismalat* (*ikar* knowers), and *kanturkana* (directors of girls' puberty rites). The women sit on backless benches either on both sides of the 'chiefs' and 'spokesmen' or on one side only (this varies from village to village). Around the women are the men, including the 'policemen,' who sit on benches against the walls. Thus the 'chiefs' are literally in the center of their village. The women are surrounded by the men. And the entire assemblage is surrounded by the 'policemen,' the watchful caretakers of the village.

As people wander into the 'gathering house' and after they have arrived, before the 'chief' begins chanting, certain issues are publicly discussed. If there are no such issues, people talk informally among themselves. Usually there is at least a public discussion of work allocations for the next day on community projects, such as the village-wide banana and coconut farms. The person in charge of such projects, or a village secretary, calls out the names of individuals who are to work the next day. There might also be a public discussion of economic or social matters of concern to the entire community, such as whether or not the village should purchase a boat, contributions to a Catholic missionary hospital on the mainland, or the Panamanian school system and its relationship to the village. Or problems that have arisen during the day, such as thefts or arguments, will be resolved. These are typically reserved for evenings when 'chiefs' do not chant, but they might also be discussed or even resolved before the 'chief' begins to chant.

The chanting itself is the most formal and ritual part of the Kuna 'gathering.' When all other business has been handled, the 'chief' who is to chant usually exits in order to urinate, often in the company of other 'chiefs' in a single file. When they return, the chanting begins in the form of a ritualized dialogue between two 'chiefs,' in the presence of and for the benefit of the audience. The two 'chiefs' straddle their hammocks in what the Kuna call the *nai* (hanging position), their feet barely touching the ground. For the entire duration of the chanting their arms are fixed at their sides; they stare into space and do not change their facial expressions. The 'chief' designated to chant begins in a soft voice. After each verse,[1] the second 'chief,' the *apinsuet* (responding chief), replies with a chanted *teki* (thus, it is so, indeed)[2] or *eye* (yes). The first part of the chant consists of a ritualized opening or greeting in which the chanting 'chief' reports on the state of health of his family, his village, and himself. As in chapter 2, the chanting 'chief' is labeled cc; the 'responding chief,' rc.

cc: Yes you appear as always.
rc: Indeed.
cc: In truth.
    You still appear.
    In good health.
rc: Indeed.
cc: In truth here.
    In truth I am.
    In good health.
    I utter.
rc: Indeed.
cc: In truth evil spirits.
    In truth I do not want.
    I utter.
rc: Indeed.
cc: Powerful evil spirits, see.
    Then I do not want them to enter.
rc: Indeed.
cc: Now I am still in good health, say.
    In truth still this way.
rc: Indeed.[3]

The performer of this chant, Chief Muristo Pérez of Mulatuppu, has just returned from a week's visit to several villages, where he participated in an interisland ritual 'gathering' involving continuous chanting by many congregated 'chiefs.' Because of his absence, the state of his health has become even more relevant than usual. Health is a topic of great concern to the Kuna, and it is frequently a focus of discourse of all kinds.

After this opening, the principal topic or theme of the chant begins. The chanting becomes louder and louder, most 'chiefs' eventually booming out their lines. During the chanting, the village 'policemen' walk about, waking people up and calling out in a loud voice *kapitamarye, nue ittomarye* (don't sleep, listen well). Most individuals, women and men, smoke pipes or cigarettes, an activity very rare during the day. The smoke and smell of the pipes, cigarettes, and kerosene lamps permeate the 'gathering house' and, though not an official part of the ritual, clearly lend a special aura to it. Add to this the symbolic seating arrangement in which the women are grouped together in a colorful array, dominated by the rich red of molas and headkerchiefs in the misty darkness, and the overall impression is that of a dramatic chiaroscuro, all under the towering roof of the 'gathering house,' which forms an intricate pattern of bamboo and palm.

The chanting, which usually lasts from one to two hours, is followed by a spoken reformulation and interpretation by a 'chief's spokesman' in colloquial Kuna, in the formal speechmaking style particular to the interpretations of chants (see chapter 2). The 'spokesman' stands and faces the audience, now the direct receivers of the message which was first performed as a dialogue between the two 'chiefs.' Some 'spokesmen' stand stiffly with their hands at their sides; others punctuate their speech with gestures. The 'spokesman' mentions constantly that it is the words of the 'chief' that he is repeating and interpreting. The spoken interpretation lasts about one hour; when it is completed, women and men gather their belongings and go home to sleep. The 'chiefs' and their 'spokesmen' sometimes stay a while longer to talk and joke. Then they go home as well and the 'policemen' lock the 'gathering house' for the night.

## The Typology of Chanting

It is difficult to present a clear, neat typology of the chants of Kuna 'chiefs.'[4] There are regional as well as individual differences. And there are overlaps between types. Since all chants are performed in the same linguistic variety, *sakla kaya* (chief language), with individual, creative development of metaphors, the distinguishing criterion for a typology is topic—the contents and themes of the chants. One type of chant is mythical-cosmological-historical. Some of these chants present myths and legends—the origin of the Kuna tribe, its ancestral heroes, and mythohistorical events. There are the stories of the many Kuna culture heroes, such as Ipeorkun and Tatipe. One series of legends deals with the great *nelekana* (seers) of the past, such as Nele Sipu (the White Seer).

cc: Friend the great seers of ancient times who came to see this world.
    We will hear their story.
rc: Indeed.
cc: Thus we will hear the story of the White Seer.
    Indeed say see.
rc: Indeed.

cc: Friend since this story is very long to chant say.
I will tell a little here and a little there say.
rc: Indeed.

This chant was performed by a 'chief' from the western region of San Blas who was visiting in Mulatuppu for a few days. The chant of the 'White Seer' is one of the mythological themes which are performed in the western region.[5] Since 'chiefs' from the west criticize those from the east (which includes Mulatuppu) for not knowing and performing such myths, the visiting 'chief' rather pointedly includes the following observations in his introduction to the chant.

cc: There are many ancestors who left their traditions.
rc: Indeed.
cc: There are many traditions which exist in my village say.
rc: Indeed.

The story of the 'White Seer' thus provides a challenge to the Mulatuppu 'spokesman' who will have to stand up and interpret it after the 'chief' finishes chanting. The chant describes how the 'White Seer' explored the various levels of the spirit world in order to observe, learn, and report back to others. The report, presented in the form of direct quotations which are developed and interpreted by the chanting 'chief,' includes advice on proper modes of behavior.

cc: Thus in truth then 'one level down I [the 'White Seer'] descended,' I utter.
rc: Indeed.
cc: Thus ' "this is the level of the golden dirt."
The man [the guide of the 'White Seer'] said to me,' I utter.
rc: Indeed.
cc: 'God placed the dirt's mother here.
God placed the dirt's father here.'
rc: Indeed.
cc: 'At the level of golden dirt,' say.
'The dirt people come to life,' I utter.
rc: Indeed.
cc: 'In the place of the golden dirt God left many golden flags God.
Left many golden bells.'
rc: Indeed.
cc: 'The golden streets of the place of the golden dirt shine brilliantly like gold,' I utter.
rc: Indeed.

CC: 'Women, listen to me well.'
    The White Seer chanted I utter.
RC: Indeed.
CC: 'Women, clean your house well,' say.
    'Don't leave [dirt] around for me.
    You must throw away the dirt.'
RC: Indeed.
CC: Thus 'along the mouth of the river,' say, 'you must place the dirt
    for me,' say.
RC: Indeed.
CC: Thus 'there the dirt people come to life.'
    The White Seer chanted.
RC: Indeed.[6]

Another type of history deals more generally with the formation
of Kuna society and culture, without referring to the exploits of particular culture heroes.

CC: Thus our ancestors came here before us I say.
    Thus it was I utter.
RC: Indeed.
CC: Thus our ancestors came before us I say.
    They came to the Kanela River.
RC: Indeed.
CC: Our ancestors came before us I say.
    They were great young men utter.
RC: Indeed.

In this type of chant, it is common to list various elements of
Kuna plant and animal ecology, in a series of parallel lines.

CC: Thus our ancestors came in the middle of fruit say utter.
RC: Indeed.
CC: Thus they came in the middle of banana roots I say they came
    in the middle of corn.
RC: Indeed.

It is also typical of this type of chant to mention the various roles
in Kuna society, each in a separate, parallel line. This process and
structure lengthen the chant considerably. It also reminds the audience of the unifying social function of both the 'gathering house' and
the chant itself.

CC: Thus in truth specialists in the way of the hot pepper [a chant
    used against high fever] came say.

Medicinal specialists came utter.

RC: Indeed.

CC: Thus in truth knowers of the way of birth [a chant used for difficulty in childbirth] came say.

Thus it was utter.

RC: Indeed.

CC: Thus knowers of the way of cocoa [a chant used against fever] came say utter.

RC: Indeed.

CC: Thus young great men came say.

Men with five hats [roles, abilities] came.

RC: Indeed.

CC: The makers of *inna* [the fermented drink consumed at girls' puberty rites] came say.

Thus it was utter.

RC: Indeed.

While this chant tends to stress continuity with the past, it also points to differences.

CC: Our ancestors had yellow skin they had long hair.

RC: Indeed.

CC: Our ancestors' hair came all the way down to their buttocks I say.

Thus it was utter.

RC: Indeed.

CC: Our ancestors cooked on stones I say utter.

RC: Indeed.

The ancestors serve as concrete models for ideal behavior today.

CC: Thus our ancestors strengthened their bodies say utter.

RC: Indeed.

CC: Thus our ancestors were hard workers say utter.

RC: Indeed.

CC: Thus our ancestors competed I say.

Thus it was utter.

RC: Indeed.

CC: Thus our ancestors killed eight peccaries at one time utter.

RC: Indeed.

CC: Thus our ancestors shot eight curassows at one time utter.

RC: Indeed.

CC: Thus our ancestors shared their food utter.

RC: Indeed.

CC:  God did not leave us this world to be stingy.
     Thus it was say.
RC:  Indeed.[7]

These chants provide continuity between past and present Kuna culture and society. They validate through history the present organization and structure of the Kuna world. And, by glorifying the exploits and abilities of the ancestors, they are an incentive to the audience in their performance of these same activities.

Another type of history is more local, dealing with a particular village, such as Mulatuppu or Sasartii—the other village on the island of Sasartii-Mulatuppu—its previous location on the mainland, and its great leaders of the past.

CC:  Thus.
     Thus there were two ancestors.
     There were two learned men.
RC:  Indeed.
CC:  Thus.
     These men governed us.
     These learned men.
RC:  Indeed.
CC:  Thus.
     We follow after them listening to their shadow.
     Say I utter.
RC:  Indeed.
CC:  A long time ago they were at the Sasartii River utter.
RC:  Indeed.
CC:  There were many great ancestors.
     Say I utter.
RC:  Indeed.
CC:  In the times of our ancestors then this river was not ours utter.
RC:  Indeed.
CC:  We are from the place where the sun rises.
     Say I utter.
RC:  Indeed.
CC:  There was Inanakinya [a great 'chief' of Sasartii-Mulatuppu in
     the past] I utter.
RC:  Indeed.
CC:  There was Inapakinya [the most often mentioned of the past
     Sasartii-Mulatuppu 'chiefs' and a regional leader].
     Say I utter.
RC:  Indeed.

cc:  Why did we come here?
     Say I utter.
rc:  Indeed.
cc:  The white men were punishing the Indians on the other side of
     the mountain.
rc:  Indeed.
cc:  Inanakinya came to the Sasartii River.
rc:  Indeed.

This chant ties the performer, Chief Pinikti of Sasartii, to renowned local traditionalists of the past and stresses his own line of prestige. This was very important to the now deceased Pinikti, who enjoyed his reputation as the leading traditionalist on the island of Sasartii-Mulatuppu. Since both Sasartii and Mulatuppu claim that their traditions derive from Inanakinya, this chant, which Pinikti performed with great frequency, emphasized his renown as senior to both villages on the island.

cc:  The shadow of Inanakinya's tongue.
     Say I utter.
rc:  Indeed.
cc:  Inanakinya chanted.
     At the Paya River.
rc:  Indeed.
cc:  Wipaillele [another renowned 'chief' of the past] learned this
     utter.
rc:  Indeed.
cc:  Inanakinya chanted.
     At the Tappalis River.
rc:  Indeed.

A final type of history presents Kuna versions of the Bible, the founding of the New World by Europeans, exploits of European and South American explorers, and relations between the Kuna and such figures as Christopher Columbus and Simón Bolívar.

cc:  Christopher Columbus mistreated our ancestors utter.
rc:  Indeed.
cc:  Christopher Columbus mistreated our grandmothers utter.
rc:  Indeed.

The sufferings of the past are stressed, sometimes quite graphically.

cc:  Our grandfathers were treated badly our grandmothers were
     treated badly.

RC:  Indeed.
CC:  Our grandmothers' bellies were cut open utter.
RC:  Indeed.

By directing attention to the Spaniards' cruelty, the chant stresses Kuna ethnic identity and solidarity as well as Kuna-Spaniard antagonism. This antagonism is still relevant today, the contemporary Spaniards being the Panamanians, who, like the Spaniards, are called *waka*.

CC:  The Indians arrived with great suffering at the Ukkurkana River.
RC:  Indeed.
CC:  The Spaniards discovered our fathers say.
RC:  Indeed.
CC:  Our ancestors arrived finally at the Ukkurkana River where they suffered.
RC:  Indeed.
CC:  The Spaniards treated our grandmothers badly treated our grandfathers badly say.
RC:  Indeed.[8]

There is a certain degree of mutual antagonism and competitive criticism between practitioners of each of these types of history. The specialists in truly Kuna mythology argue that non-Kuna history belongs in schools and in books, not in Kuna 'gatherings.' The other side claims that it is bringing historical and religious knowledge to the Kuna people by means of the 'gathering' chants. This latter tradition tends to be associated with the eastern portion of San Blas, the former with the western; there are overlaps, however.

Another type of chant is the report of a 'chief' to his village of some experience which he has had. This experience might be a dream he had the night before or a trip he has just returned from, typically for the purpose of chanting. Since a 'chief' often travels to other villages for visits, to chant and to listen to chants, he has something new to report when he returns. In fact, such chants are an important way to relate news—a 'chief' tells not only his personal experiences but other news he has learned as well. An example from the first chant in this chapter is illustrative. Muristo Pérez has just returned from a week-long interisland ritual 'gathering.' Such 'gatherings,' to be discussed in greater detail below, are attended by 'chiefs' representing various villages, each taking turns chanting during morning and evening sessions. In his chanted report to his own village, Chief Muristo describes his trip from Mulatuppu to the village where the interisland ritual 'gathering' is to be held. He focuses on minute details, of both a personal and a phenomenological nature.

CC: Now the day arrived to go to the meeting place of the village leaders see.
I was still in good health.

RC: Indeed.

CC: The day arrived see I say.
And I left see.

RC: Indeed.

CC: Thus it was dawn when I left I say hear.
Thus it was see.

RC: Indeed.

CC: Thus I arrived early at the village of Kanirtuppu I say hear.
I saw the brothers [men of the village] going off to the mainland [to work].

RC: Indeed.

CC: Thus I did not stop at Kaletonia I say see.
Thus I passed by.

RC: Indeed.

CC: In truth just as I arrived at the island of Ortup I met a Colombian boat I say.
And my friend [traveling companion] was carrying some coconuts along.

RC: Indeed.

CC: In truth he raised up [sold] six hundred coconuts I say hear.
Then I continued on.

RC: Indeed.

CC: At the village of Karetto there was another boat I say see.
Then we approached it.

RC: Indeed.

CC: In truth he raised up another six hundred coconuts see.
In truth I continued on again.

RC: Indeed.

CC: In truth I arrived at the village of Anachakkuna see say hear and the village leaders were already waiting for me see.
In truth see.

RC: Indeed.

CC: The village leaders said to me, 'just a while before you came a group left,' see say hear.
'They have probably gotten as far as the Pitto River,' say.

RC: Indeed.

CC: I did not wait I say hear and I quickly swallowed a cup of beverage see.
In truth then I left.

RC: Indeed.

CC: In truth I set foot on the beach I say I walked along the long beach say.
I moved my feet along say see.

RC: Indeed.

CC: Thus I did not stop to rest and then I crossed the Pitto River hear I say see.
And I passed it.

RC: Indeed.

CC: Thus a short walk later see I say I reached Waksakla I say hear.
In truth it was thus.

RC: Indeed.

CC: Thus there was also a woman and her two children walking along say walking along slowly.
The sun was setting on us.

RC: Indeed.

CC: Thus I saw my policeman waiting for me say hear.
He had moved ahead rapidly to wait for me.

RC: Indeed.

CC: The sun was setting on the leaders' village say see.
I saw some women at the mouth of the river.

RC: Indeed.

CC: In truth I saw that my friends the chiefs were already there before me bathing in the river say hear.
Already before me they had changed clothes see.

RC: Indeed.

CC: Thus then I quickly bathed also I say hear.
I arrived at the gathering house utter.

RC: Indeed.

CC: Then in truth the sisters [women of the village] were walking in the streets calling the visitors to come and eat hear.
The sun had set see.

RC: Indeed.

CC: Thus the brothers ['policemen'] were going about crying out, 'thus go to the gathering house to listen see.'
The policemen cried out.

RC: Indeed.

CC: Thus everyone entered see I say each of the friends took turns chanting hear.
Each one was heard for a while see.

RC: Indeed.

In this report, attention is paid to bathing, changing clothes, and the ritual drinking of beverages, all very important in the lives of the Kuna. Muristo reports on the chants of the other 'chiefs' who attended the 'gathering.'

CC: Thus friends now a little of what the chiefs chanted there I will tell you hear.
　　In truth you will hear their words.
RC: Indeed.
CC: In truth the message is not very long and a little of it I will tell you hear.
　　In truth I will tell you a little of their words.
RC: Indeed.
CC: In truth this story is difficult for me to grasp I say hear.
　　I keep forgetting it utter.
RC: Indeed.
CC: Afterward my friend Armando [the 'spokesman' who accompanied Muristo on the trip] will tell you the parts I forgot I say hear.
　　In truth thus it was utter.
RC: Indeed.[9]

The reference to Armando's filling in of missing aspects of the chant is a kind of joking modesty on Muristo's part. But, at the same time, Armando in his role of 'spokesman' is indeed a repeater, reformulator, translator, interpreter, corrector, and editor, all wrapped in one.[10]
　One of the chants Muristo reports on is in turn a report of a chant by another 'chief' of a dream he had. In this dream the improper behavior of still another 'chief,' from another village, is reported and criticized.

CC: Thus friend Juan Sittu [a 'chief'] chanted a story about Nele War Tummat [another 'chief'] say hear.
　　He saw stick dolls in his dream say see.
RC: Indeed.
CC: In truth there are parts I did not hear well and there are parts I heard well as I lay [in my hammock] I say hear.
　　Thus it was utter.
RC: Indeed.
CC: The friend [Juan Sittu] said,[11] ' " 'it is true the village of Armila [near the Colombian border] is a bad place see say hear.
　　It is a small village see utter.' " '
RC: Indeed.

CC: ' " 'In truth there is no organization among the chiefs see say hear.
They do not govern properly say.' " '

RC: Indeed.

CC: ' " 'Thus my friend the first chief is behaving improperly see say hear.
He keeps going into the houses of others [without asking permission] utter.' " '

RC: Indeed.

CC: ' " 'Thus when he goes to the river [where women bathe, wash clothes, and get fresh water] in truth he insults the women see.
That is the way this chief is,' say hear.
That is what the stick dolls said." '

RC: Indeed.

CC: 'In truth he stands up in the middle [of the 'gathering house'] and criticizes the children of the others.
This chief see utter.'

RC: Indeed.

CC: 'For this reason great hurricanes will come to you,' see say hear.
That is what the stick dolls said.

RC: Indeed.[12]

In this way, through the mediation of the reporting, retelling, and quoting process, Muristo, in a chant to his own village, is able to publicly but indirectly criticize 'chiefs' from other villages. By having others (both humans and spirits) relate the inadequate and improper behavior of other 'chiefs,' the Mulatuppu 'chief' calls attention to his own exemplary behavior. While Muristo had been a 'chief' for some time and is respected for his knowledge of tradition, at the time of the performance of this particular chant he had just recently been named head 'chief' of Mulatuppu. It was a period of considerable competitive infighting among the Mulatuppu 'chiefs,' and Muristo is able to use this report of his trip to strengthen his own image and to warn his fellow leaders of the dangers of not cooperating with him. As with other types of chanting, such reporting might come under criticism from practitioners of different types, especially when it is a question of reporting dreams, a topic considered by some individuals to be improper for 'gathering house' chanting, though not for other forms of discourse.

Another type or topic of 'gathering house' chanting is the *kwento* (story). 'Stories' can be told, in spoken form, at home or in the 'gathering house' as a form of verbal recreation and amusement. They are often humorous and are always told in humorous ways. In the 'gathering house,' 'stories' are typically told on days when people do not work because of a visiting 'chief' or a festival of some sort. There is constant activity in the 'gathering house,' and the telling of 'stories' is part of a complex of verbal behavior which occurs on these occasions. 'Stories' can also be chanted, such chanting being more common in the eastern portion of San Blas than in the western portion.[13] When 'stories' are chanted by 'chiefs,' the purpose is pleasure, but there is also a serious moral which both 'chiefs' and 'chief's spokesmen' can develop. There are many 'stories,' including animal trickster motifs such as those found in many American Indian societies—thus the episodes of agouti and his uncle the jaguar in which the nephew causes the uncle to fall for a number of tricks. There are 'stories' about the animals of the sea as well as about animals acquired since contact with Europeans, such as chickens. There are also 'stories' about human beings and relations among them.

An interesting illustration is *kaa kwento* (the story of the hot pepper), which describes how a young boy, asked by an old woman to care for her plum tree, is buried alive by her when the plum tree fails to produce fruit. The boy is later discovered by his sister and parents because of a hot pepper plant which grows on the spot where he is buried. The parents, after hearing the boy call from beneath the pepper plant, dig him out of the ground. The boy then punishes the old woman by throwing her into the place of eternal burning. When chanted, 'the story of the hot pepper' is flexibly adapted and, especially, interpreted as relevant to current issues in Kuna life. It is interpreted at the most general level as having to do with the treatment of people, at a more particular level with the treatment of children, and at the most particular level with the treatment of babies at birth, especially when they have defects. In this last interpretation, the old woman represents a midwife and the boy represents a baby. A clever 'chief' can perform the 'story' for amusement and draw one or several moralistic interpretations at the same time.[14]

Another theme or topic for chants and their subsequent interpretations by 'spokesmen' is a reflexive and metacommunicative description of the event itself as it occurs—the setting, the participants, the topic, and the purpose of 'gathering house' chanting. Here is the opening interpretation by a Mulatuppu 'spokesman' of the chant of a 'chief' who is visiting from another village.[15]

Now.
For a while thus.
We are seated listening a bit to you see.

Now thus, today thus, for a while then you are chanting a bit for us
you don't hear say.
Now thus we have all been called.
All of us thus have arrived at the listening house, see say.
Now thus, in order to listen again a bit to the way of God, we have
been called see.
Now thus everyone has really entered you don't hear say.
Now thus early thus.
The chief began to chant for us you don't hear say.

The 'spokesman' continues this introduction to his interpretation
of the chant by listing by social role, as did the 'chief,' all the individuals and groups present or potentially present at the event, in an order which reflects, in part, their relative ranking in Kuna society.

Thus now thus 'you have entered here with me,' the chief says to us
see.
'The people with names [named roles, important individuals] thus.
Have entered this house,' see say.
'All the chiefs thus really arrived.
All the spokesmen see.'
The chief informs us see.
'Thus all the policemen,' see say.
'All the hot pepper specialists thus really have entered.
Into this house,' you don't hear say see.
Thus then.
'The medicinal specialists thus really have arrived,' see say.
'To God's listening house,' you don't hear say see.
'God thus left us this listening house.
So that we may speak his name,' you don't hear say you don't hear
say.
'"One day thus you will call a bit thus to me."
God called,' see say.
'The great mother called,' you don't hear say say see.
'God thus in this house thus.
Left us thus good benches.
To these benches we still come,' he says to us you don't hear say.
Now thus 'the women have entered.
You who have names thus have entered here with me.'
The chief informs us you don't hear say.
Now thus.

'One by one you entered with me thus.

Those who know how to make hammocks have arrived,' see say.

'Those who know how to make molas thus have arrived.

To this house,' you don't hear say see.

Now thus 'those who string beads have arrived,' see say.

'The ritual haircutters have arrived, the ritual water carriers have arrived.'

The chief informs us see.

'All those thus with names,' you don't hear say say see.

'For this reason thus, to the listening house now we have come,' he says you don't hear say.

Now thus, 'which *ikar* shall I open [chant] for you?' the chief informs us you don't hear say.[16]

Such reflexive chanting or speaking typically serves as an introduction and a conclusion to one of the topics or themes listed above. However, it is also possible for a reflexive topic to be expanded and developed metaphorically into the central theme of an entire chant.

Still another topic for chanting is the *uanaet* (counsel), which is offered by 'chiefs' from time to time to the community at large or to various members of the community, for example, women, children, or ritual specialists. Such direct 'counsel' is often spoken rather than chanted, but it might be chanted as well.

The various topics and themes of chanting are not mutually exclusive within a single evening. Although one of the topics or themes is typically the central motif of a chant, several others can also be woven in as introductory, concluding, or linking elements.

### The Purpose of Chanting

What ties the different types and topics of 'gathering house' chanting together? The primary and quite explicit purpose of Kuna 'gatherings,' especially those attended by men and women together, is social control and social cohesion. Social control and social cohesion occur at various levels. At the most immediate and direct level, a chant, such as a 'counsel,' is aimed at particular persons, perhaps at the community at large, and advocates an appropriate mode of behavior—concerning, for example, the raising of children, the curing of disease, or the direction of puberty rites. Mythical and historical chants are models of appropriate behavior in that they provide examples from the past of both proper and improper actions. At the same time they remind and inform the audience of their own historical and religious heritage. Similarly, reports, such as that of Chief Muristo above, point out good and bad, proper and improper behavior of 'chiefs' or of others and are thus verbal instruments of social control. And 'stories' are also transformed into lessons in living by the chants of the 'chiefs.'

In all this it is important to recognize and stress the latitude a Kuna 'chief' has in performing his chant. He does not have a fixed text which he recites line by line. Rather, he begins with a basic idea, a basic theme, whether this be a myth, an experience, a 'story,' or a series of metaphors; he adapts it and transforms it to fit the situation at hand or the point he is trying to make. In this sense his power is a power of words. His popularity and success reside in his ability to develop moral positions, argue for modes of behavior, and espouse particular points of view through creative, innovative, and often indirect language.

There are social control and especially social cohesion in the very structure of the 'gathering'—where men and women, young and old, political leaders and ordinary villagers all sit together for hours at a time and listen to their cultural traditions being publicly performed. Within this structure, there is an interesting interplay between individual creativity and group solidarity. Each 'chief' has a unique repertoire of knowledge and experience to draw on for his chants. He performs in an esoteric language, phonologically, syntactically, semantically, and lexically distinct from colloquial Kuna. And he personally exploits and develops this language in the form of creative metaphors. This means that, while the audience may follow the story in its general outline, details might be obscure. And in the case of the truly great 'chiefs,' the great knowers and manipulators of tradition and of the 'gathering house' language, especially its metaphorical and allusive aspects, obscurity may outweigh clarity.

At the same time, since these chants are intended for social control and cohesion by means of the use of tradition, experience, and metaphor as lessons and models for proper behavior for the group at large, it is crucial that the audience understand every detail. Thus the role of 'chief's spokesman': the translator and interpreter. In his speech, following the chant, the 'spokesman' explains its message to the audience from the general to the particular. To the best of his ability, he translates and explains every word, every metaphor. Sometimes he is in doubt about certain points, though he tries not to show it. The more eloquent the 'chief,' the more developed and obscure his metaphors, the harder the task of the 'spokesman.' In exceptional cases, two 'spokesmen' are needed to explain the chant of a single 'chief.'[17]

## Visiting 'Chiefs'

The arrival of a visiting 'chief' is a special event.[18] On the island of Mulatuppu, when a 'chief' arrives from another village, the Panamanian flag is raised on the flagpole in front of the 'gathering house.' It remains there during his visit. The 'chief' and his entourage, typically consisting of his wife, his 'spokesman,' and one of his 'policemen,' proceed directly to the 'gathering house' on their arrival. From there they are taken by a Mulatuppu 'policeman' to someone's house, where they bathe in order to wash off the salty water of the sea. Then they return to the 'gathering house,' where the visiting 'chief' and one of the host village 'chiefs,' sitting beside one another in hammocks, perform *arkan kae* (literally handshake), the ritual greeting.

Like all 'gathering house' chanting, *arkan kae* is in the 'chief language.' And, also like 'gathering house' chanting, it is in the form of a ritualized dialogue between two 'chiefs.' But in *arkan kae* the 'chiefs' take turns. First the visiting 'chief' chants and his host serves as responder, chanting *teki* (indeed) after each verse. Then they switch. And finally they switch once again. The topic is that common to all Kuna extended greetings—the state of health of the 'chief,' his family, and his village, the route he has taken to arrive in the host village, the places and people he has seen along the way— all presented in the minutest detail. Here is the opening portion of the ritual greeting chanted by a visiting 'chief' from the village of Niatuppu to a host 'chief' from Mulatuppu. Health, sickness, and disease receive considerable attention.

cc: Thus God left much disease.
    Among us.
    All over utter.
rc: Indeed.
cc: Then bad days.
    Some bad months.
    We have had in my island village.
    Utter.
rc: Indeed.
cc: Thus God said see.
    'Children in this world.
    I have left diseases for you,' utter.
rc: Indeed.
cc: Thus see.
    God left in this mountain [world] with all its levels.
    All kinds of disease.
    God left in this world utter.

RC: Indeed.
CC: Thus God see.
In this world left small animals [that eat coconuts] see.
God left many kinds of disease in this world.
RC: Indeed.
CC: 'For this reason in this world see.
You will not pass through without sickness.'
God said utter.
RC: Indeed.

The visiting 'chief' goes on to describe the details of his trip, which, in addition to his state of health, is the primary theme of this chanted ritual greeting.

CC: Then see.
Of the brothers' entering [that there would be an interisland ritual 'gathering'] see here.
Indeed I learned utter.
RC: Indeed.
CC: Thus then.
I changed heart [decided] hear.
And came here see utter.
RC: Indeed.
CC: Thus among good friends.
I will spend some time see.
I think utter.
RC: Indeed.
CC: Thus then see.
I will feel good thus see utter.
RC: Indeed.
CC: Then see.
Then I left my superiors utter.
RC: Indeed.
CC: Then I was ready see.
I entered the boat see utter.
RC: Indeed.
CC: Thus then I stood up [announced in the 'gathering house'].
To my people I said, 'I myself [would attend],' utter.
RC: Indeed.
CC: Thus 'it is good,' they said see.
That is what happened see utter.
RC: Indeed.
CC: Now then from my stronghold [village] see.
I separated myself from my superiors utter.

RC: Indeed.
CC: Thus everyone is in good health see.
    My superiors are thus utter.
RC: Indeed.
CC: Thus see my spokesmen are in good health.
    In my village utter.
RC: Indeed.
CC: Thus all my policemen are in good health.
    In my village see utter.
RC: Indeed.
CC: Thus see my aunts [women] are in good health.
    In my land utter.
RC: Indeed.
CC: Thus see a little little bit.
    The playful ones [children] do have some sickness in my village
        utter.
RC: Indeed.
CC: Thus the grandfathers [older men] see.
    Have some sickness such as colds utter.
RC: Indeed.
CC: Thus see there are no other problems see.
    That is how it is see utter.
RC: Indeed.
CC: Now see.
    I left my stronghold of Niatuppu at noon utter.
RC: Indeed.
CC: Thus as God see.
    Left many islands see.
    I saw them as I came utter.
RC: Indeed.
CC: As God see.
    Left many river throats [mouths] for our people I saw them
        utter.
RC: Indeed.
CC: Thus God also.
    Left the waves [sea] and I saw them as I came utter.
RC: Indeed.
CC: Thus as the sun set see.
    I rested at the earth [village] of Ailikantii see utter.
RC: Indeed.
CC: Then see.
    Indeed at dawn hear I continued my trip utter.
RC: Indeed.

cc: Thus then I have sweated [come] out from my stronghold utter.
rc: Indeed.
cc: Then little by little our boat stopping see.
    In every village see utter.
rc: Indeed.
cc: Thus see there was thunder and lightning.
    As we arrived at this stronghold see utter.
rc: Indeed.
cc: Now the captain of the boat said to me.
    'Here we will rest and continue our trip tomorrow,' utter.
rc: Indeed.
cc: Thus 'it is a good idea,' I said to him see utter.
rc: Indeed.
cc: Thus that is how it has been see utter.
rc: Indeed.
cc: Thus like that.
    Say see you hear.
rc: Thus I hear you too.[19]

The two 'chiefs' then switch roles, and the host 'chief' proceeds to chant about his health and that of his village and the activities they have been involved in. There is no official audience for this ritual greeting, as there is for regular 'gathering house' chanting. During the performance some men enter the 'gathering house' and sit down. They might listen. But they talk to each other as well, sometimes in rather loud voices, and they joke among themselves and with the entourage of the visiting 'chief.' In fact, at times the chanting 'chiefs' must make an effort to pay attention to their own ritual greeting rather than focus on the surrounding informal greetings, conversations, and joking talk.

Women from the host village who have been assigned this task come to the 'gathering house' with buckets of beverages—coffee, cocoa, Kool-Aid, matunnu (made from ripe bananas, coconut, cacao, and sugar), or sweet corn juice. These are passed around to chanters and onlookers alike as the beginning of the special drinking and eating patterns that will be characteristic of the visit of the 'chief' and his entourage. When the chanting of the ritual greeting is finished, there is no translation or interpretation—as there is no official audience no interpretation is needed, since the two 'chiefs' share the ritual language of the greeting. And the greeting is intended for no one else but them. After this, the 'chief' and his entourage go off to bathe and eat in the home of a friend or a designated host.

Since the purpose of his visit is to chant, the 'chief' chants on almost every evening of his stay and sometimes in the morning as well—because he is a guest and does not work, he is available for morning chanting. These morning sessions are understood as being especially for women, but they are also attended by men—several 'chiefs,' 'spokesmen,' and 'policemen,' as well as some older men who do not go to work. As in the evening, the women bring their mola baskets and sit cutting and sewing molas. The evening 'gathering' at which a visiting 'chief' chants follows the same pattern as that described above for usual evening chanting, except that certain elements combine to make it even more special. There is an effort to get the greatest possible attendance; this occurs naturally as well, since the chant of a visiting 'chief' is more interesting, bringing news, a different story or myth, and a renowned performer with a unique style. Women choose an even nicer mola than usual and wear all their jewelry. Often, during or after the chanting, beverages are served to the entire 'gathering' by 'policemen.' These same 'policemen' make an even greater effort than usual to make sure that members of the audience pay attention and do not fall asleep.

## Interisland Ritual 'Gatherings'

The custom of 'chiefs' visiting other islands is formalized in interisland 'gatherings.' For the purpose of such 'gatherings' nine or ten villages, usually neighboring, are grouped together. At regular intervals, each village in the ritual group serves as host to all the others, and a representative 'chief,' 'spokesman,' and 'policeman' from each village gather together. This event lasts five or six days, during which each of the 'chiefs' will chant.

During the day of the opening of the 'gathering,' the 'chiefs' and their entourages arrive. They proceed to the 'gathering house,' where the 'chiefs' will sleep in the many hammocks strung up in the center for this purpose—they will spend much of their time sitting and lying in these hammocks. The entire host village is mobilized for the event. Members of the visiting entourages are housed with friends and relatives. Much food and many beverages have been prepared, and the guests are served both in ample quantities during their entire stay. The chanting begins in the evening about 7:00 P.M. and lasts well beyond midnight. Every morning and evening there is a session; the morning sessions are mainly for women, but some men attend as well. The afternoons are designated for rest and relaxation. There is a great deal of eating, with 'chiefs' and their entourages going from home to home to eat meal after meal. These individuals have to acquire the art of not eating too much at a time so that they always have room for a little more at the next home they are invited to. People sit around the 'gathering house,' talking, joking, and rest-ing. They also visit the homes of friends and relatives, in order to pass the time of day or to tend to any business they have in common.

During the interisland 'gathering,' each of the chanting sessions follows the same basic pattern described above for regular evening chanting, with more elaboration. During each session, two different 'chiefs' chant. And, following each chant, there are usually two dif-ferent 'spokesmen' who rise and interpret, one after the other; these 'spokesmen' are not from the same village as the 'chief' whose chant they interpret. The need for two 'spokesmen' to interpret a single 'chief' is an indication of the especially complex, esoteric nature of these chants. But there is also a competitive, almost tournamentlike atmosphere during the 'gathering,' in which 'chiefs' and 'spokes-men' perform one after the other, striving to demonstrate their own abilities and implicitly challenging others to either interpret their performance or do better. It is in the context of such 'gatherings' that 'chiefs' and their 'spokesmen' acquire prestige and renown. At the same time, the interisland ritual 'gatherings' are occasions for the sharing of knowledge and experience, excellent settings for learning Kuna traditions as well as news to bring back home.

The interisland 'gathering' is the most ritualized, the most formal, the most elaborate of the Kuna 'gatherings' for the purpose of chant-ing. It is the most heavily attended. The 'policemen' are most active in keeping people from sleeping, often screaming out their warnings with great frequency and flair. The women wear their most beautiful molas and their best jewelry. 'Policemen' pass through the 'gather-ing house' serving beverages to performers and audience.

It is during the interisland 'gathering' that new 'chiefs' and other village political leaders are inaugurated. This is done in the form of a 'counsel' to the new official by the elected 'chief' of the 'gathering.' It usually occurs during the first evening session. The host village has already chosen its new leaders, but these are not publicly or of-ficially known to anyone but a few of the village political leaders. The individual, 'chief' or 'spokesman,' is suddenly grabbed by 'po-licemen' and brought, together with his wife, to the center of the 'gathering house,' where they are made to sit on a small bench in front of the hammocks of the 'chiefs.' The individuals in question pretend that they are blind. The head 'chief' of the 'gathering' then proceeds to perform the 'counsel,' which is spoken or chanted.

This 'counsel' consists of a series of metaphors dealing with 'chiefs,' their duties, and appropriate behavior. These metaphors are developed and elaborated to fit the situation. Thus a quite common set of metaphors for village political officials involves a description of a Kuna house in terms of poles and walls, in which the center pole is the 'chief,' the second largest poles are the 'spokesmen,' the poles along the side walls are the 'policemen,' and the side walls are the nonofficials who nonetheless talk a lot at 'gatherings.' The idea is that, while the strongest and largest pole supports the house, the others are needed as well to aid in the task.[20]

Now if, as is fairly frequent, the new 'chief' had once been a 'chief' but was removed from office for some misdeed, the metaphors are manipulated in order to fit the case. Thus an advising 'chief,' in his 'counsel,' might describe the poles of a house and point out that sometimes the main pole becomes rotten and has to be taken down. The rotten part is cut away and the pole is left to lie a while in order to make sure that all the rot has been successfully removed. Then this same pole is once again available for use. These metaphors are often developed in very individual and personal ways. Here, Chief Muristo Pérez of Mulatuppu, in a spoken 'counsel,' advises his own younger brother, who has just been named 'chief' of Sasartii.

Well one pole then.
We are about to plant see.
And if we do not plant it well.
If we plant one that has holes say.
In one year then the small bug people will be chanting within the
    hole and you will hear them you don't hear.
Poisonous spiders will be chanting and you will hear them.
Cockroaches will be chanting and you will hear them see say.
The scorpion, then, the big scorpion will be chanting.
And from his hole you will hear him see say.
The sisters [women] will be frightened see.
The time will come then to take it [the pole] out you don't hear.
That is why the elders say see.
'A good pole then must be planted, without holes and without
    splits.'[21]

During the interisland 'gathering,' every morning when they awake, the 'chiefs'—who have been sleeping next to one another all night long in hammocks—ritually greet one another with *arkan kae*. Simultaneously adjacent pairs of 'chiefs' chant this ritual greeting. The result is a spectacular overlapping fugue of chanting. Each 'chief' recounts to his neighbor how he spent the night, how he feels, and what dreams he has had.

The interisland ritual 'gathering' is in every way a magnification and intensification of the ordinary Kuna 'gatherings,' held on alternate evenings, when 'chiefs' chant to their villages. In interisland 'gatherings' there are more 'chiefs' and a larger audience; there are more and longer chants and interpretations; there are more formalization, ritualization, and spectacle at all levels.

## When 'Chiefs' Speak

While at 'gatherings' attended by men and women it is most common for a 'chief' to chant, there are occasions when he will *sunmakke* (speak) rather than *namakke* (chant). He does so standing beside his hammock and using the formal *tule kaya* (everyday Kuna) speechmaking style, though including the metaphors characteristic of 'chief language.' His speech is followed by an interpretation by a 'spokesman' or by a series of similar speeches by other 'chiefs' as well as 'spokesmen.'

There are various reasons why a 'chief' will speak rather than chant. One has to do with the structure of 'gathering house' chanting as a ritual dialogue between two 'chiefs.' If, as happens more often in smaller villages, there is no second 'chief' to serve as responder, because other 'chiefs' are ill or are visiting elsewhere, it is not formally possible for chanting to occur, and the one 'chief' present must speak. Another reason why a 'chief' will speak rather than chant is simply that he chooses to do so. This is especially the case in certain types of 'counsel.' Thus, when counseling married couples or particular members of the community or the community at large, a 'chief' will most probably speak. This may be because there are no established chants for these topics as there are, for example, for mythical history. The 'counsel' given at an interisland ritual 'gathering' to a new 'chief' or 'chief's spokesman' and his wife may be spoken or chanted; it is usually spoken.[22]

It is interesting to speculate upon why a 'chief' chooses to speak a 'counsel' rather than chant it. In chanting, a 'chief' does not address the community directly. Rather, he ritually converses with another 'chief' in front of the community as audience and secondary addressees. In speaking, on the other hand, he directly addresses either particular individuals, such as a new 'chief,' a married couple, or a curing specialist, or the village at large. The spoken pattern is then a more direct form of communicative counsel than is a ritual chant. It is performed in response to some misdeed, or because someone has achieved a new position in life, or because someone is going on a trip to study or to represent the village.

Finally, 'chiefs' will speak rather than chant when for some reason evil spirits are circulating in the village and, as a result, the village is susceptible to disease and misfortune. At such times, chanting becomes inappropriate and is replaced by speaking (see chapter 7).

## Men's 'Gatherings': Village Affairs, Reports, and Relaxation

On evenings when 'chiefs' do not chant, women stay home and only men assemble in the 'gathering house.' Not all the men necessarily attend—attendance depends in large part on the issues being discussed or debated. When there is an extremely lively issue, the 'gathering house' is packed with men, and women stand and listen outside, peeping in through the doors and bamboo walls.

Many topics are discussed at men's talking 'gatherings.' Some of these have already been mentioned as topics which might be dealt with at chanting 'gatherings,' before the chanting begins. Thus, there is ordinary, rather mechanical business, economic in nature, which affects the village at large—for example, the calling out of names of individuals who will work the next day on the communal coconut or banana farms or who owe money for particular projects. There might also be discussion of village-wide ventures. In Mulatuppu, several years ago, there was much discussion in the 'gathering house' concerning whether or not to purchase a large boat for the village. Several of the larger islands of the San Blas possess boats which travel to Colón and throughout San Blas, carrying passengers and cargo and bringing income to the villages which own them. Mulatuppu has had particularly bad luck with boat ventures, which have therefore been the subject of much heated debate in the 'gathering house.' There is also frequent discussion concerning cooperation with the Panamanian government or missionary organizations with regard to such matters as schools, hospitals, and clinics.

A most common and time-consuming topic for discussion at men's 'gatherings' concerns various types of wrongdoing, usually involving stealing but at times involving violent arguments, fighting, or marital and sexual misconduct. In these cases, the defendant is called before the 'gathering' and sits on a small stool in front of the first 'chief' of the village. They are expected to defend themselves and do so in a long speech, in the 'gathering house' speechmaking style. Eloquence, fluidity, and creativity are highly valued in these speeches and count in the ultimate evaluation. Witnesses for and against the defendant also speak. Consensus is reached by the 'gathering,' not by any vote but rather when, after discussion on all sides, the 'chief' senses a group feeling. He expresses this and sums it up in the form of a 'counsel' to the wrongdoer. This is frequently interpreted afterward by one or more 'chief's spokesmen.' The 'chief' also sets a punishment. In the past, guilty individuals were slapped with stinging nettle on various parts of the body by 'policemen.' Now it is more common for them to be fined—either to perform some duty for the village, such as bringing a certain amount of sand or stones from the mainland to the island for various uses, or to pay a certain sum of money to the village.

Cases involving sexual misconduct are particularly lively and heated. Several years ago in Mulatuppu, a man was accused of sexually molesting a young girl. Since he had a reputation for such behavior, he was generally assumed to be guilty. There was a long discussion, including the performance of severe, reprimanding 'counsels.' Late in the evening, a large fine was levied and the guilty individual was required to go immediately to his house and bring the money back. He did so, publicly gave it to the village, and the 'gathering' ended.

Discussions of misconduct involving village leaders, such as 'chiefs,' are most dramatic. Long and heated arguments are brought to bear, especially with regard to possible removal from office. Compromise solutions result from public discussion. In 1971, a 'chief' of Sasartii, at that time a separate village from Mulatuppu although both are located on the same small island, traveled to a village at the other end of San Blas for a meeting of many 'chiefs' and other political leaders. Shortly after his return, a letter, written in Spanish, was sent to all the villages of San Blas to be read aloud in the 'gathering houses.' The letter accused the Sasartii 'chief,' while he was attending the meeting, of molesting a young girl who was sleeping in a hammock adjacent to his in his host's house; it demanded that he be removed from office. The men of Sasartii met until two o'clock the next morning to decide what to do. The 'chief' defended himself by claiming that he had eaten much seafood and could not control himself. This was not sufficient for his opponents, who insisted that he be removed from office. His defenders pointed to his extensive knowledge of Kuna history and tradition. The long speeches were listened to by the packed 'gathering' as well as by men from Mulatuppu and women from both Sasartii and Mulatuppu, standing outside and peeking in through the doors and walls. Finally, it was decided that the 'chief' would be removed from office and no longer permitted to enter the 'gathering house.' But his 'spokesman' and student, who was named the new first 'chief' of Sasartii, insisted on the right to continue to study with his old teacher, in the privacy of his house. Several years later, the deposed 'chief' died. His photograph now hangs in the Sasartii 'gathering house,' alongside those of other renowned deceased 'chiefs,' and his anniversary is ceremonially celebrated.

If a crime has been committed and the guilty party is not known, there will be a long discussion in the 'gathering house' in order to try to solve the case. At times, especially for serious crimes, such as the theft of coconuts or money, a *nele* (seer) will be called in, perhaps even from another village. The 'seer' reports his or her findings, revealed by spirits, to the 'gathering.' The long discussions of such cases may last several days and are always reserved for evening 'gatherings,' either before chanting, if there is to be chanting, or during a men's talking 'gathering.'

Another topic for men's 'gatherings' are reports of various kinds—by those who have worked in the Canal Zone, Panama City, or elsewhere; by students or teachers who have made trips; by ritual specialists who have traveled to other villages in order to acquire more knowledge; or by any individual who has had an unusual experience during the day. What is interesting about such reports is that their purpose is not solely to provide news to the community, though this is part of it. Frequently, many members of the community, especially family and friends of the news bearer, already know the news and have spread it during the day through conversation. Rather, the 'gathering house' report is a public performance of this news for the benefit of the assembled group, including the 'chiefs' and other village leaders. As in all 'gathering house' speaking, verbal artistry is expected and appreciated. Such reports are long, involved, and often suspenseful and humorous. The narrators hold the attention of their listeners even though the facts may already be known in considerable detail. Two examples of such reports are illustrative.

In 1970, Olowitinappi, a 'medicinal specialist' and '*ikar* knower,' was awarded a scholarship by the village of Mulatuppu to travel to an interior jungle village along the Río Bayano in order to learn snakebite medicine and curing. This was very important, since Mulatuppu, a densely populated island, had no renowned snakebite specialist at the time. On his return to Mulatuppu, Olowitinappi came to an evening men's 'gathering' and reported on his trip. By means of his long spoken report, he publicly announces that he too can now be called on as a snakebite specialist, as a curer as well as a teacher of others. Through the speech, he validates himself and gains prestige and recognition. Thus the act of having learned snakebite medicine, while important, is not sufficient in itself—it is essential for Olowitinappi to publicly inform his community of the experiences he has had, the type of medicine he has learned, and how much he will charge patients and students. This particular speech was well received. The report contains a description of Olowitinappi's travels, including a stop in Panama City. The audience expects and enjoys hearing about minute details, which involve direct quotations of conversations.

When I arrived in Panama City, I went to the bank to take out some
    money I had been saving.
I took out thirty dollars.
I wanted to have some eyeglasses.
'Twenty-six dollars and thirty cents,' they say.
Then they took the money out for me.
'You can get them in three days,' they say.
Friend Adriano [a man from Mulatuppu who happened to be in Pan-
    ama City at the same time] said to me.
'As you choose,' he says.
'If you want to go now,' he says.
'After you leave I will go and get them for you,' he says.
I gave him all the papers.
I paid everything.

The actual learning process is described in considerable detail, alternating understatement and exaggeration. Conversations between Olowitinappi and his teacher are quoted.

Well the friend [teacher] began to teach me, I see.
'First you will learn the magic secret,' he says.
'That is what I will teach you first, see,' he says.
'Fifteen dollars,' I will pay for it, see say.
'All right,' I say to him.
Then I paid.
Well thus at first [what he told me] I did not understand.
I could not catch it.
I did not know what to do.
I was ashamed not to be able to do it.
I did not understand, not even a little bit.
Well 'keep on, keep on, keep on,' he says.
Secretly he was speaking.
I was surrounded with shame.
Like little kids.
As if I did not know how to pronounce the words.
Then the next day when we woke up.
'Today we won't leave the house,' he says.
'All day we will stay in the house,' he says.

Attention is given to financial aspects of the endeavor, always important but particularly significant in this case, since Olowitinappi's village is paying for his training.

Well one day as we were clearing his banana farm.
There, as we were talking.
'This [the snake's] secret incantation will cost three dollars,' he says.
I paid him again.
'The other one is his boat [part of the secret incantation],' he says.
I paid him again.
The entire expense had reached thirty dollars.
When I left here I bought some things.
Red cloth.
Pencils.
Notebooks.
Such purchases.
All, all small, small expenses.
I also paid for the outboard motor [for the trip down the river to the village] three dollars.
These things together came to ten dollars.
The total of everything was thirty dollars.
'But that is what I came for,' I say to him, 'why should I save the money?'

In the words of his renowned teacher, Olowitinappi announces how much he will charge his own students and patients.

'Therefore then when you have a student you will teach him the same.'
He says to me.
'And the student that you get, he will help you only [will not pay money] see say.
When you have something that is a little hard see say.
When you clear a banana farm,' he says.
'Or a coconut farm,' he says.
'Whatever thing you have to do,' he says.
'Everything see say.
As for people from other islands [villages],' he says.
'The money that you spent [here].
The money you will spend, they will give you see say.
Therefore friend do not raise the price see say.
There are people then who raise the price very high see say.
As if their teacher had told them to do so see.'
The friend [teacher] counseled me.

Finally, Olowitinappi reports how and why his teacher instructed him to make this speech and shows the 'gathering' a letter sent by the teacher, validating the training and serving as a diploma.

'Therefore now the *ikar* [chants plus knowledge] you came here to learn, it is a good *ikar* see say.
Therefore your village will think very highly of you you don't hear say,' he says.
'Therefore you must do well see,' he says to me.
'Therefore thus then [when you arrive home] you must say all this well to your village see.
Now therefore so that no one contests you now I am also sending this letter for you see,' he says.
'Now since you do not know how to write.
You did not write it yourself, I say.
They cannot accuse you of that.'
He says to me.[23]

The second illustration involves a man from Mulatuppu, Arango López, who, while out fishing one day with his wife, came upon an old hulk of a boat floating about and brought it back home. Of course, he was seen by many people and talked to them, so his discovery was well known by evening. Nonetheless, that evening in the 'gathering house,' after the usual business, cries of 'López' went out—and sure enough López was there. He rose and, in a long, dramatic, and humorous way, recounted the incident—how he found the boat and brought it back, whom he thought it might have belonged to, what he would do to get it into proper shape, and whom he might sell it to. López is an excellent storyteller and the audience loved his performance. The men assembled in the 'gathering house' roared with laughter throughout.

Humor is extremely difficult to translate from one language to another. A significant aspect of Kuna humor is that it always occurs intimately bound together with serious purposes and contexts— with such serious matters as hosting a visiting 'chief' or reporting news at a men's meeting, as is the case with López' narrative. The alternation of fast and slow speech and loud and soft speech is important, as are the dramatic moments of silence between spoken lines. Sounds of noises, actions, and voices are imitated. As in all forms of Kuna discourse, conversations are quoted directly, including minute and circumstantial particulars of questions, answers, requests, and commands. Experiences are described in great, exaggerated, and repetitive detail. While not funny in themselves, the detailed verbal descriptions of personal experience actualize for Kuna audiences the humorous potential inherent in the banal foibles and pratfalls of everyday life.

First López sets the scene.

We woke up early early in the morning.
Then we left early.
There was no wind you see.
So we went paddling.
On the high sea the wind came up and we raised our sail.

He describes his struggle with a fish.

One came to me, ah.
I caught a big one I see.
I could feel it.
I said to her [my wife], 'this is jackfish see,' I said to her.
'I'm not going to leave it,' I said to her.
'This one,' I said to her.
'This boy is wild.'

Then he discovers and inspects the empty boat on the high, rough sea and tries to bring it along with his own. He describes how he and his wife are almost killed.

My wife got carried away, had the sea been rougher she would have been knocked against the rocks.
Since she could not reach me I could not see her, ah.
Ready swoosh.
I jumped into the water.

He describes his great fear as both his own boat and the boat he is trying to bring with him fill with water.

I kept bailing out water do you hear?
I cannot anymore.
I could not anymore.
I said to my wife, 'it's your turn, my arm can't anymore see.'
I said to her.

Finally the wind and sea calmed down, and López and his wife were out of personal danger. But then it was difficult to bring the two boats back together.

Then I tied it.
Then I tied it tightly on top.
Now we started to move.
Barely.
My boat was full of wood.
And I was pulling the other one.
So we came slowly.

Behind came the other one.
We came slowly.
And there was no wind.
My wife was seated paddling, paddling, I saw her behind me as we
    moved along.
'Night is coming,' I said to her.
'We won't get there, see.'
Already the sun had set.
'I'll leave you here,' I said to her.
'You alone a little bit,' I said to her.
'Then I'll send you our son,' I said to her, 'in the other boat, to get
    you,' I said to her.
'Thus I'll take the poles back.
I'll leave you here,' I said to her.
'Yes,' she says.

López describes the boat, finally obtained by his and his wife's efforts.

It is a smooth well-made boat.
It is a good boat.
Because it is covered with metal.
The metal is all loose.
On top now, and also below.
Because, it hit against the rocks.

He finishes his very long speech by describing what he will do to the
boat.

I'll put wood on top and then I'll hammer it on to repair it.
Thus I got a boat, a boat for nothing I got a boat.[24]

It is noteworthy that Arango López is not an active participant in
the Mulatuppu 'gathering house,' not an officially recognized leader,
not publicly involved in Kuna verbal life. But, when called upon to
report on his experience of the day, he does so at great length and
with much verve and exuberance, weaving together seriousness and
humor and demonstrating the verbal ability characteristic of most
Kuna men, women, and children. Both Olowitinappi's and López'
reports are characterized by the fine-grained attention to detail—
including geographical, conversational, and financial matters—that
is a feature of all Kuna 'gathering house' discourse.

Finally, evening 'gatherings' are a place for verbal relaxation. Playful joking is common, 'stories' of all kinds are told, and conversation
abounds. Such discourse always has the 'chiefs' at the center and is
always directed toward and through them, with 'spokesmen' and
others commenting as well.

## The 'Gathering House' as Informal Meeting Place

The chanting and speaking of 'chiefs' and 'spokesmen,' the performance of myths, legends, and history, and the use of poetic, especially figurative and metaphorical, language are the most marked
features of the Kuna 'gathering house.' They will be referred to here
as 'gathering house' tradition, in contrast to the two other primary
ritual verbal traditions, those associated with medicinal curing and
magical control (chapter 4) and with girls' puberty rites (chapter 5).
But the 'gathering house' is also an informal meeting place. From
the time it is opened it attracts large or small groups of people. Every
afternoon, after returning from work in the jungle or from fishing,
having bathed, changed clothes, eaten, and relaxed a bit in their
homes, the men of the village gradually begin to congregate there.
There are generally one or more 'chiefs' and other village leaders, as
well as other men who wander in and out. The atmosphere is very
informal. Some men sit and weave baskets as they chat or listen to
others talk. Others come in and relate an experience or joke for a
while, always finding an attentive audience. People constantly pass
through or by to see if anything interesting is going on. There are
always wit, joy, and life.

Any important news, such as the arrival of a 'chief' from another
village, is reported in the 'gathering house.' Outside visitors come to
the 'gathering house' almost immediately upon their arrival. There
they report news from their own village and learn what is happening
locally. Any visitor is a potential bearer of interesting anecdotes. In
1973, the blind son of Nele Kantule, the famous 'chief' of the village
of Ustuppu who died in 1944, visited Mulatuppu for several days. He
sat in the 'gathering house' for hours at a time, entertaining passersby with stories about his father and other political leaders, experiences he had during his own life, and recent news from Ustuppu.
He stopped talking when Mulatuppu men came in to discuss press-
ing local matters; then he picked up again, never tiring, always
lively.

On days when people do not work at all, because of a village or a
national holiday, a heavy rain, a solar or lunar eclipse, or the presence
in the village of important visitors, the 'gathering house' is open all
day long and there is considerable attendance there. Women assigned
to do so bring large containers of beverages they have prepared and
serve them to all present. There tends to be a great deal of speech play
at such all-day 'gatherings,' including joking and storytelling.

On evenings when 'chiefs' do not chant or there is no important
business, or after chanting and business, there is always informal

verbal activity. Someone has a story to tell, a humorous incident to recall, or a little verbal joke to play on someone else, before finally, usually late at night, everyone goes home to sleep and the 'police-men' lock up the 'gathering house' until the next day.

## The 'Gathering House' as Verbal Nerve Center

The Kuna 'gathering house' is thus the setting for a range of activities, from ritual to everyday, from political and economic to playful and recreational. It is a men's meetinghouse, similar in some ways to the men's meetinghouses found in various parts of tropical forest South America. It is the place where men assemble as a group, physically and socially isolated from women, to discuss and carry out men's business. But it is also the place where men and women gather as a unified community to listen to the 'chiefs' relate tribal tradition and history to everyday concerns.

The 'gathering house' is the place where the 'chief' leads his village. But he does not do so alone. Decisions are made by the community as a whole. The 'chief' mediates and channels community views, summing them up and focusing them in his 'counsels.' While he is the verbal leader of the community, anyone who speaks in the 'gathering house' can and does become a man or woman of words, creatively using language in a public performance. Speeches are long, involved, animated, and eloquent.

The 'gathering house' is the nerve center of a Kuna village. It serves to bring people together on a regular basis. It is a place to see and be seen, to learn the latest news, often as it is happening. Whether we focus on the informal events or on the more formal and ritual events that occur within it, the 'gathering house' is, as the Kuna themselves often say, a chanting house, a talking house, a performing house, a listening house. Here, through language and speech, the Kuna learn about and maintain their traditions, are reminded of and counseled about proper ways of behaving, learn about the past and present world around them, solve their problems, joke, enjoy words, and relax.

This examination of Kuna 'gathering house' speaking and chanting sharpens our understanding of the role of language and speech in social and, especially, political life in tropical forest South America. Pierre Clastres has pointed to the importance of oratory in political success among South American Indian societies. His personal experience is with the Guaranian Aché, but the central role of oratory in leadership has also been described for the Tupian Urubu and the Gê Shavante. Clastres notes that in these groups leaders do not have ab-solute power but, rather, rule through reasoning, consulting, and convincing. Oratory is both the condition and the means of political power.[25]

For the Kuna, political success, not only of community leaders but of all women and men, depends on the ability to speak well in the village 'gathering house.' Kuna 'chiefs' are not dictators who rule autocratically but verbal focal points through whom community opinion is expressed—successful 'chiefs' are able to lead by creatively summing up and directing the desires of their villages. Nonetheless, a really successful 'chief' must be an excellent and often extraordinary speaker; he must master an extensive, specialized body of tribal literature, legend, and tradition and perform it, usually by chanting, in the 'gathering house.' Kuna 'chiefs' thus contrast with political leaders in societies such as that of the Yaruro of Venezuela, in which no specialized verbal knowledge or ability is required of chiefs, who consult with rather than verbally lead their communities.[26] A still sharper contrast is provided by the Abipones and other groups of the Gran Chaco, among whom political leaders were selected for success in warfare rather than for verbal abilities.[27]

From a more general, cross-cultural perspective, a number of researchers have investigated language use in the politics of various societies around the world which, like the Kuna, profess an egalitarian ideology. These researchers have found that such societies often develop indirect means of expressing personal and group tensions, conflicts, and differences.[28] As I have shown, indirectness is a feature of the suggestive, figurative, and metaphorical language of Kuna 'chiefs' and other political leaders, and the egalitarian ideal is an important aspect of the highly developed oratory of which all Kuna seem capable.

# 4. Curing and Magic: Counseling the Spirits

Unlike curing and magic in other societies, in particular many North and South American Indian groups, Kuna curing and magic involve no drugs, no trances, and no spectacular tricks or sleight of hand. Rather, Kuna magical actions are achieved solely by means of verbal communication between humans and spirits. According to Kuna belief, there is a world of spirits which underlies and animates the concrete world of humans, plants, animals, and objects. The spirits behave in every way just like real, living Kuna. Their family and social organization is Kuna. Their needs and desires, such as eating and drinking, are expressed and satisfied according to Kuna practice. And, like all Kuna, they have a great appreciation for verbal artistry and verbal play. There are spirits of good and spirits of evil. Both are controlled by means of a set of *ikarkana* (ways, texts) which are addressed by *ikar wismalat* (*ikar* knowers) directly to them. *Ikarkana* are used for curing, disease prevention, advising and counseling medicine, acquiring special abilities, in certain rites of passage, and, in general, for magical control of the spirit world.

Kuna curing and magical events share with events of the *onmakket neka* (gathering house) a focus on language and speech. It is through language and speech that medicine becomes effective, the spirits of good are put to work, and the spirits of evil are neutralized and disarmed. At the same time, the use of language and speech in magic is significantly different from that in 'gathering house' ritual. Curing and magic constitute a separate ritual tradition from that of the 'gathering house,' with regard to social organization, setting, linguistic variety, and the overall structure of events.

There is no Kuna word for magic, just as there is no Kuna word for politics, or religion, or law. I use the term magic here, following anthropological tradition, to refer to the causation of supernatural actions by means of special power. For the Kuna the special power is verbal—communication with spirits through the performance of *ikarkana*. While *ikarkana* are used primarily for curing and disease prevention, they are also used more generally in order to cause or insure the occurrence of a wide variety of actions. For this reason I stress a close association between curing and magic throughout this chapter.

## Curing Events

When a Kuna woman, man, or child is ill, a member of the family is sent to a *nele* (seer), who decides what the cause of the sickness is and what cure is needed. Through her or his ability to communicate with the spirits, the 'seer' is able to determine what the patient's problem is. If the cure involves actual medicine, this medicine must be acquired from an *inatulet* (medicinal specialist), who also serves as a diagnostician in the absence of a 'seer.' The 'medicinal special-ist' gathers plants of medicinal value from the nearby jungle. Before giving these plants to the patient's family, he counsels them in order to activate them and give them life; that is, he transforms the plants into usable medicine. This activation process is carried out by di-rectly addressing the spirits of the plants and telling them what they need to know in order to carry out their work.

In addition to the administration of physical medicine, curing, es-pecially of serious diseases, often involves the performance of appro-priate *ikarkana*. An *ikar* is performed by an '*ikar* knower' for the benefit of the sick person but addressed directly to the spirit world, in the form of a box of *suar nuchukana* (stick dolls), the representa-tives of the spirits of good, whose role it is to counter the evil spirits causing the disease. The sick person lies in a hammock in his or her house, and the '*ikar* knower' sits alongside on a bench. Under the hammock is the box of 'stick dolls,' as well as a pot of burning hot peppers and burning hot cacao, also used to fight off disease.

The '*ikar* knower' makes no physical gestures during the perfor-mance. He stares vaguely into space and, from time to time, smokes tobacco in his pipe. Others in the house either go about their usual business or sit beside the sick person and the '*ikar* knower.' The '*ikar* knower' performs the long (typically one hour or more) *ikar* in the late afternoon or early evening, after he has finished his other work for the day; he then leaves the house of the patient. He carries his walking stick and wears beads, signs of his role, and sometimes a tie. Performance of a curing *ikar* is usually repeated on four succes-sive days.

## The Typology of *Ikarkana*
### *Curing and Disease Prevention*

There are a variety of diseases or infirmities for which a particular named *ikar* is used. Most common is *kapur ikar* (the way of the hot pepper), used in the curing of high fever and diseases accompanied by high fever. Another is *kurkin ikar* (the way of the hat), used in curing headaches. Others are *muu ikar* (the way of birth), used in difficult childbirths; *aplis wiloet ikar* (the way of blood strengthening), used to augment the blood; *serkan ikar* (the way of the deceased persons), used to avoid having nightmares about dead spirits; *purwa ikar* (the way of the wind), used against epilepsy; *nika ikar* (the way of strength), used to give the patient strength; *nia ikar* (the way of the devil), used for mentally deranged persons; *akkwanele ikar* (the way of the magic stone), used to return a lost soul to the body of the patient; and *tala kannoet ikar* (the way of eye strength), used to improve the sight of the patient.

Immediately related to the *ikarkana* used in curing diseases is another set, used in the prevention of disease or other evils. According to Kuna belief, some people are likely to succumb to certain diseases or are marked to fall prey to certain calamities. Some of these proclivities can be noted by the midwives at the birth of a child; they inform the child's family so that it can have the appropriate medicine and *ikar* administered.

'Seers,' because of their great mental powers, are subject to headaches; the performance of *nele kurkin ikar* (the way of the seer's hat) prevents them from getting such headaches. *Ukkunakpe ikar* (the way of the rattlesnake) is performed for individuals who have a propensity to be bitten by snakes, in order to prevent this from happening. The rattlesnake is counseled to attack other snakes and thus protect the marked individual. Also used against snakes is *wekko ikar* (the way of the hawk)—the hawk eats snakes and in this *ikar* it is counseled to do just that. *Purpa oteket ikar* (the way of the bringing down of the soul), also called *tampoet ikar* (the way of the cooling off), is performed for children so that they do not die, especially when other children have died in the same family or when the child in question keeps getting sick. *Pinnuwar olaet ikar* (the way of the felling of the *pinnuwala* [*Anacardium* species] tree), also called *suar olaet ikar* (the way of the felling of the tree) or *mortup okwaet ikar* (the way of the changing of the clothesline), is performed next to felled trees, where disease-causing spirits are located. In this *ikar* the spirits of good are counseled to in turn counsel the evil spirits residing in the tree to move to another tree. If the evil spirits do not move, they become angry and dangerous.

No doubt the most spectacular of the *ikarkana* involved in curing and disease prevention is that used for the mass exorcism of evil spirits. This *ikar* is called *apsoket ikar* (the way of the mass curer) or *ukkurwala ikar* (the way of the balsa wood). Its performer is called an *apsoket*; his title is derived from the verb *apsoke* (to converse). In this *ikar*, the 'mass curer' converses with both good and evil spirits in order to defeat the evil spirits. The whole event is called *nek apsoket* (mass-curing ritual, literally to converse with the place), place having the sense of the world, the environment, and conditions in general, ultimately referring to the spirits who inhabit the world and its environment and cause conditions. It is also called *nekuet* (smoking the surroundings), which refers to the smoking of tobacco by members of the community who participate in the ritual; this smoking is an essential feature of the efficacy of the exorcism.

The 'mass curer' is the most respected of all medicinal and curing '*ikar* knowers.' 'The way of the mass curer' is extremely long and takes many years to learn. Furthermore, it is used not for the benefit of a single individual but, rather, for the well-being of an entire community. All the aspects of ordinary curing rituals are more elaborate in the 'mass-curing ritual.' The entire community is present in the 'gathering house,' in which this *ikar* is performed. It lasts for eight days, beginning each day in the late afternoon and continuing until midnight. Enormous balsa wood figures are brought into the 'gathering house' and placed against the benches of the *arkarkana* (spokesmen); these are large versions of the 'stick doll' representatives of the spirits of good which are used in all curing events.

From the center of the 'gathering house' the 'mass curer' addresses these figures in his *ikar*, while the other members of the community sit silently and smoke tobacco, literally smoking out the evil spirits. Large quantities of cacao, hot peppers, and other medicine are also burned as part of the smoking-out process. All members of the community (not just the ritual performer, as in ordinary curing ceremonies) must refrain from sexual relations during the entire eight-day period. Quiet is maintained during the daytime and the village is under strict quarantine—no outsiders are allowed in. The 'mass-curing ritual' is used to cure whole communities of epidemics, to clear new lands of dangerous sicknesses in preparation for habitation and farming, and generally to rid an area of disease, danger, and evil.[1]

### *'Medicine Counsels'*

Intimately related to the curing and prevention of disease is *ina uanaet* (medicine counsel), a set of *ikarkana* used to advise and counsel various types of medicine in order to activate them and render them effective. Certain objects in nature—for example, plants in the nearby mainland jungle—are inherently of medicinal value.[2] Nonetheless, in order to be effective, to be given life, these potential medicines must be told how to carry out their cure. This is precisely what occurs in 'medicine counsel' when the 'medicinal specialist' addresses the spirits of these plants directly. 'Medicine counsel' is performed in the jungle, at the moment of the cutting of the particular plant, and/or later on, in the home of the 'medicinal specialist.' The 'medicinal specialist' either sits or stands, with the medicine he is addressing placed directly in front of him. In addition to plants, such objects as pieces of glass, sticks, stones, phonograph needles, old shoes, or bars of soap can become medicinally effective if counseled. So while medicine is effective because of a combination of internal medicinal properties and power rendered through language, it is the verbal 'counsel' which is ultimately supreme, since without it nothing is effective and with it anything can become effective.

'Medicine counsels' are performed frequently and relatively publicly. They are typically performed by the 'medicinal specialist' when he returns from his morning's work in the jungle. Many men have some knowledge of traditional medicine so that, even when they go to the jungle primarily for the purpose of farming or cutting wood, they often bring some medicine back with them. As a result, if you wander through a Kuna village at midday, through the bamboo walls of many houses you will hear the voices of men performing 'medicine counsel' to their just gathered medicine. These voices are often mingled with other voices and noises—the preparation of midday meals, children playing after their morning session at school, ordinary conversations, and radios.

There are various 'medicine counsels,' depending on what the medicine is to be used for and where it comes from. *Muu ina uanaet* (birth medicine counsel) advises medicine used in childbirth. *Ina pukkip ikar* (the way of much medicine), performed in the home of a sick person, counsels all the medicine in the jungle to come to the patient's aid. *Ina ulukanki* (medicine in the trunks) counsels a whole medicinal laboratory; it is performed either in the home of the 'medicinal specialist,' in front of his collection of medicine, or in the home of a sick person. *Ina tiikinet ikar* (the way of the medicine in the water) counsels the medicine located at the bottom of a river.

## The Acquisition of Abilities

Another set of *ikarkana* is performed for the purpose of enabling one to acquire particular abilities or achieve particular goals. *Pisep ikar* (the way of the basil) is performed for the benefit of a man who wants to become a great hunter or is about to set out on a particular hunting expedition. This man makes a potion out of basil and other fragrant plants; then 'the way of the basil' is performed to the potion by a 'knower,' who addresses the spirit of the plant directly and explains to it what animals will be hunted. The hunter then bathes in this perfume and, as a result, becomes fragrantly attractive to animals, who fall in love with him and approach him, enabling him to kill them. During the period of the efficacy of the potion, the hunter is not permitted to have sexual relations;[3] the interdiction of sex is characteristic of all the *ikarkana* discussed here and is an aspect of their magical power. Also used in hunting is *yauk ikar* (the way of the sea turtle), performed to a potion which is used in the hunting of these turtles. *Ikarkana* such as 'the way of the basil' and 'the way of the sea turtle' are directly related to economic concerns. There are always a need and a demand for meat within San Blas. A number of years ago, there was a great demand for sea turtles, since their shells were being purchased for very high prices. These shells often reached Japan, where they were used to make frames for eyeglasses. At that time many men were asking to have 'the way of the sea turtle' performed for them or were learning it themselves. Still another *ikar* performed to a potion is *mutup ikar* (the way of birth string); in this case, bathing in the advised potion makes a man attractive to women.

Other *ikarkana* are used for the acquisition of other types of abilities. An example is *neloet ikar* (the way of seeing), which is performed for 'seers' while they are still children, in order to develop their potentially extraordinary mental abilities.

## Rites of Passage

There are *ikarkana* whose role is to assure passage through stages in the Kuna life cycle. Many of these focus on young girls and women. For example when a girl is two or three years old, a hole is pierced in her nose, and from that moment she begins to wear a gold nose ring (Kuna women wear nose rings throughout their lives). In order to assist in the nose-piercing process, *ikko ikar* (the way of the needle) is performed.

Other *ikarkana* are directly involved in girls' puberty rites and in the preparation and consumption of *inna*, an alcoholic beverage, during these rites. Several days before the rites and associated fes-

tivities begin, the men and women of the village communally prepare the *inna*, under the supervision of a specialist. After its preparation, *inna sopet ikar* (the way of the making of *inna*) is performed to
render the drink stronger. It is performed by the *inna sopet* (*inna*
maker) and is addressed to the spirit of the *inna*. Another *inna*-
related *ikar* is *wipoet ikar* (the way of sobering up), used during
puberty rites by an extremely inebriated individual in order to sober
up. Other *ikarkana* are performed for the benefit of various objects
and persons involved in the events which occur during the girls'
puberty rites (see chapter 5).

Two *ikarkana* are performed after a death to assure proper travel
to and through the afterworld. The very long *masar ikar* (the way of
the bamboo cane) is addressed by a 'knower' to the spirit of cane
while the corpse lies at home; it is continued during the trip to the
cemetery and at the cemetery. It assures safe passage into and through
all parts of the afterworld. *Orpatte ikar* (the way of the golden eleva-
tor) aids passage to the afterworld. Like all *ikarkana*, these must be
paid for. However, the family of the deceased individual does not always have the means or the desire to pay for the performance of such
a long and expensive *ikar* as 'the way of the bamboo cane.' Part of
the expense often involves bringing a specialist from another village,
sometimes rather distant, since there are relatively few 'knowers' of
this *ikar* in San Blas.

### Magical Control

A very interesting set of *ikarkana* is related to the carrying out of
magiclike feats, such as grabbing a dangerous snake, holding a hot
iron harpoon, or surrounding oneself with bees without being at-
tacked by them. The addressees of these *ikarkana* are the spirits of
the objects to be controlled—the snake, harpoon, or bees. However,
such controlling activities are often carried out, not by performing
the longer *ikar*, but by either intoning or thinking a short charmlike
incantation called a *sekretto*, which is associated with the particular *ikar* and magical act. The *sekretto* is the 'secret' of or the key to
the object.

There is a large set of such 'secrets.' Some have to do with controlling—touching or being near—otherwise dangerous animals or objects, such as bees, wasps, scorpions, spiders, vipers, poisonous ants,
or hot harpoons. Others can cause extraordinary events to occur,
such as water not draining through the holes of a sieve or a rattle
bursting open by itself. Some are used in the curing of sick individuals, such as persons who have fainted or who have tumors or boils.
Some are used to achieve success in certain activities, such as at-

tracting women or hunting. Finally, some are used by certain individuals for protection in the afterworld. Thus, if a man has had sexual relations with the *iet* (haircutter) at girls' puberty rites, he will want to know the *tisla sekretto* (the scissors secret), in order to prevent giant scissors from cutting him in the afterworld. 'Medicinal specialists' must know the medicine 'secret' in order to cross a lake of medicine in the afterworld.

'Secrets' are in a linguistic variety quite distinct from that of the *ikar*. In fact, 'secrets' are not really in any particular linguistic variety at all. Rather, they are combinations of words from various languages—Kuna (modern and archaic), Choco, English, Spanish, and Latin. They have no referential content but evoke a mystical magic through their rhymes and rhythms. I cite a few lines here for illustrative purposes but do not present a complete example, because of the incantations' very secretive position within Kuna genres of speaking.

santa lusia e pasato.
kona leche.
pita se kayó.
wes pasarió.
paitera amen.

Sounds and sound oppositions are manipulated, almost playfully, as in the following lines.

elis elis ihelis.
iklesia iklasia.
matté mattéus.
temones teppottes.

'Secrets' are intended to inform the spirit of the object in question that the performer knows its origin and is therefore able to control it. Understanding Kuna magical control requires paying attention to the relationship among *ikarkana*, 'secrets,' and another verbal genre, *purpa* (soul).[4] Associated with almost every *ikar* is a 'soul,' a relatively short text in everyday though somewhat esoteric Kuna. The 'soul' describes the origin of the object to be controlled by the *ikar* in explicit terms and is an essential aspect of the learning of an *ikar*. The choice of whether to use an *ikar*, a 'soul,' or a 'secret' on a particular occasion depends on the circumstances or activity involved and on what a particular specialist happens to know. For most diseases and disease prevention, it is most common to use the long *ikar*. For ailments which require quicker, more direct results, 'souls' are used. For the control of such objects as bees and snakes, where a rapid magical demonstration of power is called for, the short 'secret' might be employed.

It is interesting to ask why there exist long *ikarkana* for the magical control of objects when short 'secrets' would seem to suffice and in fact are sometimes used in the actual magical act. However, the long *ikarkana* are always an important element in the process of controlling objects and spirits—they are a reminder of the power the '*ikar* knower' has over them, including the fact that he can also control them with 'secrets.' These *ikarkana* are also part of the knowledge of the specialist, necessary to his work, and are learned only after hard study. But *ikarkana* are also pleasurable verbally in and for themselves. They can be performed for the enjoyment and benefit of the 'knower' himself or for his family or friends and are appreciated for their aesthetic qualities, even if some of the listeners understand little of the referential content. Spirits as well appreciate the verbal artistry of these *ikarkana* and in part follow the directions of the performer because of the pleasure they derive from this verbal play and poetry.

Becoming an expert and specialist in a particular area of Kuna curing and magic—curing fever, preventing snakebite, aiding women in childbirth, or benefiting hunters—thus involves learning a complex of verbal skills and the traditions associated with them. This complex includes a set of related *ikarkana*, a set of 'souls,' and a set of 'secrets.' The more of this verbal complex a specialist knows and performs, the greater his prestige and renown.

### Contexts for the Performance of *Ikarkana*

It is characteristic of all *ikarkana* (but not 'souls' or 'secrets') that they are performed in a variety of contexts, in addition to the primary one of curing, preventing disease, improving abilities, or magical control. These other, secondary contexts include the practicing of an *ikar* by a 'knower,' the learning and teaching of an *ikar*, and the chanting of an *ikar* for the pleasure of the 'knower' and his human and spirit listeners during certain festivities (especially those associated with girls' puberty rites). On all these occasions, performers are usually said to *namakke* (chant) the *ikar* rather than *sunmakke* (speak) it—the latter is the appropriate way to perform *ikarkana* in their primary context for their primary function. There are ambiguities in this distinction, however, in that each performer has his own style of both *namakke* and *sunmakke*, depending on whom he learned the *ikar* from.

One distinguisher between performances in the principal primary context and performances in secondary contexts is the tightening of the larynx in secondary contexts, resulting in a voice quality considered to be aesthetically pleasing. The 'knower' begins these secondary performances of an *ikar* with the words *wai sae*, which tightens the larynx. The Kuna show a certain lack of agreement concerning the *namakke-sunmakke* distinction, generally using *namakke* to label secondary contexts but alternating between *namakke* and *sunmakke* for the labeling of primary performances, which are definitely tuneful and melodic. This contrasts with the chanting of *saklakana* (chiefs) in the 'gathering house,' which is consistently called *namakke*.

When chanted for practice or for the personal pleasure of the 'knower,' *ikarkana* are performed in his home or that of a member of his family, usually late at night after the evening 'gathering' or even while this 'gathering' is taking place, if the 'knower' does not attend. Learning and teaching are carried out in the house of the 'knower' at night. The process is as follows. The teacher first performs the *ikar* completely. Then the student learns it by a line-by-line repetition. When the student becomes more familiar with the text, he begins the session by performing the *ikar* himself. The teacher corrects the student when he makes mistakes. (See chapter 8 for a more complete discussion of learning and teaching.)

During the festivities associated with girls' puberty rites, 'knowers' perform *ikarkana* either in the *inna neka* (*inna* house) or in a private home. These are not official parts of the ritual. (Official and unofficial aspects of puberty rites are discussed in chapter 5.) Rather, they are one of a number of pleasurable activities that people engage in while drinking *inna* and other alcoholic beverages. The performer, usually quite drunk himself, sits surrounded by other men, equally drunk, who listen. Performer and audience, as well as spirits, enjoy the event immensely. Members of the audience often provide a bottle of rum to consume during the performance—this willingness to spend money indicates the degree to which the verbal art is appreciated.

These secondary purposes or contexts for the performance of *ikarkana* are of great significance in Kuna society and should not be viewed as marginal in any sense. Obviously the performance of *ikarkana* in learning and teaching is the process by which they are passed on from generation to generation. But performing for practice and personal pleasure is also important. And, while the Kuna clearly enjoy *ikarkana* for purely aesthetic reasons, there are other motivations and functions for such performances as well. This is most evident with regard to *ikarkana* which are rarely used for their primary purpose or are performed for their primary purpose in a place where they cannot be heard. It may be, as in the case of 'the way of the devil,' used for mentally deranged individuals, that it has been some time since anyone had the disease or, as in the case of 'the way of birth,' used for difficulty in childbirth, that outsiders are not permitted to be present when it is performed or, as in the case of 'the way of the bamboo cane,' used to guide a dead person's soul into and through the afterworld, that it has been a while since anyone died who left a family willing to pay for the performance. Thus how can an *ikar* knower' remind members of his community that he is indeed a specialist in a particular *ikar*? The best way is to perform the *ikar* in secondary contexts.

An illustrative example is Manuel Campos, a now deceased Mulatuppu *'ikar* knower' who was the only person in his large village who knew 'the way of the bamboo cane.' He would often practice it at night on evenings when men were talking in the 'gathering house.' Of his many relatives' homes, he would often select that of a daughter who lived near the 'gathering house.' Thus, as they talked, the men could hear the booming voice of Campos practicing 'the way of the bamboo cane' for hours at a time. Who could deny that he indeed knew it, that he fully deserved the credit and respect associated with it?

### *Ikar* Structure and Content

Since the purpose of *ikarkana* is to counsel and control representatives of the spirit world, their various themes or topics can be seen as subservient to that purpose. At the same time, they have a narrative structure in their own right.

One frequent *ikar* theme is the description of the conception and birth of the object to be controlled; this description may be quite graphic, as in 'the way of birth' or 'the way of the basil.' The actual labeling of the body parts and acts involved in conception and birth is in a vocabulary particular to the *ikar*. If the words have meanings in everyday Kuna which are different from the meanings they have in the *ikar*, the result is metaphorical, achieved at the intersection of two linguistic varieties. Here is the description of the birth of the plant in 'the way of the basil.'

Inapiseptili [the spirit name of the plant] in the golden box is moving.
In the golden box is moving.
Inapiseptili in the golden box is swinging from side to side.
In the golden box is swinging from side to side.
Inapiseptili in the golden box is trembling.

In the golden box is trembling.
Inapiseptili in the golden box is palpitating.
In the golden box is palpitating.
Inapiseptili in the golden box is making a noise.
In the golden box is making a noise.
Inapiseptili in the golden box is shooting out.
In the golden box is shooting out.[5]

On the other hand, the *ikar* might merely state that the '*ikar* knower' is acquainted with the object and its parts, its origin and its 'secret.' It is understood, especially by the spirit of the object, to which the *ikar* is addressed, that this knowledge involves detailed understanding of conception and birth. An example is *pulu ikar* (the way of the wasp), used to attract and control wasps.

The specialist knows your secret origin.
The specialist says.[6]

*Nakpe ikar* (the way of the snake), used to grab a dangerous snake and raise it into the air, first announces that the '*ikar* knower' is in complete control of knowledge about the snake's origin.

Machi Oloaktikunappinele [the spirit name of the snake] calls [to the specialist].
'How well do you know the abode of my origin?'
Machi Oloaktikunappi calls.
The specialist counsels Machi Oloaktikunappi.
'Indeed [I] already know the abode of your origin.
Indeed [I] have come to play in the abode of your origin.
Indeed I have come to encircle the abode of your origin.'

This same *ikar* then lists, in a series of parallel lines, all the parts of the snake, thus enabling the '*ikar* knower' to display his anatomical knowledge about the snake's origin.

The specialist says.
'Indeed how your lips were placed on.
The specialist knows well.'
The specialist says.
The specialist says.
'How your chin was put in place.
How your lower chin was formed.
The specialist knows well.'
The specialist says.
Indeed the specialist says.
'How your pupils were formed.

The specialist knows well.'
The specialist says.
The specialist says.
'How the point of your tongue was put in place.
The specialist knows well.'
The specialist says.
He counsels Machi Oloaktikunappi.
Indeed the specialist [says].
'How your golden arrow [fangs] was put in place.
How your golden arrow was buried in.
The specialist knows well.'
The specialist says.[7]

There is a great deal of secrecy and taboo surrounding conception and birth among the Kuna, this being the most sensitive of all topics for them; thus there is power in knowledge about this area. The intersection of taboo and power with regard to knowledge of and speaking about conception and birth is deeply embedded in Kuna beliefs and practices, from the most everyday to the most ritual and magical. There is an interdiction on talk about conception and birth in everyday interaction, especially in the presence of children. This is an area of vocabulary in which euphemisms abound. At the same time, by revealing to a spirit in an *ikar* that he knows its origin (that is, its conception and birth), an '*ikar* knower' is able to control it.

Some *ikarkana* contain taxonomies of plants or animals—of the objects whose spirits are addressed in the *ikar*. These taxonomies, at times rather long and complicated, are usually in the special lexicon of the linguistic variety of the spirits and of curing and magical *ikarkana*. The presentation of these taxonomies is related to the highly parallelistic structure of *ikarkana*. It is also intimately associated with the statement of the origin of the object to be controlled in that it shows the place of the object in nature, its origin and essence, in truly structural terms. Taxonomies are either localized in a particular portion of an *ikar* or dispersed throughout as a recurrent theme.

A taxonomy of hot peppers appears in 'the way of the hot pepper,' used in calming high fever. The spirits of these peppers are called into action in the fight against disease; fifty-five parallel stanzas are used to name fifty-five plants.

The specialist is calling.
He is calling to the mountains.
He is calling the spirits.
Nele Pinaisepa Nele [hot pepper].

Ulu Sankwali Nele [*sankwa*-type pepper].
Ulu Tipyana Nele [toasted pepper].
Ulu Opirpa Nele [ground pepper].
Upikkwa Nele [well-ground pepper].
Alakkwa Nele [almost ground pepper].[8]

This taxonomy includes pepper types as they are found in nature as well as types that have been transformed by human action.

In 'the way of the basil,' the spirits of a taxonomy of fragrant plants are addressed. The hunter bathes in a potion made of these plants so that animals fall in love with him and are attracted to him. The spirits of the plants are named in a set of parallel lines, each of which ends and thus punctuates a parallel stanza.[9]

Pisep, I am advising you . . .
Achueryala, I am advising you . . .
Kokke, I am advising you . . .
Nopar, I am advising you . . .
Aksar, I am advising you . . .
Pakla, I am advising you . . .

The spirits of the plants are provided with a taxonomy of animals to be hunted. These animals are of two types, *tulekala* (walking) and *ullukka* (flying). This animal taxonomy is presented in a set of parallel lines, each of which opens a parallel stanza.

The specialist's hat makes noise like a *tulekala yaya* [an agouti] . . .
The specialist's hat makes noise like a *tulekala manikwillosakpia* [a collared peccary] . . .
The specialist's hat makes noise like a *tulekala punayai* [a white-lipped peccary] . . .
The specialist's hat makes noise like a *tulekala ukkusalu ekwilamakkatola* [a tapir] . . .
The specialist's hat makes noise like a *tulekala narwalipe* [a rabbit] . . .
The specialist's hat makes noise like a *tulekala tukkwa* [a squirrel] . . .
The specialist's hat makes noise like a *ullukka sitoni* [a curassow] . . .
The specialist's hat makes noise like a *ullukka kwami kwami* [a wild bird] . . .
The specialist's hat makes noise like a *ullukka mormolipe* [a wild bird] . . .
The specialist's hat makes noise like a *ullukka kokorkwana* [a wild bird] . . .[10]

In addition to those of plants and animals, there are other taxonomies. For example, a taxonomy of directions occurs in a version of 'the way of the basil,' performed by a different *'ikar* knower.'

Your branches are pointing to where the sun rises.
Your branches are pointing to where the sun sets.
Your branches are pointing to where the sun is highest.
Your branches are pointing to where the sun rises halfway.[11]

Another topic or theme of these *ikarkana* is the detailed description of the day-to-day life of the objects being addressed. Since these objects, especially animals, have spirits with social organizations and daily activities identical to those of humans, these texts provide fascinating insights into the Kuna perception of their own daily round of activities—sleeping, waking up, drinking, eating, hunting, and conversing with family and friends. In 'the way of the rattlesnake,' used as protection against dangerous snakes, the rattlesnake gets ready to go hunting while, just as happens every morning as real Kuna farmers and hunters go off to the mainland jungle to work, his wife prepares a beverage for him.

Puna Inakunipyaisop [the spirit name of Rattlesnake's wife] responds [to Rattlesnake].
'You are going hunting for me,' she says.
'I will prepare your beverage for you.'
The wife says.
She lights the fire.
She turns the firewood.
In the fireplace the fire begins.
The fire burns brightly.
On top of the fire she places a pot.
Inside the pot she places the fruit.
She lowers the liquid [to the fire].
The liquid begins to boil.[12]

Some *ikarkana* depict in detail Kuna cultural activities which are associated with the object being addressed and the functions of the *ikar.* 'The way of the bamboo cane,' used to guide the soul of the deceased, describes in great and gory detail the sickness, death, funeral, and passage to the afterworld of an individual. In the following passage the patient, in the final moments of his life, converses with his family. He is surrounded by his wife and female relatives, who have already begun their *poe* [tuneful weeping] for him. They will continue their 'tuneful weeping' after his death. This *ikar* reflects such basic Kuna concerns as the ability of 'medicinal specialists' to care for the sick and the inheritance of the property of the deceased. It is noteworthy that the concerns and conflicts of everyday life are expressed in a fixed, ritual text in an esoteric language.

The patient says.
'The medicinal specialists cannot help me.'
The patient's wife says.
'It is very serious; he is going to die.'
The relatives speak.
The female relatives say.
'There is much medicine under the hammock.
Cups of medicine are lined up.
There are many cups of medicine.'
The patient cannot speak.
The patient is very congested.
His throat makes a rasping noise.
The patient's mouth tastes bitter.
He has no taste in his mouth.
The patient's tongue is pale.
His tongue is white.
The patient's eyes are weak.
His eyes flutter.
He does not open his eyes.
The patient says his last words.
'I left you enough.'
The patient says his last words.
'I planted enough for you.
After my death you will take care of it.
I planted enough coconuts for you.
After my death you will take care of them.'[13]

In 'the way of the making of *inna*,' used to render the alcoholic beverage consumed at girls' puberty rites stronger, all activities—personal, cultural, and social—relating to the preparation of the beverage are described in detail. Here the Kuna perception of their own activities is reflected in the depiction of Kuna actors in a narration addressed to spirits.

The *inna*-making specialist awakens.
The cock crows.
The owners of the *inna* [members of the community] are making a lot of noise.
There is much commotion.
The owners of the *inna* are grinding sugarcane.

The *inna*-making specialist calls his group together.
He calls his assistants together.
He calls his *inna* tasters together.
His wife says.
'Let us change clothes, blouses, pants.
We will go to the river to bathe.'
They go to the river to bathe.
They stand up in the river.
The water makes waves.
The water really makes waves.
The water is splashing.
The water is gushing.
The river sardines leave their smell in their hair.[14]

Some *ikarkana* narrate mythic struggles, epic battles between opposing forces, as in war. In these struggles between the spirits of good and the spirits of evil, the spirits of good eventually win out, simultaneously eliminating the patient's disease. Here is a portion of 'the way of the balsa wood,' used to exorcise evil spirits in the 'mass-curing ritual.'

The balsa wood spirit leaders are climbing.
They have all of their equipment.
The balsa wood spirit leaders are climbing.
They are at the mouth of the Opakki River.
They fill the *inna* house.
They stuff the *inna* house.
The spirits are ready to fight.
The balsa wood spirit speaks.
'You are going to the place of evil spirits.'

In these battles, the physical characteristics and clothing of the spirits are described.

The balsa wood spirit leaders are massing.
The balsa wood spirit leaders are marching.
Their golden hats are almost touching each other.
Indeed their golden hats are almost touching each other.
The balsa wood spirit leaders are marching.
The balsa wood spirits' golden shoes are almost touching each other.
Indeed their golden shoes are almost touching each other.
The balsa wood spirit leaders are marching.
Through the streets of the people.

Conversations among good spirits and between good and evil spirits are quoted. In fact, what is involved are more trickster-type foolery and conversational chicanery than actual gory battles. The spirits of good utilize such ploys as including in their ranks a drunken spirit (made from 'drunk wood') who, because of his inebriated state, fights furiously.

The balsa wood spirit leader speaks.
'Friend drunk wood spirit.
Do not worry so much.'
The balsa wood spirit leader speaks.
'We will place friend drunk wood spirit in the rear' [to back up the
    ranks with his attack].
The balsa wood spirit says.
'For the good of human people.
To eliminate evil spirits.
Let us examine everything well.
Let us clear out everything.
To the sixth level underground.
Let us dig.
I say.'
The balsa wood spirit leaders descend.
To the first level underground the balsa wood spirit leaders descend.
The evil spirit boat owners speak.
'For what reason have you entered my house?'
The balsa wood spirit responds to the evil spirit boat owners.
'My people have many sicknesses.'[15]

Finally, *ikarkana* can be viewed as 'counsel' to objects and especially to spirits on how to behave, on what to do in order to carry out the biddings of the performer, the specialist 'knower,' and this fact is repeated over and over, addressed directly to the spirits.

The specialist counsels Machi Oloaktikunappi [the spirit name of
    the snake].[16]
The specialist is again counseling Puna Olosemaktili [the spirit
    name of the wasp].[17]

Curing and magical *ikarkana* consist of a series of themes, topics, and episodes which are strung together. While a primary characteristic of these *ikarkana* is that they are putatively fixed or unchangeable in form, and thus must be learned by rote memorization, there is some variation. Depending on the particular origins of the disease or on the particular object of several possible objects to be controlled, choices are made in the selection of topics or themes. In 'the way of the basil,' for example, verses relevant to the particular animal the hunter is desirous of killing or to a combination of these are chosen. *Ikarkana* can also be made longer or shorter, according to the selection of appropriate episodes and themes. Once the selection has been made, however, the '*ikar* knower' proceeds according to a line-by-line, fixed text. This is quite different from the chanting and speaking of 'chiefs' and other political leaders in the 'gathering house,' in which a theme or an idea is taken as a point of departure and then elaborated in a fresh, spontaneous way.

### Parallelism

A pervasive feature of the structure of curing and magical *ikarkana* is parallelism—the patterned repetition of sounds, forms, and meanings. Many types of parallelism are found; in every *ikar* certain crucial lines are repeated identically or almost identically throughout the text, punctuating it and marking the boundaries of sections within it.[18] In 'the way of the snake,' for example, used to enable a specialist to grab a dangerous snake, the snake's spirit is continually reminded that the '*ikar* knower' is advising it. Likewise, in 'the way of the cooling off,' used to cool and calm a feverish patient, the medicine spirits are repeatedly told to cool off the patient's spirit.

Adjacent lines of *ikarkana* are linked by various types of parallelism. Two or more lines may be identical, with the exception of the deletion of a single word, as in 'the way of the basil.'[19]

Inapiseptili in the golden box is moving.
          In the golden box is moving.[20]

Two or more lines may differ in nonreferential morphemes (in addition to the possible deletion of a word), as in 'the way of the snake.'

The specialist is sharpening [*nuptulu-makke-kwichiye*] his little knife.
          Is sharpening [*nuptulu-sae-kwichiye*] his little knife.

Notice that the verb stem formative *makke* of the first line is replaced by the verb stem formative *sae* of the next line.

Two or more lines may be identical except for the replacement of a single word, the two or more words having slightly different meanings within the same semantic field. Here are several examples of paired lines from 'the way of the snake.'

He is cutting small bushes.
He is clearing small bushes.
The specialist moves a little.
The specialist advances.

His [the snake's] hooks open and close.
His [the snake's] hooks open and close repeatedly.[21]

Here are two examples of series of such parallel lines from *nakrus ikar* (the way of the cross), used to scare away the devil.

The specialist is calling you.
The specialist is naming you.
The specialist is listing you.
The leaders are carrying the silver crosses.
The leaders are walking with the silver crosses.
The leaders are turning around with the silver crosses.
The leaders are moving their hands with the silver crosses.
The leaders are moving their hands rapidly with the silver crosses.
The leaders are holding the silver crosses.
The leaders are making signs with the silver crosses.[22]

The result of this type of parallelism is a slow-moving narration which advances by slight changes in referential content, added to repeated information. Extreme attention is paid to minute and precise detail.

Sometimes the pattern underlying the parallel structure involves not a single sentence or line but, rather, an entire set of lines, a verse, or a stanza, a frame which is repeated over and over with changes in one or more words. For example, in 'the way of the cooling off,' the patient's illness is described as follows.

Our child has a feverish spirit.
We must cool off his spirit for him.
We must really cool off his spirit.
Our child has feverish blood.
His blood is very feverish.
We must cool off his blood for him.
We must really cool off his blood.
Our child has feverish skin.
His skin is very feverish.
We must cool off his skin for him.
We must really cool off his skin.
Our child has a feverish body.
His body is very feverish.
We must cool off his body for him.
We must really cool off his body.
Our child has a feverish head.
His head is very feverish.

We must cool off his head for him.
We must really cool off his head.

Our child has feverish hair.
His hair is very feverish.
We must cool off his hair for him.
We must really cool off his hair.[23]

Each of these examples involves a quite similar process, namely, the projection of a paradigm or taxonomy onto a fixed verse structure or frame. In addition to this poetic function,[24] clearly an aspect of these *ikarkana* and appreciated as such by the Kuna, the process of projecting paradigms and taxonomies onto fixed verse structures has other functions. Since it is important for these *ikarkana* to be long, length being a major aspect of their magical power, such projection enables one to generate a long text or portion of a text. Since 'ikar knowers' have to memorize these texts, the taxonomy is related to the memorization process. That is, the memorization process involves the learning of the taxonomy together with the fixed verse pattern. And, since the *ikar* is learned line by line as a text and not, as might be expected given its underlying structure, in two parts—taxonomy plus fixed verse pattern—it is an interesting question whether the taxonomy helps one learn and remember the *ikar* or whether the *ikar* helps one learn and remember the taxonomy or both.[25]

The parallelistic structure of curing and magical *ikarkana* is found at all levels, from the most macro—repetition of whole verse and stanza patterns—to the most micro—repetition of words and morphemes. The result is an overlapping intersection of various parallelistic patterns. An excellent example is provided by the opening of 'the way of the basil,' in which the plant's birth is described.

Inapiseptili olouluti tulalemaiye.
⠀⠀⠀⠀⠀olouluti tulallemaiye.
Inapiseptili olouluti sikkirmakkemaiye.
⠀⠀⠀⠀⠀olouluti sikkirmakmamaiye.
Inapiseptili olouluti wawanmakkemaiye.
⠀⠀⠀⠀⠀olouluti wawanmakmainaye.
Inapiseptili olouluti aktutumakkemaiye.
⠀⠀⠀⠀⠀olouluti aktutulemainaye.
Inapiseptili olouluti kollomakkemaiye.
⠀⠀⠀⠀⠀olouluti kollomakmainaye.
Inapiseptili olouluti mummurmakkemaiye.
⠀⠀⠀⠀⠀olouluti mummurmakmainaye.

Inapiseptili in the golden box is moving.
        In the golden box is moving.
Inapiseptili in the golden box is swinging from side to side.
        In the golden box is swinging from side to side.
Inapiseptili in the golden box is trembling.
        In the golden box is trembling.
Inapiseptili in the golden box is palpitating.
        In the golden box is palpitating.
Inapiseptili in the golden box is making a noise.
        In the golden box is making a noise.
Inapiseptili in the golden box is shooting out.
        In the golden box is shooting out.[26]

If this text is represented as a series of the following symbols, the overlapping patterns of parallelism become much more striking.

a: Inapiseptili
b: golden box
c, d, e, f, g, h: various verb stems
W, w: *makke, mak*: verb stem formative endings
x: *mai*: verbal suffix, 'in the process of, in a horizontal position'
y: *nae*: verbal suffix, 'go to a location'
z: *ye*: verbal suffix, 'optative, emphatic'

The text can now be rewritten as follows.

```
a b c     x     z
  b c     x     z
a b d W x       z
  b d w   x x   z
a b e W x       z
  b e w   x y   z
a b f W x       z
  b f     x y   z
a b g W x       z
  b g w   x y   z
a b h W x       z
  b h w   x y   z
```

### Figurative Language and Speech

As in the chanting and speaking of the 'gathering house,' curing and magical *ikarkana* contain instances of figurative and metaphorical speech. But in these *ikarkana*, as distinct from those of the 'gathering house,' the metaphors are fixed; they are not elaborated, manipulated, or individually developed by the performer. Furthermore,

**Table 11.** Figurative Vocabulary in Curing and Magical *Ikarkana*

| Word | Meaning in *Ikar* | Colloquial Meaning |
|------|-------------------|--------------------|
| *kurkin* | brainpower | hat |
| *inna ipet* | Kuna person | owner of the *inna* |
| *urwetule* | evil spirit, sickness | angry person |
| *alulukwale* | red | firelike |
| *ansuelu* | fangs of snake | hook |
| *siku* | fangs of snake | arrow |
| *puti* | fangs of snake | blowgun |
| *kole* | to speak | to call |

they are, with a few exceptions, completely different from those of the 'gathering house.' The figurative language of curing and magical *ikarkana* can be approached in two ways. The first way is lexical. There are words in curing and related *ikarkana* which exist in colloquial Kuna as well but which in the *ikarkana* have distinct, derived, figurative meanings. Table 11 lists some examples.

At times a single word in the colloquial language is used with distinct meanings in different *ikarkana*. For example, *mola* (shirt or blouse in colloquial Kuna) signifies leaves in 'the way of the hot pepper' and skin in 'the way of the cooling off.' From a sociolinguistic point of view, these examples are part of the special lexical system of the 'stick doll' linguistic variety (described more fully in chapter 2).

Second, the figurative speech found in curing and magical *ikarkana* occurs in the form of whole descriptive passages which are to be understood as symbolic representations or as statements of analogous relationships between the spirit and the physical world. Thus the description of the movements of the plant in 'the way of the basil' represents the actual birth of the spirit of this plant. The description of the house of *muu* in 'the way of birth' is to be understood as a simultaneous description of the body of the childbearing woman and a real spirit house.[27]

While figurative-metaphorical language is clearly an aspect of Kuna curing and magical *ikarkana*, it is not as crucial to the functioning of these *ikarkana* as it is in 'gathering house' discourse, where metaphors are creatively adapted and manipulated. Thus Kuna magical language cannot be productively analyzed by focusing exclusively on metaphors and metaphorical relationships, as Tambiah has analyzed Trobriand magical language, Rosaldo Ilongot magical language, or Howe Kuna 'gathering house' language.[28]

## What Makes Curing and Magic Work

In describing the Kuna system of curing and the related magical control of spirits and objects, I have focused on the verbal properties of curing and magical *ikarkana*. It is also useful to ask what makes the system effective, what makes it work. The Kuna share with other American Indian societies the existence of curing specialists who perform their duties by means of communication with the spirit world. But whereas in many of these societies, especially in tropical forest South America, specialists make extensive use of drugs and induced trances, the Kuna employ neither. Rather, the spirit world is controlled solely by means of the performance of *ikarkana* by their specialists, the *'ikar* knowers.'

One way in which the *ikarkana* are conceived is as an *apsoket* (conversation) between the 'knower' and the spirits. The name of the most spectacular of all these *ikarkana*, that of mass curing and the exorcising of evil spirits, is derived from the word *apsoket*. The *ikarkana* are also 'counsel,' explicit directions on how to carry out the bidding of the performer. In this 'counsel,' the performer speaks directly to the spirits in their own language. He demonstrates intimate knowledge of them by describing their origin, their home, their various names, the parts of their bodies, and their daily activities. Having convinced them in this way that he knows them, the specialist is able to control them. This is achieved by describing and narrating a series of events. Because of this narration and simultaneous with it, the events described occur in the spirit world.[29] As a result of the performance of the *ikar*, the spirits then bring about the desired result in the physical world—the calming of a fever, the disappearance of a headache, a successful hunt, or the grabbing of a snake. Verbal control is magical control.

Kuna magic involves no abracadabra, hocus-pocus, unintelligibility, or weirdness, as Malinowski thought should be everywhere characteristic of magic.[30] Although not understood by noninitiates, curing and magical *ikarkana* are definitely understood by spirits and are clearly intelligible in the sense that they can be analyzed phoneme by phoneme, morpheme by morpheme, word by word, line by line, verse by verse, and stanza by stanza. In these *ikarkana*, grammar, rhetoric, speech play, poetry, and magic intersect. In the verbal mediation among humans, nature, and the world of spirits, grammar becomes poetry and poetry becomes magic.

This is how the *ikarkana* work with regard to interaction between the *'ikar* knower' and the spirit or object. What about Kuna individuals and Kuna society more generally? How does Kuna curing work psychologically and sociologically? Those who are not '*ikar* knowers' do not generally understand the *ikarkana*, which in any case are not addressed to them. Yet they have ample opportunity to see and hear them performed, either in actual curing, whether for their own benefit or for that of friends or members of their family, or in the learning, teaching, or practicing by '*ikar* knowers' or students. So the existence, efficacy, verbal artistry, and general importance of these *ikarkana* are constantly brought to public attention. And, while ordinary Kuna may not understand an *ikar* in absolute detail, they are quite aware of its purpose and general structure. And to varying degrees they understand some of the *ikar*, ranging from a few words here and there to whole passages.

Thus, the psychological efficacy of *ikarkana* depends on individuals' knowledge of and belief in the general features of the process rather than on a comprehension of its minute referential and symbolic details. Furthermore, the repetitive, incantatory, and euphonic nature of these *ikarkana* renders them mentally relaxing. Performed by a specialist in whom the patient has the utmost confidence and combined with the administration of actual medicine, the *ikarkana* usually prove to be quite effective. Thus Lévi-Strauss' interesting analysis of a Kuna curing text is both wrong and right. Lévi-Strauss is incorrect in his assumption that the patient understands the language and symbolism of the text. But he is no doubt correct in the more abstract sense that the patient's general knowledge of the nature of the text and how it works is psychologically effective.[31]

So, while the Kuna curing and magical system is the specialty of certain ritualists, it is also a public affair, a constant part of Kuna life for all to see, appreciate, and respect. And since for the most part it does not contradict but complements the changing world—with its new diseases, medicines, and hospitals—it is quite adaptable.

### Variation and Adaptation

Given that *ikarkana* are passed on by rote memorization from teacher to student, they constitute a most traditional aspect of Kuna life. Viewed in this way, Kuna curing and magical events seem to contrast with events of the 'gathering house' with regard to flexibility and adaptability. And to a certain degree this is true. The most striking aspect of 'gathering house' chanting as well as speaking is their focus on creative adaptation, on the ability of individuals— 'chiefs' and followers, women and men, young and old—to perform verbally for long periods of time, on the spot, with no preparation, taking a theme, an idea, or a metaphor and developing it to make it fit the particular issue at hand. In curing and magical *ikarkana*, on the other hand, the texts appropriate for particular diseases or other purposes are putatively fixed, and the '*ikar* knowers' make changes, really choices, in these fixed texts only according to the origin of the disease or the particular goal of the *ikar*.

Nevertheless, as is characteristic of Kuna life in general and speaking in particular, there is room for change and adaptation within the tradition of continuity. This is possible because of variations (both in the approach to disease and related matters and in the existence of differing traditions of the same *ikar*), conflicts, new situations, and a generally eclectic attitude on the part of the Kuna.

Varying approaches to curing can cause differences of opinion. A particularly good example has to do with snakebite. This is a very sensitive area in that the Kuna are agriculturalists and the jungle mainland is populated by a number of very dangerous snakes. There are curing specialists who believe that in the treatment of snakebites, because evil spirits abound, the entire village must be involved. In extreme cases this might mean the prohibition of work in the jungle and the prohibition of noise in the village, especially at night. Radios are silenced, people are told to walk barefoot, and 'gatherings' are either canceled or held in a whisper; no chanting is permitted. Other specialists, however, disagree. They hold that if a curing specialist is adequately trained, if he is truly an expert, he should be able to cure a snakebite victim rapidly without the need to disrupt village life—medicine, *ikarkana*, and 'secrets' should suffice.

These differences can lead to conflict, especially when the principal exponents of the different approaches live in the same village. Just such a situation occurred in 1970 in Mulatuppu, when the village gave a scholarship to a respected curing specialist, Olowitinappi, to permit him to study snakebite medicine with a renowned expert in a distant village (see chapters 2, 3, and 8). Just after his departure, a man was bitten by a snake on his evening hunting trip to the jungle. The victim was placed in the care of another curing specialist, who insisted on the village-wide measures described above. When the patient did not get better, there was considerable tension on the island. Evening 'gatherings' heatedly (though in a whisper) debated whether the methods were effective. Some men argued that, when Olowitinappi returned, he would be able to handle such cases without all the village-wide fuss. Finally, the man's family decided to take him to a missionary-run hospital in another village, six hours away by motorboat.

The case of the snakebite victim is a good illustration of the role of variation in the Kuna curing system. On the one hand, variation is a source of conflict, both between individual specialists and between factions within the community. On the other hand, both variation and conflict provide opportunities for change and adaptation. And both relate to empirical reality—the important fact that sometimes cures do not work. Another case provides a useful illustration.

In March of 1979, Armando, a Mulatuppu 'chief' and an active political leader in the eastern region of San Blas, fell seriously ill. His friend Richards was called on to perform 'the way of the hat' for him. Richards is a respected curing specialist who often publicly affirms his abilities, especially claiming that he is the best performer of an *ikar* on the island or that his version is the best. At the same time, other versions of 'the way of the hat' are known in Sasartii-Mulatuppu; in fact, it is commonly known. While each version is, from an official point of view, equally effective, there is always the possibility that on a particular occasion one version or one performer might be more successful than another.[32] The performance of long *ikarkana* such as 'the way of the hat' is, furthermore, time-consuming and tiring. It was thus decided that Richards and another 'medicinal specialist' and 'knower,' Mastayans, would alternate performing the *ikar* on successive afternoons. In this way, potential conflict between the two respected specialists, while not necessarily avoided, was channeled into a cooperative, if nonetheless competitive, medical team. As it turned out, Armando was slow to recover, his illness became the subject of a 'gathering house' discussion, and it was decided that he should go to the local government-run hospital. The argument was that, while the Kuna approach is effective, it takes longer than Panamanian medicine; since it was important for Armando to resume his official duties and responsibilities as soon as possible, it was best that he go to the hospital. Armando was thus cured by an effective combination of native Kuna specialists and a modern Panamanian hospital, all potentially in conflict with one another.

A good example of variation and especially adaptation which functions to maintain tradition within the Kuna curing system is 'medicine counsel.' This set of *ikarkana* is used not only for traditional Kuna medicine but for any object or substance which is to be used as medicine. It is the 'medicine counsel' which renders the medicinal potential inherent in an object effective and gives it life, by explaining to it how to go about its work. This openness with regard to the class of medicine and its relationship to 'medicine counsels' makes it possible to accept and welcome non-Kuna, western medicine. From the Kuna point of view, it is quite possible for there to be medicine other than the plants that 'medicinal specialists' gather in the jungle; many objects are potentially medicinal. The skill of the 'medicinal specialist' consists not only in knowing what plants have medicinal value but in being able to counsel them and thus empower them. Similarly, the *ikarkana* used in the curing of disease are not in opposition to the medicine which is also used in the cure—they are complementary. The *ikar* advises the spirits of good to struggle against the spirits of evil. The *ikar* and the medicine work together. The more the patients have going for them, the better. So a cure can be effective by using Kuna medicine, Kuna *ikarkana*, and non-Kuna medicine, all at the same time. This is something which the Kuna understand perfectly well but outsiders have trouble grasping. An incident is representative of this situation.

Recently a hospital was built on the mainland near Mulatuppu. After it began operating, the Panamanian minister of health visited it to see how things were working out. He was greeted by a local 'chief,' to whom he made long speeches explaining how lucky the Indians were to have a government which built them schools and hospitals, supplied them with medicine, and so on, so that they could progress. The 'chief' responded that he agreed and that his people were most thankful. The minister of health then took off in his goverment helicopter, in time to have lunch in the capital. The 'chief' set off on his typical morning chore, gathering medicine in the jungle—he is also a respected 'medicinal specialist' in the community.

There are also various ways in which new *ikarkana* can develop, if the need arises. And needs do arise—new diseases occur, old diseases get harder to cure, and people need new skills. Although *ikarkana* are primarily transmitted through teaching, there is another way as well. Certain specialists, especially 'seers,' can learn *ikarkana* in their dreams. In such dreams, the 'stick doll' representatives of the spirit world or *serkan* (deceased persons) teach the 'seer' the *ikar*. The 'seer' is then capable of teaching it to others, who become 'knowers' as well. It is because the *ikarkana* are in their language and are in their realm of knowledge that the spirit representatives are able to teach them to 'seers.' But, while these *ikarkana* are traditional in theme, form, and content, they can be new, either new versions of existing *ikarkana* or totally new.[33] They might thus be effective in ways that old *ikarkana* no longer are.

The learning of *ikarkana* in dreams is not always believed or accepted by all members of the community. Specialists who have learned their *ikarkana* by the long, tedious, and difficult method of apprenticing themselves to a teacher are particularly skeptical. It is in moments of crisis especially that representatives of the spirit world tend to appear in the dreams not only of 'seers' but of other village leaders and ritual specialists as well, in order to comment on and criticize aspects of Kuna life and behavior and to propose solutions to village problems.

Thus curing and magic can be seen as an essentially traditional aspect of Kuna life, involving a set of ritual specialists, a secretive, somewhat archaic language, and a set of *ikarkana* passed on from 'knowers' to their students. These *ikarkana* derive their efficacy from the belief that the spirits of good and evil can be controlled when properly advised, in their language with the appropriate memorized text. At the same time, the system is not frozen. There are openness and adaptability; there is always the possibility for change and development in order to meet new situations and new problems in the context of tradition.

# 5. Puberty Rites and Festivities

The focus of the third Kuna ritual tradition is an important stage in the life cycle of a woman, puberty. Girls' puberty rites—called *inna* rites, after the fermented drink which is consumed in large quantities during them—are sharply distinguished from the other two Kuna ritual traditions, the *onmakket* (gathering) tradition and the curing and magic tradition, by means of a separate ritual language, *kantule kaya* (*kantule* language); a particular setting, the *inna neka* (*inna* house); a distinct social organization, at the center of which is the *kantule*, the director of the ritual; and a special set of events and activities, official and unofficial, serious and playful. Many societies, including those of tropical forest South America, are reported to have both curing and magical rituals and puberty rituals. Belief in the existence of spirits and in the possibility of human-spirit communication is also common. What is special and significant about the Kuna is that curing and magic on the one hand and puberty on the other centrally and crucially involve human-spirit communication as well as two distinct speaking traditions and organizations. At the same time, these two traditions are also joined within the context of the puberty rites and festivities, during which both humans and spirits are intensely involved.[1]

## Puberty Events

Until she reaches puberty, a Kuna girl wears her straight hair long and flowing down her back. At puberty, her hair is ritually cut very short; it is kept short for the rest of her life. If he chooses to and if he can afford to, the girl's father provides food for village-wide festivities. The entire community—which assists and cooperates by providing bananas and some fish—participates in eating this food and in drinking *inna*, as well as rum and beer. The central form of discourse at puberty rites is a long *ikar* (way, text) which is performed by the *kantule* and his student-assistants and addressed to the spirit of the *kammu*, a long flute, in the presence of the community, which drinks freely and participates in many types of activities and festivities. The most full blown and spectacular of the various puberty rites, in terms of length of time and degree of ceremonial activity, are the *inna tunsikkalet* (short *inna*), which lasts two days, and the *inna suit* (long *inna*), which lasts three or more days. There are no puberty rites for Kuna boys, although perhaps there used to be.

The puberty festivities are the only occasions on which the Kuna are permitted to drink alcoholic beverages in large quantities (some San Blas villages allow a beer at a store on ordinary evenings). When a girl's father announces in the *onmakket neka* (gathering house) that he is planning to provide food for the festivities, the preparation of the *inna* begins (in a more general sense, these festivities are planned months and sometimes years ahead of time, and preparations also begin well ahead). On a set day, all the men of the village are required to gather sugarcane, each returning with a specified amount. The cane is then squeezed into juice in wooden squeezers or mills located outdoors throughout the village. Under the supervision of the *inna sopet* (*inna* maker) and his student-assistants, the *inna* is prepared in the '*inna* house,' which contains the caldrons, long dugout river canoes, and jars used for this purpose.

The '*inna* house,' like the 'gathering house,' has exactly the same structure as all traditional Kuna houses and is built with the same materials. And, also like the 'gathering house,' it is a huge version of a Kuna house, capable of including the entire population of a village and outside visitors as well. On the island of Sasartii-Mulatuppu, the '*inna* house' is located between and parallel to the 'gathering houses' of the two separate villages of Mulatuppu and Sasartii. The three structures, all opening onto a large plaza, constitute an important and impressive central focus of the island. The '*inna* house' physically and symbolically links the two villages; both use it to prepare *inna*, and both participate together in the rituals and festivities within it. The '*inna* house' is kept closed during most of the year. It is opened and used only during the preparation of *inna* and food for the village-wide rites and festivities and during these rites and festivities.

The '*inna* maker' directs all the details of its preparation—the mixing of the ingredients, the cooking in large iron caldrons, the stirring in the long wooden pirogues, and the tasting. This specialist also performs, either in the presence of the fermenting sugarcane juice or in the privacy of his own home, *inna sopet ikar* (the way of the making of *inna*), a long chant addressed to the spirit of the *inna* which advises it to ferment properly. Like other magical *ikarkana* (see chapter 4), 'the way of the making of *inna*' demonstrates to the *inna* spirit the performer's knowledge of its origin and essence and causes desired events to occur by means of a narration of them. This is one of several magical chants which are performed in order to insure that the various preparations for the puberty rites and festivities are properly carried out. *Kammu suet ikar* (the way of the getting of the flute) is performed as part of the preparation of the *kantule*'s very important flute. *Kaspak ikar* (the way of the hammock rope) is performed as part of the preparation of the hammock used by the *kantule*. And a curing-magical *ikar* often performed during the festivities themselves is *wipoet ikar* (the way of sobering up); addressed to the spirit of the *inna* by inebriated individuals, it functions to sober them up.

'The way of the making of *inna*' describes in detail the preparations for the puberty rites and festivities as well as the rites and festivities themselves. It is an excellent and precise verbal reflection of how these events actually proceed. Here the '*inna* maker' tastes the *inna* and decides when it will be strong enough to drink.

The *inna*-making specialist opens the door of the *inna* house.
The door of the *inna* house makes noise.
The different tones cannot be distinguished.
He enters the door of the *inna* house.
There are many golden benches in place.
There are many silver benches in place.
On his golden bench.
The *inna*-making specialist sits down.
On their silver benches.
The *inna* tasters sit down.
The *inna*-making specialist says to the owners of the *inna* [the parents of the young girl for whom the festivities are to be held].
'Bring me water to rinse out my mouth.'
The owners of the *inna* pour this very water.
They give this water to the *inna*-making specialist.
The *inna*-making specialist rinses out his mouth with the water.
The *inna*-making specialist says to the owners of the *inna*.
'Bring me sugarcane juice [*inna*].'
He tastes the sugarcane juice.
He tastes it.
The *inna*-making specialist lines up the jars in order of strength.
The jars are lined up in order of strength.
The jars are in a straight line.

The *inna*-making specialist says to the owners of the *inna*.
'In three days you will have the festivities.'
The *inna*-making specialist says.

The '*inna* maker' goes to the '*inna* house.'

The *inna*-making specialist takes his cane [a sign of his office].
The *inna*-making specialist's tasters take their canes.
The *inna*-making specialist walks around his house.
He leaves.
He goes out the door of his house.
He plays his *korki* flute [announcing the beginning of festivities] on
    the way to the *inna* house.

He directs the details of the preparations for the ritual activities.

The *inna*-making specialist says.
'Put up the balsa wood shelves [used in the *inna* ritual].'
The owners of the *inna* nail up the shelves with palm wood.
The *inna*-making specialist is watching, inside the *inna* house.
On the shelf next to the jars of *inna*, the flute specialists [ritual offi-
    cials] put the wood for the flutes.
The caretakers of things [ritual officials] are inside the *inna* house.
The owners of the *inna* put a *karpa* basket on the shelf, a small
    *karpa* basket.
They place a *sikki* cup [a small drinking cup] in the *inna* house.
The *inna*-making specialist is watching.

The various ritual officials arrive at the '*inna* house' for the event.

The *inna*-making specialist is watching, inside the *inna* house.
The *kanturkana* are weaving are stepping toward the *inna* house.
The *inna*-making specialist is watching, inside the *inna* house.
The caretakers of things are weaving are stepping toward the *inna*
    house.
The *inna*-making specialist is watching.
The caretakers of the incense burners [ritual officials] are weaving
    are stepping toward the *inna* house.
The *inna*-making specialist is watching.
The *inna* servers are weaving are stepping toward the *inna* house.
The *inna*-making specialist is watching.
The caretakers of the hammock rope are weaving are wandering are
    walking toward the *inna* house.
The *inna*-making specialist is watching.
The haircutters are weaving are stepping are walking toward the
    *inna* house.

Finally, all members of the community have entered the '*inna* house' and the festivities are in full swing.

The owners of the *inna* [now referring to the entire community] make much noise.
The owners of the *inna* drink much *inna*.
The owners of the *inna* drink more *inna*.
The owners of the *inna* make much noise.
'This is how we want to feel.'
The owners of the *inna* shout.
The owners of the *inna* make so much noise that the different tones cannot be distinguished.
The owners of the *inna* make much noise.
The owners of the *inna* are drunk with *inna*.
The owners of the *inna* make much noise.
The owners of the *inna* empty the benches.
They scatter the benches all over the place.
The *inna*-making specialist is watching, inside the *inna* house.[2]

After five or six days of fermentation, the *inna* is tasted in order to decide when it will be ready to drink. The tasting is a public event; it takes place in either the '*inna* house' or the 'gathering house' and is attended by the '*inna* maker' and his assistants, who sit on a bench in front of the *inna*, as well as by many men who come in to observe. There is a lively, festive atmosphere, including considerable verbal play and amusement. The event is an appropriate precursor to the full-blown letting go of the actual festivities to follow.

When it is decided that the *inna* is ready to drink, the rites and festivities begin. A special enclosure is constructed for the young girl outside the '*inna* house' and she is placed within this enclosure and buried in the sand with only her head above ground.[3] Within the enclosure, the *iet* (haircutter) and her assistants cut the girl's long hair according to prescribed techniques. The women perform the nonverbal aspects of the ritual; the men perform the verbal. The rites include various official activities which are performed only on these occasions, as well as various unofficial activities which are associated with the festivities. One of the important official events is the selection of a secret *nuka sunnat* (true name) for the girl by the *kantule*.

Central to the whole affair is the performance by the *kantule* and his student-assistants in the '*inna* house.' (While the prestigious role of *kantule* takes many years of hard work and expenditure to acquire, his students have official roles within the puberty ritual and perform the *ikar* along with him, thus affording them an oppor-

tunity to gain public prestige while still in the apprenticeship stage.)
These individuals, both standing and sitting or lying in a large hammock, two at a time shout the very long *kantule ikar* (the way of the
*kantule*), shaking rattles and blowing on the long flute (*kammu*) as
they shout.[4] The shouting of the *kantule*—called *kormakke* in
Kuna—is quite different in performance style from the chanting of
*saklakana* (chiefs) or the chanting of *ikar wismalat* (*ikar* knowers).
Apart from the *kantule* and his assistants and the flute, there are no
official participants in this event. The *kantule* role is named for the
flute (*kantule* < *kammu - tule* = flute man). And 'the way of the
*kantule*' is addressed to the spirit of the flute, in the special linguistic variety shared by the *kantule* and this spirit. The *kammu* is one
of several Kuna flutes which are used during the puberty rites and
associated festivities. Made by Kuna specialists from a type of bamboo, which is a very important plant in the everyday and ritual life of
the Kuna, the flute is a most significant element and participant in
the puberty rites.

The members of the community who are present in the '*inna*
house' do not listen to the shouting of the *kantule*. They are typically quite drunk and involved in many sorts of activities. However,
they are aware of the general content of 'the way of the *kantule*' and
of its purpose and significance—they know that successful completion of the puberty rites depends on its performance and that they
should be present.

### The Structure and Content of 'The Way of the *Kantule*'

Puberty rites and festivities are considered by the Kuna to be the
most traditional of all their ritual activities. From a linguistic point
of view, especially with regard to vocabulary, the language used in
'the way of the *kantule*' is most different from everyday colloquial
Kuna; it is the most difficult of all ritual linguistic varieties for the
noninitiated to understand. There is at the same time a general similarity between the overall structure of 'the way of the *kantule*' and
the structure of the curing and magical *ikarkana* described in chapter 4. In both a narrative describes various acts associated with the
event. In both the performance of the *ikar* is necessary in order for
these acts to occur. And both have a unique secretive and metaphorical vocabulary, pervasive syntactic and semantic parallelism,
and a line and verse structure.

The *kantule*'s long *ikar* is the most immutable of all Kuna ritual
discourse. It is repeated identically, including every single phoneme
and morpheme, each time it is performed. The extremely realistic
*ikar* precisely reflects the set of events in which it plays a central,

organizing, and directive role. It describes in minute detail every aspect of the puberty rites and associated activities and festivities, from the preparation of the participants to the cutting of the young girl's hair to the eating of a special meal and drinking of the *inna*. Here is a description of the young girl going to the jungle river in order to bathe in preparation for the ritual.

The girl goes quietly.
Along the path of the river.
Walking along the path of the river.
She arrives at the river.
She stands up in the river.
She bathes in the river.

The young girl undresses and bathes.

She carries her *karpa* basket.
She carries her *sile* basket.
The girl takes off her belt.
The girl takes off her underwear.
The girl takes off her coin necklace.
The girl takes off her bead necklace.
The girl takes off her beads.
The girl takes off her mola.
The girl quietly bathes.

Here is a description of some of the drinking utensils used for the *inna*.

There is the strainer.
There is the large *inna* drinking cup.
There is the small *sikki* cup.
There is the *nokmur* drinking cup.
There is the mouth-rinsing cup.

Here is a description of the carrying into the enclosure of the cosmetics and utensils used in the ritual haircutting.

The women carry in the *makep* dye.
The women carry in the *nisar* dye.
The women carry in the comb.
The women carry in the scissors.

Here is a description of the 'haircutter' drinking *inna*.

They take the cover off the *inna* jar.
They scoop up *inna*.
The haircutter begins to drink.

The haircutter greets people as she drinks [a special ritual greeting
 used only while drinking *inna*].
The haircutter swallows.
Her throat makes a loud noise.
The *inna* makes her burp.

Here are descriptions of the cutting of the girl's hair.

They arrange her hair.
They comb her hair.
The hair is all arranged.

They open the hair.
They raise the hair.
The cutting of the hair makes noise.
It can be heard far away.

The hair doubles over.
The hair piles up.[5]

As is characteristic of each of the Kuna ritual varieties and *ikar-kana*, there is a lexicon particular to 'the way of the *kantule*.' Table
12 provides some examples, showing how the same meaning is ex-
pressed in colloquial Kuna and in 'the way of the *kantule*.' (See also
chapter 2 for a discussion of the Kuna sociolinguistic system in general and the relationship among varieties.) Words in 'the way of the
*kantule*' are usually completely different in form from the corresponding words in colloquial Kuna. It is for this reason that this linguistic variety is so difficult for noninitiates to understand.

As in all ritual *ikarkana*, there is a great deal of overlapping grammatical and semantic parallelism in 'the way of the *kantule*,' rendering the narration long and slow-moving. Here is but one of many examples, a description of the women who participate in the ritual and
its associated festivities.

*yaikana uuparpa imakte.*
The women's underwear makes noise.
*yaikana uuparpa pukki nite.*
The women's underwear can be heard far away.
*yaikana kala tere imakte.*
The women's coin necklaces make noise.
*yaikana kala tere pukki nite.*
The women's coin necklaces can be heard far away.
*yaikana kala purwa imakte.*
The women's bead necklaces make noise.
*yaikana kala purwa pukki nite.*
The women's bead necklaces can be heard far away.[6]

**Table 12.** Words in Colloquial Kuna and 'The Way of the *Kantule*'

| English | Colloquial Kuna | 'The Way of the *Kantule*' |
|---|---|---|
| woman | *ome* | *yai* |
| girl, maiden | *yaakwa* | *yainua* |
| chicken | *kannir* | *ila koke* |
| river | *tiwar* | *ipe ansui* |
| path | *wala* | *kuna pilli* |
| chicha | *inna* | *waalina* |
| native red cosmetic dye | *makep* | *nia topa* |
| plant which produces *makep* | *nisar* | *kiki yai* |
| strainer | *pukpu* | *saksa tule* |
| light, lamp | *kwallu* | *ipe kanni tule* |
| to feel happy | *yer ittoe* | *ana pina kine, ana kine* |
| broken | *pichisa* | *tupya* |
| *sile* basket | *sile* | *tarpa tarpa* |
| bead necklace | *winkwa* | *kala purwa* |

Associated with the parallelistic structure is a clearly defined poetic line structure. In this passage, every line begins with the noun *yai-kana* (women) and ends with the tense-aspect and also line final marker *te* (then).

'The way of the *kantule*,' like curing and magical *ikarkana*, can be performed in several contexts. When performed for its primary function, as part of the puberty rites, the *ikar* is *kormakke* (shouted) and accompanied by the blowing on the special flute, to whose spirit the *ikar* is addressed. When performed for learning, teaching, and practicing, in the home of the *kantule*, the *ikar* is *namakke* (chanted) in a melodic form quite distinct from the shouting of the actual performance but distinct as well from either 'gathering house' chanting or the performance of curing and magical *ikarkana*.

## Official and Unofficial Activities

The verbal performance of the *kantule* and his assistants, the ritual drinking and eating, the cutting of the hair of the young girl, and the various games and dances are the official events of the puberty rites. Drinking of alcoholic beverages by adults, otherwise taboo, is expected and encouraged.[7] This drinking, especially in its early stages, is done according to ceremonial rules. At dawn, the '*inna* maker' and his assistants, sitting on a long bench and drinking out of tiny cups, taste the *inna*. Individuals stand in a long line and drink out of small cups. Special greetings are exchanged by the drinkers.

As the morning wears on, more and more people enter the '*inna* house.' Drinking rounds and competitions are held, making use of drinking gourds of different shapes and sizes. People often drink to the point of passing out—it is typical to see a man, stone-drunk, being carried home from the '*inna* house' by his wife and daughters.

The puberty festivities are a total time out from ordinary Kuna life; the elaborate recreational and carnivalesque activities associated with the rites provide a break in the routine of everyday life, a moment of needed relaxation and recreation for the entire community, both human and spirit. No one goes to work in the jungle, and there is no evening 'gathering.' The entire community is mobilized for and oriented toward the ritual and the associated festivities. From early morning to late evening, everyone is involved in some way. A whole set of ritual officials and experts perform such functions as preparing various flutes, stringing up the *kantule*'s hammock, serving *inna* and meals, and cutting the young girl's hair. Within the '*inna* house,' women and men participate in a series of ritual games and dances that are played and performed on no other occasion. Most members of the community, as well as people from both nearby and distant villages who come just for this occasion, spend a great deal of time in the '*inna* house' and in the homes of friends.

In addition to these official events, there are many activities which are associated with them. Both men and women engage in long and intimate conversations in which their faces almost touch. Men especially speak in languages, such as Spanish and English, which they barely know. Verbal and even physical disputing and fighting, which the Kuna severely interdict and which are quite rare on most occasions, are frequent. Serious wounds and lasting injuries sometimes result, although quite rarely. Loud talking and joking, yelling and screaming, touching, and a lack of attention to how or where one walks, sits, or lies are all the rule. Pairs of men spend hours at a time playing songs on their panpipes. A holiday atmosphere pervades the village, radiating from the '*inna* house.' Puberty festivities are an occasion for letting go, for both humans and spirits—the drunker and more playful humans become, the more spirits enjoy the festivities.

During the festivities, specialists in particular curing and magical *ikarkana* perform them for a group of individuals, who typically purchase a bottle of rum which is consumed during the performance. Certain *ikarkana* which are especially poetic and dramatic are very popular in this regard, for example, *nia ikar* (the way of the devil). Even if the small audience understands the details of the text only to varying degrees, there are general appreciation and respect for the performer, who, in a state of great inebriation, rattles off his text. In addition, the spirit world, which is also participating in the festivities, enjoys listening to the performance of *ikarkana*.

There is another set of *ikarkana* which, like curing and magical *ikarkana*, are addressed to spirits but which have no direct curative or magical function. The purpose of this set of *ikarkana* is both to inform and remind the spirits that the performer knows about them, about their lives and their environment, and to amuse them and give them pleasure; humans also take pleasure in performing and listening to them. These *ikarkana* are often performed during puberty festivities. Snakes and snake spirits, a source of great danger and fear to the Kuna, are the focus of several such *ikarkana—nakpe tuttu* (the snake's flowers), *nakpe panter* (the snake's flags), *nakpe mesa* (the snake's table), and *nakpe kalu* (the snake's stronghold). Here is the opening of 'the snake's flowers.'

Machi Olowintupippi [the spirit name of the snake] is planting a row of golden *panapki* flowers.
Machi Olowintupippi Nele is planting many rows of golden *panapki* flowers.
Around Machi Olowintunappi Nele's [another spirit name of the snake] stronghold.
At the mouth of the Oloupikuna River.
Machi Olowintunappi Nele causes golden *panapki* flowers to be born.
Machi Olowintunappi causes many golden *panapki* flowers to be born.
Around Machi Olowintunappi Nele's stronghold.
At the mouth of the Oloupikuna River.
Machi Olowintunappi Nele's *panapki* flowers are budding out.
Machi Olowintunappi Nele's *panapki* flowers are budding out all over.
Around Machi Olowintunappi Nele's stronghold.
At the mouth of the Oloupikuna River.[8]

Another set of *ikarkana, totoet ikarkana* (play *ikarkana*), are performed by both men and women during puberty festivities; the humorous memorized texts are chanted. The language of 'play *ikarkana*' is a mixture of colloquial Kuna and the linguistic variety of the spirit world. It shares some syntactic features and vocabulary with the *ikarkana* used in curing and magic. For this reason, 'play *ikarkana*' are only partially intelligible to young people who have had relatively little exposure to curing and magic. In addition to their human audience, 'play *ikarkana*,' like curing and magical *ikarkana*, have a spirit audience which also appreciates and enjoys playful and humorous language, especially during puberty festivities. 'Play *ikarkana*' deal with the exploits of humans, animals, and such supernatural beings as the devil. Examples are *yaukka ikar* (the way of the sea turtle), *tapkala ikar* (the way of the heron), *ulur ikar* (the way of the howler monkey), and *iskwir ikar* (the way of the cockroach).[9] Here is the opening of 'the way of the sea turtle,' the story of Machi Esakunappi, a man who loses his wife to a sticky sea turtle.

Machi Esakunappi speaks to his wife.
He says.
'There is the sea's mother [the sea turtle's 'play name'].
Let us go see the sea's mother.
It is the moment to do it.'
Machi Esakunappi speaks to his wife.
Machi Esakunappi pursues the aunt-niece [another name of the sea turtle] toward the waves [the sea].
Thinking about the aunt-niece.
Beside his wife he is turning about on the waves.
Thinking about the aunt-niece.
And then the aunt-niece comes rising on the waves.
Machi Esakunappi watches.
Machi Esakunappi says to his wife.
'Let's find out.
How strong she is.
First you find out.'
Machi Esakunappi says to his wife.
His wife touches the aunt-niece.
She sticks to the aunt-niece sees Machi Esakunappi.
Machi Esakunappi thinks.
'This is one of those [sticky turtles] the elders chant about [in the 'gathering house'].
I should not touch my wife.'
His wife raises her arm.
On the waves, on the waves, the aunt-niece descends.
Machi Esakunappi watches the waves.
The waves fall.
He watches his wife.
Out on the waves his wife is floating.
The aunt-niece is floating.
And Machi Esakunappi sees his wife.
'I am leaving you.'

The wife says to Machi Esakunappi.
His wife says different kinds of things on the waves.
'The devil will take you.
I am leaving on the waves.'
She says as she goes.[10]

## Tradition and Variation

Kuna puberty festivities share certain features with carnival and holiday rites of reversal found throughout the world, including those of tropical forest South America.[11] There is a general sense of looseness and letting go which is in direct contrast with ordinary Kuna etiquette. While many types of behavior and activity are permitted and encouraged, there is a special focus on speech play and verbal art. In addition to being rites of reversal, with a loose (at least for the highly moral Kuna) carnival atmosphere, the puberty rites and festivities are a most serious and punctilious occasion, celebrating the passage of a young girl into womanhood and involving both the human and the spirit worlds to a very full extent. It is these striking combinations of human and spirit, seriousness and play, and carnival and ritual which so mark these rites and festivities.[12]

The most complete and spectacular puberty rites are the 'long *inna*,' which lasts three or more days, and the two-day 'short *inna*,' which I have described here. However, before this official passing into womanhood, the life of a Kuna girl is punctuated by a series of events.[13] This existence of different life-cycle rituals, involving a variety of periods of time and types of events, allows for varying degrees of village and personal mobilization, time off, drinking, and expense.

*Ikko inna* (needle *inna*) celebrates the piercing of holes in the nose of a two- to three-year-old girl; these holes are for the gold nose rings which Kuna women wear all their lives. If the girl's father chooses to, he provides food for a one-day festival. During 'needle *inna*,' there is ritual and ceremonial drinking, but the *kanturkana* do not perform and there are no official games or dances.

When a Kuna girl has her first menstruation, this fact is announced in the 'gathering house' by her father. The next day, the men of the village are required to go to the mainland and gather thatch for the construction of a hut within the house of the girl's family. The girl resides in the hut during her menstruation, as part of a series of rituals and activities. She is painted black with *saptur* (*Genipa americana*), a native dye which is used to counteract evil spirits. The dye is gathered by a specialist, who also counsels it in a special *ikar* in order to render it effective.[14] As part of a ritual known as *tii wee* (water carrying), female relatives and friends bring water into the house and bathe the girl. While she is isolated and does not talk, the relatives and friends sit together in the house, drinking oatmeal, sweet corn, and other beverages, talking, and making molas. In addition to its official place in the ritual cycle of a Kuna girl's life, 'water carrying' provides a several-day occasion for women from different households to get together for gossip and verbal play.

*Inna muttikkit* (night *inna*) is a village-wide celebration of a young girl's first menstruation. It is an abbreviated version, along several dimensions, of the full rites and festivities that I have described here. There is ritual and ceremonial drinking, which begins at dawn and lasts throughout the day; other ritual events include smoking locally made cigars and blowing the cigar smoke on the ritual specialists. *Kanturkana* do not perform, and there are no ritual games or dances. Unofficial activities, such as the playing of panpipes, the performance of curing and magical *ikarkana* and of 'play ikarkana,' and long intimate conversations in Kuna and other languages, do occur.

Of the three Kuna ritual traditions, the puberty tradition is publicly practiced and performed least frequently. In Sasartii-Mulatuppu, two or three full-scale puberty rites are typically held during a single year, contrasted with the daily occurrence of chanting or talking 'gatherings' and the common performance and practice of curing, medicinal, and magical *ikarkana*. At the same time, the Kuna accord great significance to the puberty rites and associated festivities, and as a result they are the focus of an enormous amount of village-wide and individual energy, time, and money. They are anticipated long in advance and are discussed both in private homes and in public 'gatherings.'[15]

In spite of the fact that puberty rites are in many ways the most traditional of all Kuna ritual activities, there exist flexibility and adaptability in them as in all other aspects of Kuna life. According to the Kuna, in the past there was considerable geographical variation in the language and text of 'the way of the *kantule.*' It is said that there were twelve distinct traditions. Today there are three—*nia* (devil) *kantule*, *ipe* (sun) *kantule*, and *sulu* (monkey) *kantule*, distributed geographically. Sasartii-Mulatuppu, which has two *kanturkana*, belongs to the 'monkey' *kantule* tradition. Puberty specialists take an interest in this geographical variation. Specialists from different villages invite one another to perform and participate as guests and thus observe and listen to the differences in the way each performs the ritual.

There are also flexibility and adaptability with regard to the preparation and celebration of puberty festivities. Some men take jobs in Panama City or the Canal Zone, precisely in order to earn enough money to pay for their daughters' puberty festivities. And some men, with enough money but not enough time to expend on the effort, have the ritual performed and the festivities prepared and carried out in a village different from their own, literally catered by specialists. In this way, a traditional village is able to gain economically and in prestige by performing puberty rites for other villages, which also contribute to the maintenance of tradition by having them catered. This pattern is part of a larger picture—each village, especially small ones, cannot always have an entire set of ritual specialists, even though this might be a goal, and therefore each needs to go to other villages for certain ritual services.[16] There are both cooperation and competition among villages as a result.

# 6. Everyday Speech: From Morning to Night, from Birth to Death

The boundary between Kuna ritual and everyday speech is by no means always a sharp one. Rather, a set of continua and intersections characterizes the relationship between the ritual and the everyday. The linguistic dimensions of this situation were analyzed in chapter 2, in which the Kuna linguistic varieties and styles were presented. Aspects of the relationship between the ritual and the everyday with regard to the settings for and the social organization of speaking, as well as with regard to genres of speech and their structure, were discussed in chapters 3 to 5, in the context of the presentation of the three Kuna ritual traditions. Relationships of various kinds between ritual and everyday speech, in the broader context of a total Kuna ethnography of speaking, will be focused on and elaborated in chapter 7.

Kuna everyday speech is a combination of the following features: frequent rather than rare, ordinary rather than special, routine rather than carefully programmed, unscheduled rather than scheduled, relatively personal rather than communal, and private rather than public. Everyday speech tends to be in the colloquial style of Kuna (see chapter 2) and to be spoken rather than chanted. At the same time, there is some overlap with other varieties and styles of Kuna, and some everyday speech is chanted and tuneful.

There has been considerable interest in recent years in the ordinary and especially the conversational use of language. Analysis has tended to focus on (actual or idealized) conversations in middle-class North American society.[1] The various lines of research have developed the notion of the speech act, revealed the existence of rules for conversational turn taking, analyzed the various kinds of cohesive relations that link utterances within a single discourse, and shown the degree to which understanding what is actually said depends on unsaid but shared principles and assumptions. In general this research has indicated that underlying everyday speech (in fact all speech) is a highly intricate structure which is not obvious from or necessarily encoded in surface forms.

This exploration of Kuna everyday speech contributes to more general interests in several ways. Since the Kuna are a nonindustrial, nonliterate society, they contrast sharply with the literate U.S. society which has been the source of most conversational analysis to date. I investigate a wide range of communicative behavior, including conversations but also greetings, leave-takings, commands, requests, verbal and nonverbal pointing, lullabies and 'tuneful weeping,' and various forms of play with language. These forms of discourse are analyzed in and for themselves as well as in terms of the systematic relationships among them and between them and more ritual speech. In addition, in keeping with the ethnographic perspective which is the organizing principle of this study, Kuna everyday speech is always examined in relation to the social and cultural realities in which it is situated.[2]

The best way to explore everyday speech among the Kuna is to approach it simultaneously from several directions and dimensions—in terms of the settings, the occasions and locations, in which everyday speech occurs; in terms of the speech acts, events, and situations of everyday life; in terms of the communicative and social interactional activities and strategies involved in speaking; and in terms of the general patterns of speaking that cut across and interrelate settings, events, activities, and strategies.

### A Focus on Setting: Times and Places for Talking

A Kuna day begins early, typically before dawn. Each man in a family has been assigned or has assigned himself some task the day before and sets out to do it after a drink of *matunnu* (a nutritious combination of bananas, coconut, sugar, and cacao). Men usually go off individually or in small groups to work a family plot of land—clear, burn, plant, or harvest—or, in very large groups, they work on village-owned banana or coconut farms. Other male activities, involving a single man or a small group of men, include hunting, fishing, cutting firewood, and gathering medicinal plants. All these activities are occasions for talk, especially during the travel to and from them by boat and on foot, as well as during breaks within work periods for a drink, a rest, or both. There are neither taboos against talking nor penchants for silence during such activities as hunting or fishing.[3] The Kuna love to talk, feel that talk is natural, and see no reason not to talk while working. Quite the contrary, talk helps make work a pleasure.

The same is true with regard to women's work. In fact, one of the reasons Kuna women like to go to the jungle mainland at any time of day in order to bathe, wash clothes, get fresh river water, or gather fruit is that these ostensible work activities are also occasions for fun and leisure among mothers, daughters, sisters, cousins, and friends. And such fun and leisure consist of constant chatter, including quite a bit of very playful joking. At least one woman remains at home, to watch over and clean the house, cook, and take care of young children. If more than one woman is at home, they talk constantly as they work together.[4]

The Kuna house is a major setting for talk, among both women and men, during the leisure hours of the day. These are typically after work, bathing, and eating in the afternoon but might be in the morning as well, in the case of individuals who for one reason or another did not go to work that day. This talk is first among members of the household, who discuss what they have done during the day and report any particularly interesting or special experiences and any news they have learned. The house is also the setting for visiting, by family and friends. Men are more mobile in this regard than women, who must have very particular purposes for leaving their own house and visiting another. A typical afternoon scene at home involves a group of women, usually related, making molas and talking. Mola making and talk go well together; no one is idle either verbally or economically. In the afternoon there are often quite a few men in each house as well, resting after work and talking. Men also frequently visit family and friends in other houses, to talk about particular work projects and other issues of concern or simply to pass the time of day by chatting a bit. This is especially the case with men visiting from other villages or men who have recently returned from work or travel outside the village. But there are many other pretexts for visiting, including the desire to chat for its own sake. Visits always begin with the host offering the guest something to drink—this is an important communicative act, a significant aspect of Kuna etiquette.

The house is also a place for talk at night. People chat as they get ready to go to sleep, again reporting on the day's activities or gossiping about topics they have not yet discussed with members of their family. With little access to television, radio, or newspapers, it is through talk that people are informed of events in both the nearby and the distant worlds.[5] The day ends as people lie side by side in their hammocks, often still talking to each other.

There are other places in the village where people gather to talk. Most of these places have other functions, though they can become popular spots for talk in and for itself. The docks where Colombian and Kuna boats arrive often become a place where people gather, to stand or sit or walk around and look at the boats, watching the coming and going of people and the buying and selling of goods. The docks are also a convenient place for small groups of men to converse about personal matters in private, out of earshot of anyone else. These relatively secluded settings are rare and valuable on highly populated islands such as Sasartii-Mulatuppu. The airstrip, on an island adjacent to Mulatuppu, is another place where people sit and talk, in the morning, as they await arriving friends and relatives or accompany departing ones.

Many stores, from very small to fairly large and often attached to someone's house, are scattered throughout the village. Here, especially in the afternoon, people come and buy a cup of sugar or rice, ciagrettes, some cloth or thread to make molas, or kerosene for a lamp. Some of these stores, especially those that have a bench outside where people can sit, attract small groups of individuals who gather mainly to talk with the owner, members of the household, or friends who live nearby.

There are places which become popular meeting spots because of some nearby activity. Outside the 'gathering house' but not too close to it, a group of men and sometimes women quietly talk during the evening 'gatherings,' whether these involve chanting or talking.[6] There is a certain degree of coming and going in and out of the 'gathering house,' depending on interest in what is going on, both inside and out, as well as on the personal preferences of the individuals involved. Other activities typically attract groups of people as well, whether or not they are themselves personally involved in them—work activities, such as the mending of fishing nets or the painting of a school building or library, and leisure activities, such as the daily rehearsals of the village dance group. During these activities, there are always much talking and joking.

Certain ritual activities also become focal points for talk, talk that frequently is unrelated to the particular ritual being celebrated or performed. During 'water carrying,' part of the ritual celebration of a Kuna girl's first menstruation (see chapter 5), women sit together and converse and joke as they make molas. During both the preparation and the tasting of the *inna* which is to be drunk at village-wide puberty rites (see chapter 5), men and women (during preparation) or men (during tasting) sit together and observe, talk, and joke among themselves and with the official participants.

This discussion of Kuna settings for everyday talk concludes with a return to the 'gathering house'—for the 'gathering house,' the geographical center of the village, the social and political center, is also always the center for talk. The official talk that goes on here ranges from the most ritual chanting of 'chiefs' to the everyday arguments of men and women. While purely familial issues, such as the parceling out of work tasks for the next day, are confined to private houses, these blend into areas which the Kuna consider to have public consequences and thus to be appropriate for 'gathering house' discussion. They include extramarital affairs, couples whose disagreements involve physical fighting or even loud yelling, and disputes concerning inheritances. Cases of stealing and conflicting points of view about public projects, such as purchasing a village boat or building a health clinic, can also be brought up for discussion in the 'gathering house,' as can disagreements between ritual specialist-teachers and their students.

Most serious arguments that occur during the day are not immediately discussed publicly; rather, they are brought up in the evening during the regular 'gathering.' And the 'gathering house,' whenever it is open, is a natural place for people, again mainly men, to sit and talk. Small groups gather in one corner and chat—these groups form their own locus, while at the same time being able to listen to the relaxed chatting that goes on among village political leaders, seated or lying in hammocks in the center. And this center easily becomes a focal point, a place where men go just to listen or to talk a bit themselves.

## A Focus on Discourse: Speech Acts, Events, and Situations

The speech acts, events, and situations which permeate daily life among the Kuna can be approached in terms of a Kuna day, starting early in the morning until late at night. Or one can follow the life cycle, from birth until death. Another way into Kuna discourse is to separate speech acts and events which are Kuna manifestations of more universal or general acts and events from those which are uniquely Kuna occurrences. In following each of these paths, I have selected for discussion a set of discourse forms which give a sense of what everyday life among the Kuna is like.

I begin with certain events which are probably found in every society in the world—greetings, leave-takings, conversations, commands, and requests. Such basic communicative activities as greeting, taking leave, conversing, commanding, and requesting are rituals of everyday interaction; they are the ways people manage face-to-face encounters on a daily basis. Seemingly simple and straightforward, even trivial, they often involve a considerable amount of structure and strategy.[7] Every society has its own way of structuring these events. Here is the Kuna way.

## Greetings and Leave-Takings

Kuna greetings and leave-takings can best be viewed in terms of a set of relatively discrete acts (verbal and nonverbal) which contrast along several distinct but intersecting dimensions—social relationship (especially degree of closeness) of individuals, setting, and time elapsed since last interaction. The set of Kuna greetings is shown in table 13.

The shortest greeting forms, verbal and nonverbal, are used between two individuals who see one another regularly within a com-

**Table 13.** Kuna Greetings

| Communicative Events Consisting of Two Acts (Initiation and Response) | |
|---|---|
| Verbal | |
| Initiation | Response |
| *tekitte* (well, then, hello) | *anna, na* (utterances with no translatable meaning) |
| *anna, na* | *anna, na* |
| *iki soke?* (what do you say?) | *anna, na, suli* (no) |
| *an ai* (my friend) | *anna, na* |
| person's name or nickname | *anna, na* |
| *pia pe nae?* (where are you going?) | *sappurpa* (to the jungle) |
| *pia pe tanikki?* (where are you coming from?) | *arpae* (work) |
| Nonverbal | |
| Initiation | Response |
| pointed lip gesture | pointed lip gesture |
| hand and finger pointing | hand and finger pointing |

| Communicative Event Consisting of a Single, Nonverbal Act |
|---|
| handshake |

| Communicative Events Consisting of Several Verbal Acts |
|---|
| questions and replies about one's state of health and travel experiences (when chanted, and between 'chiefs,' called *arkan kae*) |

| Silent Communication |
|---|
| mutually acknowledged copresence |

munity, as they pass each other or as they begin to interact. There are certain times of the day, especially early in the morning as people leave for work or in the afternoon as they return, when the atmosphere is literally punctuated with *pia pe nae?* (where are you going?) and *pia pe tanikki?* (where are you coming from?). Greetings are not obligatory, except in the mainland jungle, where in addition to *tekitte* (well, then, hello), *anna*, and *na* individuals exchange questions and replies about their activities.

The longer greeting events are used by individuals from the same community, in close social relationship (kin or friendship), who have been separated for some time; individuals from separate communities visiting one another; or two 'chiefs' from separate villages on an official, ritual visit, in which case the greeting is public. The chanted greeting between two 'chiefs,' *arkan kae* (literally handshake), is performed when a visiting 'chief' arrives in a host village and, if he spends the night, in the morning upon awaking (see chapter 3). Always performed in the 'gathering house,' it is the only member of the set of Kuna greetings which is explicitly labeled. There is no Kuna word for greeting in general. Handshakes are used between men only after a period of separation; they are limited mainly to village officials. Two 'chiefs,' the chanter and the responder, sometimes shake hands just before beginning to chant in the evening.

When two close friends or family members have not seen one another for a significant stretch of time, because one member of the pair has spent several months or years outside the village, the two sometimes seem to avoid one another and exchange no overt greeting at all—yet they manage to be at the same place at the same time, whether this be the airstrip, dock, or 'gathering house.' And each is clearly aware of the presence of the other. This behavior is labeled "mutually acknowledged copresence" in table 13. Such avoidance is quite marked among the usually talkative Kuna. The individual who has stayed at home does not carry out the normal activities for that moment—hunting, farming, fishing, medicine gathering, washing clothes, or cooking—but rather makes it his or her business to be at the place of arrival of the returning individual. Others are present as well, so there may be much talk, but the two individuals do not directly interact with one another. Later on, in one of their homes, lying side by side in adjacent hammocks, the two will greet one another verbally, asking and replying to a series of questions about travels, activities, and health, a pattern very much like the *arkan kae* performed by 'chiefs.'

The pattern of two individuals seeming to avoid one another in some ways resembles the communicative silence that has been described for certain North American Indian groups.[8] For the Kuna, this seeming avoidance—actually mutually acknowledged copresence—should be viewed not as the absence of greeting but as a slowing down and stretching out of the total greeting process, in which the initial portion is nonverbal.[9] This slowing and stretching require interactional work and are a reflection of a more general rule, namely, the more special and significant the social relationship between individuals, the greater the amount of interaction necessary to mark and restore this relationship in greetings.[10] Thus close friends and family members prolong the greeting process by combining public nonverbal, mutually acknowledged copresence with later private questioning and answering. And two 'chiefs,' the political and ritual leaders of two distinct communities, prolong the greeting process by chanting a lengthy and public ritual greeting in an esoteric language.

The set of Kuna leave-takings is not as elaborate as that of greetings. It parallels greetings in that there are short, formulaic leave-takings; handshakes; a longer, more ritualized leave-taking used by socially close persons in anticipation of a period of separation, consisting of the giving of advice to the parting individuals; and mutually acknowledged copresence. In a daily manifestation of the mutually acknowledged copresence greeting and leave-taking pattern, Kuna wives accompany their husbands to their canoes as they leave for work in the morning and meet them as they return, often without exchanging a word.

### Conversations

Kuna conversations resemble the conversations of many societies in that two or more individuals sit or stand together in a focused group and one person tends to talk at a time. The Kuna term for conversation, *apsoket*, is best translated into English as dialogue, which reflects the fact that Kuna conversations tend to be structured in the form of two-person dialogues, even if more than two persons are involved. A set of features characterizes and structures Kuna conversations, including both those involving two participants and those involving more than two. The rule that one person talks at a time is firmly respected. Persons breaking this rule are told by others to wait their turn. The Kuna thus might seem to be more like middle-class North American whites with regard to conversational turn taking than like Caribbean blacks.[11] But there are no doubt more than just these two typological possibilities. Observers of North American conversations have noted that there are considerable overlapping and interrupting across turns and that interactional work is done in order to remedy this. Kuna speakers, in contrast, often talk for long periods of time without overlap or interruption, and extreme patience is exercised by others who wish to talk.

Within each period of talking a line structure frequently emerges, which is akin to but different from the poetic line structure of ritual speaking and chanting. This line structure involves both a particular intonation pattern and line initial and line final markers. In two-person and even multiperson conversations, one individual tends to serve as the second member of a dialogue, ratifying and literally punctuating in various ways the speaker's utterances after each line. Others present serve as audience, observing and commenting on the dialogue between the two principal participants. Conversations often involve the reporting of news or other information. In the following pages, I will provide two examples of Kuna conversations which demonstrate some of their salient characteristics. I will also interpret those aspects of the conversations which cannot be understood without explicit explanation of the social and cultural contexts in which they occur.

The first example is a conversation between two elderly Mula-tuppu men, T and O, old friends who often sit together conversing for long periods of time.[12] This example concludes with the narration of a boat accident resulting in a death. This most engaging story was learned from another person in conversation with him and was told and retold throughout Sasartii-Mulatuppu and, no doubt, San Blas as well. Explanatory and interpretative commentary is placed in brackets.

T:  Today a boat came, today a boat came.
    A Colombian one.
    Colombian.
    [The Kuna carry on a lively trade, centered on but not limited to coconuts, with boats from the Colombian ports of Cartagena and Barranquilla. The arrival of a Colombian boat is a significant event which attracts a crowd at the dock and generates conversational topics. Since the sailors are all black, they stand out sharply if they walk through a Kuna village. A Colombian sailor is just walking by, which is why T makes his remark.]
O:  I don't know, I tell you a boat.
    There's a sailor [referring to the passing sailor].
T:  There's a boat?
O:  Hello [said to a person entering the house, who will then be an observing participant in the conversation].

T: I was talking with Oloaknaikinya and he [another person] came in.

> [Oloaknaikinya, a well-known curing specialist from another village, is visiting Sasartii-Mulatuppu to discuss traditional medicine and other subjects with students as well as with other ritual specialists. By saying that he was talking with Oloaknaikinya, T thus indicates that he himself is a ritual specialist. T ends his turn at talk with the suffix -to, one of the many colloquial line final verb suffixes in Kuna.]

O: Ah. Ah.

> [O ratifies T's turn at talk.]

T: Well I'll retell to you what I was talking about with our friend.

> [This is a very common way of reporting or narrating in Kuna, namely, by directly quoting the words of someone else. T begins his turn with the word *teki* (well, then) and ends it with the verb suffix -*sunno*, both common Kuna line markers.]

O: Yes.

> [O ratifies.]

T: Our friend said.

'I tell you someone got hurt.'

> [T introduces his narrative with the topic—an accident involving injury, always a reportable topic for the Kuna.[13] The verb suffix -*ye* (emphatic) is used as a line final marker.]

O: Mm.

> [O ratifies.]

T: While he was talking about the person who got hurt, I asked him questions about it, ah.

> [T is here stating the structure of his conversation with Oloaknaikinya; namely, as is the Kuna pattern, Oloaknaikinya would report line by line and T would ratify and ask questions, precisely as O is now doing with T. Notice that T considers it appropriate to include this metacommunicative structural description as part of his conversational report.]

O: Yes.

T: Only that, ah.

He told me.

It's true, ah.

In Ukkupseni [a Kuna village to the west of Sasartii-Mulatuppu], a foreigner.

He died, I tell you an American.

> [The narrative now becomes extremely interesting and reportable, involving a foreigner in San Blas, a death, an American.]

O: Ah.

An American died.

[o ratifies with 'ah' plus a repetition of a portion of t's turn at talk.]

t: An American died.

He was speaking to me about this.

He [another person] was listening.

'There were four,' he says.

[t again inserts a metacommunicative commentary, describing the conversation in which he learned that the American died. He then concludes by returning to the actual narrative, stating that four persons were involved in the accident. He ends with *soke* (he says), a quotative and line final marker.]

o: An American.

t: 'They were coming in a motorboat,' he says.

[t again ends with *soke*. From here until the end of the narrative is essentially one turn at talk for t, with very short ratifications from o. As such narrations become more involved and developed, turns become longer and longer.]

o: Ah.

t: Probably with a sail, I think, that's my opinion.

o: Ah.

t: 'They had a motor,' he says to me.

[t again ends his line with *soke*.]

o: Ah.

t: 'The wind came up,' he said.

[t ends his line with *soke* plus the verb suffix -*sunto* (in truth), also a line final marker.]

o: Mm.

t: As they came.

It seems they were coming from Colombia.

Where were they coming from, Colombia, I think.

o: Mm.

t: Then the boat turned over.

They didn't feel anything anymore.

Lost.

[t begins his turn with the word *kep* (then), a common line initial marker.]

o: Mm.

t: One was found, dying.

o: Mm.

t: He came up on the beach, the others were lost.

o: At Ukkupseni, or at Ukkuppa?

They found one?

At Kweptii, no.

T: At Ukkupseni.
O: At Ukkupseni.

The next example is part of a public discussion in the Mulatuppu 'gathering house' concerning the theft of coconuts from a community farm. This portion of the discussion deals with obtaining an outboard motor for a trip the next day to another village in order to consult a 'seer' about the theft. The participants are labeled by letter.[14] Underlying this conversation-discussion and constantly reflected in it is a conflicting set of norms and values. On the one hand, individuals who have certain useful goods, such as outboard motors, should be willing to make them available without charge for community use, especially for use by village leaders and in particular for ritual purposes or for such situations as the investigation of a theft from a community farm. Furthermore, individuals who own motors are usually considered to be wealthy and thus can be asked for favors and contributions. On the other hand, motors are privately owned, and as a general rule their owners should be paid for their use. The owners therefore feel caught between the norm of willingly helping the community and the norm of being paid for their motors, and they are always a bit afraid that they will be exploited in the name of the village. As in the previous example, explanatory and interpretative commentary is placed in brackets.

A: [a Mulatuppu 'chief's spokesman' who has been leading the discussion about the theft of the coconuts] Now, I see there's no motor.
   [The first line of A's turn at talk begins with *emite* (now), a common line initial marker.]
   Thus Dempsey's motor 'will be gone,' he says, 'away.'
   [The second line begins with *takkarku* (thus), another common line initial marker.]
   Where to go?
   Cirilo's 'will be at Sukkunya [a Mulatuppu work village],' he says.
   [This line ends with the quotative verb *soke* (he says) plus the common line final suffix -*ye* (emphatic).]
   Whose motor is available?
B: [another Mulatuppu 'spokesman'] José's is not here?
C: [a third 'spokesman'] He went to Ustuppu [a large village to the west of Mulatuppu], to Ustuppu he went.
A: Whose do you think is available?
D: Tell those who have motors, they're not going for nothing.
   [D announces that the owners should not be afraid that the

'spokesmen' are asking them to volunteer their motors without charge.]

E: They don't want money?

[E calls into question whether this is really the case.]

F: [another 'spokesman'] The town is telling you, 'it will pay you.'

[F, speaking in the name of the village, assures the owners of the motors that the village will repay them for their services.]

G: [a 'chief'] Did you get the motor yet?

H: There are none.

[All the owners have managed not to be in the 'gathering house' or have come up with excuses demonstrating that their motors are not available.]

G: What to do?

The owners of the motors are saying 'they want to go for nothing,' they say.

[The village leaders have not been able to convince the motor owners that they really will be paid for their services. This line ends with the quotative verb *soke* plus the line final suffix -*ye*.]

### Commands and Requests

As seems to be the case in all societies, Kuna commands and requests are expressed in different ways, according to the relationship between the participants, the social context, and the setting. There is no Kuna word which neatly translates the English notion of command. The word *soke* (say) is sometimes used with the sense of command or order, as in *nekkwepur soket-pa* (by the saying [order] of the town).

One common form of command is a verb or verb phrase in the simple present tense. This form can be used either between social equals or by a higher-ranking or senior individual to a lower-ranking or junior individual. Examples are *sike* (sit down), said to a guest in one's house as an invitation to stay for a while; *take* (come in), said as an invitation to enter a house in response to the utterance of *na!* (anyone home?) by a person outside; *mel ieke* (don't forget), one individual reminding another to do something; *take* (come here), said by a parent to a child; and *naemala* (go away, all of you), said by an elderly man to a bunch of young children, including his grandchildren, who were making a lot of noise near him.

A set of verbal suffixes indicates temporal and social emphasis: *sikwele* (sit down first), said by a parent to a child; *take-ye* (I said, come here), said by a parent to a child; and *tay-ten* (so, have a look then). One of these emphatic forms is the future suffix, commonly used by persons in a higher-ranked position. For example, *kapitkuo mer nekinpapa parnao* (you will sleep, you will not walk in the streets) was said by a 'spokesman' in the 'gathering house' to a young boy, just after a 'chief' has performed a 'counsel' to the boy, reprimanding him for misbehaving. The boy is thus the recipient of two kinds of commands, uttered sequentially—first the very long 'counsel,' then the focused and emphatic verb phrase in the future tense. Another example is *'natmar' peka soko pete* ('they left,' you will tell them); in this case, a 'spokesman' in the 'gathering house' told a particular individual to tell something to someone else outside the 'gathering house.'

Declarative or interrogative forms can serve as commands or requests when the context provides such an interpretation. The social relationship is typically that of higher-ranked individual to lower-ranked individual. For example, *pia naluppa?* (where are the peach palm fruits?) was uttered by a father to his children in order to get them to bring him a basket of fruit. *Kine pane* (ready tomorrow), *pan kine a?* (ready tomorrow?) was uttered consecutively by two 'spokesmen' in the 'gathering house' to insure that M will bring his motor for a trip the next day. (See the description of this discussion above.) When M balks, one of the 'spokesmen' makes it explicit that a command was intended by saying, 'The town is telling [ordering] you, "it will pay you."'

If the action desired by the speaker is obvious from the context, a single noun can be used. Again, the social relationship is typically that of higher-ranked to lower-ranked individuals. Thus *noka* (cup) is addressed to a woman responsible for serving beverages by someone who has finished drinking and wants the cup taken away. The suffix -*ye*, illustrated above for verbs, can also be used with nouns to indicate emphasis: *noka-ye* (hurry up and take away my cup). Similarly, when the desired action is obvious and unambiguous from the context, a nonverbal pointing, to the cup for example, is a sufficient communication of the command. For the Kuna, the most common way of pointing is by means of a lip gesture, a raising of the head combined with a pursing of the lips in the direction of the object or person involved. (See below for further discussion of the communicative functions of this pointed lip gesture.)

Kuna does not have a set of explicit formulaic expressions which can be combined with command forms in order to soften them or make them more polite, the equivalent of English please, excuse me, or sorry. Nor does it offer the large choice of grammatical-stylistic alternants characteristic of polite commands in European languages (pass the salt, can you pass the salt, will you pass the salt, would you pass the salt, could you pass the salt, would you mind passing the salt). Nor is there an elaborate array of allusive expressions which are used in the etiquette of everyday commands. In this the Kuna contrast sharply with such Asiatic communities as the Javanese and Balinese, in which indirectness and allusion are highly developed in day-to-day verbal life and are a most important aspect of commands.[15] At the same time, there does exist a range of indirect ways of commanding, in addition to those that I have already described. One very common indirect command involves reporting or quoting, making it seem as though the actual speaker is not doing the commanding but is merely reporting the command of someone else—for example, *Rupen pese kolo urpa* (Rubén you are being called down below), uttered by a younger cousin. This direct quotation of others is part of a more general pattern, to be discussed in chapter 7.

Another set of forms is used to suggest that an ongoing conversation should be terminated; these forms often seem to function as indirect commands. It is typically the higher-ranked participant in the conversation or the host, if the conversation occurs in a private home, who uses these forms. For example, if A and B are conversing in A's house and A would like to terminate the encounter and have B leave, A can say something to B about a place they are sure to see one another later that same day, for example, the 'gathering house.' Thus A can say to B, 'I will see you later in the gathering house.' Or A can mention another activity he or she is about to engage in such as sleep. Or A can say *napiri* (it's true). Leave-takings then occur. Two factors are involved here: (1) the host-guest situation, in which the host has the right to control the flow of persons in and out of the house, and (2) hierarchical ranking, either social organizationally if A is more highly ranked or social interactionally if B has come to A for some particular service or at least has been allowed entrance and served food or beverages.[16]

While treated in this study as ritual and formal rather than everyday, much of the chanting and speaking in the 'gathering house' (see chapter 3) is intended to suggest a course of action or to win an audience over to a point of view and can be seen as a very indirect and often allusive way of commanding. The 'counsel' performed by 'chiefs' to a variety of persons, while long and in this sense perhaps indirect, is also a form of command. Finally, and also in the realm of ritual, the curing and magical *ikarkana* (see chapters 4 and 5) used to control the spirit world are also commands to individual representatives of that world. The command consists of a narrative which describes what the performing specialist wants the spirit to do.

In this discussion of Kuna commands and requests, I have used such concepts as politeness and directness, concepts which have proven useful for the analysis of language use, including especially commandlike behavior, in other societies.[17] While these are relevant dimensions for an analysis of Kuna speech, they do not in and of themselves provide a sufficiently rich framework to account for the particular nature of the Kuna system, which includes short, literal statements of an action desired, long narratives, direct quotations of others, allusive metaphorical suggestions, and nonverbal pointing and relates the most everyday and the most ritual contexts.

## The Pointed Lip Gesture

A very common Kuna facial gesture is so tightly integrated with everyday speech and communication, in particular with the forms of discourse that I have been exploring, that it merits extensive discussion here. The gesture (see figure 6) consists of looking in a particular direction and raising the head; during the raising of the head, the mouth is first opened and then closed with the lower lip thrust outward from the face. The gesture is completed by a lowering of the head to its original position. It is this constellation of raising the head and opening and closing the lips which gives the impression of pointing lips. Some Kuna call the gesture *kaya sui sai* (to make a long or pointed face); others have no name for it. For convenience here, I will give it a descriptive label—the pointed lip gesture.

While the Kuna use hand gestures as batons,[18] to accent the rhythm of their speech, there is relatively little gesturing of other kinds. Mediterranean-like gestures, which replace specific words, are unknown. Hand and finger pointing occurs infrequently and has a set of usages essentially identical to that of the deictic pointed lip gesture; however, the latter is more common by far.

What is striking about the Kuna pointed lip gesture is that it is used in a variety of situations and for a variety of purposes which at first seem unrelated. However, all uses of the gesture are related, precisely because pointing is involved in all of them. Differences in meaning result from the various communicative contexts in which the gesture occurs. Focusing on the integration of the nonverbal pointed lip gesture with the discourse structure of speech acts and speech events brings out the relationship of all the uses of this gesture. The pointed lip gesture is used in questions, answers, statements of information, commands, directions, comments on previous acts and interaction, and greetings. Nine distinct cases can be recognized.

1. The gesture is used as part of a question involving direction or location, with or without verbal accompaniment. Examples are:

**Figure 6.** The Pointed Lip Gesture

One woman says to another, 'What's that cloth?' and makes the plg[19] toward the cloth which is in the second woman's hand.

The first woman might have simply made the plg toward the cloth and the second woman would have interpreted the action to mean, 'What's that cloth; where did you get it?'

A group of men are in a boat on the sea. Another boat passes in the other direction. One of the men in the first boat asks a second, 'Who was that?' and makes the plg toward the passing boat.

These and similar examples show that there is a paradigm of Kuna questions involving direction or location; the paradigm consists of four possibilities.

1a. Purely verbal utterance without the use of the pointed lip gesture, direction or location being specified verbally.

1b. Verbal utterance in which direction or location is expressed both verbally and by means of the pointed lip gesture.

1c. Verbal utterance in which direction or location is expressed by means of the pointed lip gesture only.

1d. No verbal utterance; the pointed lip gesture is used alone.

The four possibilities for Kuna questions involving direction or location demonstrate that the pointed lip gesture must be included in a linguistic description of Kuna deixis or pointing. A limitation to verbal expression of direction or location would arbitrarily restrict the paradigm. This argument remains valid in the other eight cases of the gesture.

2. The pointed lip gesture is used as part of an answer to a question involving direction or location, with or without verbal accompaniment. Examples are:

A boy asks his mother where his father is and the mother replies, 'At the point,' making the plg in the direction of the spot in question, where the father is constructing a canoe.

One man questions another about a third who is not present, 'Where is Julio?' The second makes the plg toward a house and says, 'Julio is eating.'

One man asks another, 'Where is my son?' and the second responds by making the plg in the direction in which the son had gone.

Thus, analogous to questions, Kuna answers to questions involving direction or location can be studied in terms of a paradigm consisting of four possibilities.

2a. Purely verbal utterance without the use of the pointed lip gesture, direction or location being specified verbally.

2b. Verbal utterance in which direction or location is expressed both verbally and by means of the pointed lip gesture.

2c. Verbal utterance in which direction or location is expressed by means of the pointed lip gesture only.

2d. No verbal utterance; the pointed lip gesture is used alone.

Cases 1 and 2 have the following in common. In both the gesture is an essential element in a communicative event which consists of two acts—a question and an answer. In case 1 the pointed lip gesture is used as part of the question; and in case 2 it is part of the answer.

3. The gesture is used as a demonstrative in a statement of information, a direction, or a command. Examples are:

An old woman says to a young girl, 'You know how to speak Spanish,' and makes the plg to her.

Two men are sitting on a bench in the 'gathering house' when a third man walks in through a distant door. The first man says to the second, 'Your friend,' and makes the plg toward the third.

After a rain, a man who has just returned to the island from the mainland jungle passes another and says to him, 'The river is rising'; at the same time he makes the plg toward the mainland river.

Two 'chiefs' are chanting *arkan kae*, the traditional Kuna greeting, to one another in the presence of a group of men in the 'gathering house.' A few women are serving beverages to the men. The women are supposed to take the empty cups back from the men when they finish drinking. One man finishes his cup and raises it. The woman who gave it to him doesn't see it. One of the 'chiefs' then says *noka* (cup) and makes the plg toward the man who is holding the empty cup.

Two very young boys inadvertently knock over a small fence in the presence of an adult. The adult says to one of them, 'You will be punished.' The boy, thus labeled as the guilty one, turns to his young friend and makes the plg toward him, as if to say, 'He did it, not me.'

These examples illustrate that Kuna statements, directions, and commands about direction or location form a paradigm consisting of the same four possibilities discussed for questions and answers. Cases 1, 2, and 3 of the pointed lip gesture are similar in that in all of them the gesture is used as a pure deixis or pointer to indicate direction or location, either with an accompanying verbal utterance or alone. In case 4 the gesture does more than merely point; it also mocks its recipient.

4. During an event of any kind involving two individuals, one individual makes the pointed lip gesture toward the other. It seems as

though the second individual is being made fun of by the first. Examples are:

A man and a woman are conversing during the festivities associated with girls' puberty rites. Both are slightly drunk and are joking, as is customary on this occasion. The woman says something which the man considers funny. He then makes the plg toward her, as if to say, 'Got you' or 'You're something.'

Two women and one of their husbands are standing at the dock talking. A Panamanian police boat pulls up to the dock. One of the women says to the other (the one whose husband is standing there), 'They've come to get your husband.' At this point the husband, laughing, looks up at the woman who has just spoken. When they make eye contact, she makes the plg to him.

At first glance, case 4 seems quite different from 1, 2, and 3. There is not a paradigm of possibilities but simply one possibility—the pointed lip gesture. The meaning of pointing (as in direction or location) so clear in 1, 2, and 3 is not immediately obvious here. Structurally, however, 4 is rather similar to the first three cases, especially to the third. The first three cases all involve speech events consisting of two acts. In 1 and 2 the event is a question-and-answer sequence, the answer being required or in some sense demanded by the question. Thus in case 2 the pointed lip gesture is often used anaphorically, namely, to relate back to an interrogative expressed in the question. Its meaning is acquired from both its immediate referent—the object pointed to—and its discourse context—the interrogative expressed in the preceding question.

Case 3 also occurs in two-act events, although the second is not required by the first. Once the second occurs, however, its meaning is related to the first act of the discourse structure which triggered it. The examples in case 4 all involve two-act events similar to those in 3; the pointed lip gesture is triggered by the first act but not required by it. Case 4 differs from case 3, however, in that the triggering act is always comical in some way. The pointed lip gesture then relates back to the preceding humorous act. But it is also directed toward a particular individual. Its meaning is then to relate an individual to the preceding humorous act or interaction. For this reason, it seems to mock its recipient, precisely by this relationship to what came before. Thus 4 is not very different from the other cases of the pointed lip gesture investigated above. The meaning of the gesture in all cases derives from both its actual recipient or referent—the thing or person pointed at—and the communicative event in which it occurs.

5. During an event of any kind involving more than two individuals, one individual makes the pointed lip gesture toward a second, who may or may not be aware of its being made, for the benefit of a third or more. It seems as though the second individual is being made fun of. Examples are:

> One afternoon in the 'gathering house,' a 'chief's spokesman' is joking and using obscenities to a considerable degree; everyone present is laughing. One of the men present makes the plg at the joke teller, as if to say, 'How about that guy?'
>
> Three men are standing together and joking. One of them says something funny and the other two laugh. The second makes the plg in the direction of the first with the third as the intended receiver, not bothering to see whether or not the first observes it, as if to say, 'He's funny' or 'What a character.'

Case 5 differs from 4 in that more than two individuals are directly involved. The pointed lip gesture is used by one person to signify something about a second to a third. The communicative and discourse properties of 5 are, however, precisely the same as those of 4. That is, the pointed lip gesture is used to relate a particular individual to a preceding humorous act or interaction. The gesture simultaneously points and mocks.

6. During an event of any kind involving more than two individuals, one individual makes the pointed lip gesture toward a second, who is not aware of its being made, for the benefit of a third or more. It seems as though the unknowing individual is being mocked. Examples are:

> Two individuals are joking with a third, at this third's expense. The third walks away. The first individual then makes the plg toward the back of the third so that the second (but not the third) can see it being made.
>
> Two men are joking about a third's being unpleasant and irritable, in this third's presence. One of the two catches the eye of the second and makes the plg toward the subject of their discussion; the subject has his head turned at this moment and does not notice the gesture.

Case 6 is like case 5—a relevant individual is specified by means of the pointed lip gesture and thereby linked to a preceding humorous interaction. It differs from 5 since deliberate care is taken so that the specified individual is not aware of being mocked by the gesture. Thus not only are the referent and the receiver of the pointed lip gesture distinct, the referent is furthermore not permitted to know of the making of the gesture.

The six cases of the pointed lip gesture investigated thus far are all related in that the meaning of pointing is present in all. In cases 4, 5, and 6 the meaning of mocking also enters in, derived from a humorous act or interaction which immediately precedes and indeed triggers the gesture. In case 6, furthermore, the gesture enables two individuals to communicatively collude against a third by taking care that the person pointed at and mocked does not know about it. The first six cases are also similar in that they occur within the boundaries of an encounter or social interaction. It is in this respect that the remaining cases are different.

7. The pointed lip gesture is used as a greeting between two individuals. Examples are:

Two individuals make the plg to one another in passing.
One woman calls out to another who is standing at some distance, 'My friend.' (This is one of several ways of getting someone's attention in order to begin an interaction.) The second woman replies by making the plg to the first.

In case 7 the pointed lip gesture is a greeting, used in a manner similar to a nod of the head in North American society. It seems useful to consider this in terms of a paradigm consisting of the following possibilities. (See also the discussion of greetings above.)

7a. Both individuals use a verbal greeting; the pointed lip gesture is not used.

7b. One individual uses the pointed lip gesture to greet a second; the second responds verbally.

7c. One individual greets a second verbally; the second responds with the pointed lip gesture.

7d. Two individuals greet one another with the pointed lip gesture; no verbal greetings are uttered.

Since the physical gesture in case 7 is exactly the same in cases 1 through 6, it is logical to ask if the meanings are related. It is important to note, however, that the discourse properties of 7 are quite different from those of 1 through 6. In 1 through 6 the pointed lip gesture always occurs within the context of a social interaction or event that has already begun. In 7, on the other hand, it is used in the very opening of an interaction as the first act, the response to the first act, or the total encounter. As the formal marking of the opening of an encounter between two individuals, it functions as a greeting. However, it is also used here, as in all other cases, to point not to a thing but to a person. In case 7 one individual points to another as a greeting. Just as the humor of the mocking gesture in cases 4 through 6 is derived not from the gesture itself but from its immediate context, the meaning of greeting in 7 is derived not from the physical properties of the gesture but from its context; that is, it begins an interaction between two individuals.

8. Two individuals make the pointed lip gesture to one another as a greeting. This reciprocal greeting takes on a jokingly insulting or mocking aspect.

The mocking aspect of this case derives from the relationship between the two individuals involved: such semiinsulting joking must be possible. Other aspects of the event are also significant. Case 8 is often accompanied by smiling or laughing. Cases 7 and 8 are thus alike in that they are both greetings; 8, furthermore, involves mocking derived from the relationship between the two greeting individuals.

9. Two individuals in passing exchange a series of pointed lip gestures as mocking greetings.

Case 9 is a repetition of case 8. The joking relationship between the individuals which enables them to exchange a mocking greeting also permits the repetition of this greeting.

In all nine cases the physical characteristics of the pointed lip gesture are the same. I have argued that all nine cases are systematically related, precisely because pointing or deixis is involved in all. This pointing can be considered the basic meaning of the gesture. To it may be added the meanings of mocking and greeting. According to this analysis, there are three basic usages of the pointed lip gesture. First is pure pointing, as in cases 1 and 2, questions about direction or location and answers to questions about direction or location. The second usage involves a comment on a previous act or interaction, as in cases 3 through 6. Cases 4 through 6 are furthermore mocking in that they respond to a previous act or interaction which was humorous. And the third usage concerns a greeting, as in cases 7 through 9. Cases 8 and 9 are also mocking, derived from a joking relationship which exists between the two participants.[20]

### Lullabies and 'Tuneful Weeping': Two Women's Speech Events

An exploration of the Kuna life cycle finds women directly and uniquely involved in two speech events, one focused on the beginning of life, the other on its end. If you walk through a Kuna village, especially in the morning when men are at work, you hear singing coming from almost every house. These are women, from young girls to quite old grandmothers, singing to little babies to keep them calm and put them to sleep. These lullabies are often called *koe pippi* (literally little baby), named for the addressee, who is explicitly referred to. In the performance of lullabies, the singer holds the baby in her lap in a hammock or sits next to it, moving the hammock back and forth and shaking a rattle. Lullabies have certain basic themes. The baby is told not to cry, that it will soon grow up and perform adult tasks and that its father is off working in the jungle or fishing. In addition, there is improvisation to fit the actual situation of the baby and its family—whether the singer is a mother, sister, or aunt; whether the baby is a boy or a girl; whether those off at work are fathers, uncles, or brothers; whether they are farming in the jungle, fishing, or working in Panama City. The description is reflexive. The singer describes what she is doing at the moment of the performance, as well as what the relevant others are doing.

The language of lullabies is that of colloquial Kuna, with particular stylistic features. Morpheme final vowels are typically not deleted so that morphemes usually occur in full form, for example, *nana* (mother) rather than *nan*. Certain suffixes, such as *-ye* (optative), are used with much greater frequency than in colloquial Kuna. The suffix *-ye* is also used to mark the ends of lines. Stanzalike units are terminated with a long *mmmm*, whose use is particular to lullabies.[21]

The first part of the lullaby presented here describes the actual situation of the performance—the mother in a hammock singing to a young but already walking baby girl.

Little baby.
Your mother is sitting with you in your hammock.
Little baby she is sorry to see you cry.
Mmmm.
Little girl.
You can now walk.
You can run as well.
Your aunts are sorry to see you [cry].
My little baby girl can now walk.
Mmmm.

Then the baby is told what her father is doing at the same moment that her mother is singing to her.

Father is not here I see.
He went to the jungle.
'I am going to clear out the coconut farms.'
Father said as he left.
Mmmm.

The future activities of the girl, when she grows older, are described.

Little girl.
You will stay in the house.

You will make a little mola [a child's mola].
You will also sit beside your mother.

You will wash clothes.
You will go to the river.
With your relatives.
You will wash small clothes [children's clothes].
Your mother is raising you alone [as of this moment you are an only
    child].
You have already grown up a bit mother sees also.
Mmmm.

When your uncles return [from work].
You will serve beverages to your uncles.
You will serve them food.
When your uncles return.
Mmmm.
Your relatives will call to you.
'Bring me a beverage.'
Mmmm.

The lullaby ends as it began, with a reflexive description of the actual scene of the performance.

Little baby girl.
My little girl lying here.
Little baby.
Mmmm.[22]

'Tuneful weeping' is the melodic lament performed by women to a dying and then deceased individual. A large group of women, the family members of the addressee, surround the dying person's hammock and 'weep,' either one at a time or several at a time, each in her own words. 'Tuneful weeping' continues after the death of the person, while she or he remains in the hammock, on the canoe trip to the mainland cemetery, and until burial. It is in colloquial Kuna, in a sobbing yet melodic style, involving, like lullabies, the nondeletion of morpheme final vowels and the much more frequent use of such suffixes as -kue (become) and -ye than in colloquial Kuna. The suffix -ye, along with the musical shape, marks a line structure.

'Tuneful weeping' deals with the life of the dying and then deceased addressees and the performers' relationship to them. The performer improvises on a highly stereotyped basic pattern, incorporating the particular details which are relevant in each case. Here a young girl laments the death of her grandfather.

It pains me to see grandfather.
My grandfather died.
He will be underground.
I say.

She notes that he was a curing specialist.

He would always go with us [to the mainland jungle].
In order to get medicine.
'I am going to get medicine.'
He said to us.

The deceased's wife had died before him.

You will climb along God's path together with grandmother.
My grandmother died before you.

This melodic lament ends with a quite literal statement of what will happen to the deceased's body.

I am sorry to see you, grandfather.
Lying in the hammock, dead.
Under the ground you will rot, grandfather.[23]

Lullabies and 'tuneful weeping' share several features which make it appropriate to group them together. They are both performed by women and are melodic. They are both addressed directly to an individual who is present and have to do with his or her life and situation and relationship to the performer. And they both involve basic themes which are manipulated and improvised in order to fit particular situations. It is furthermore interesting to compare these two verbal genres with the melodic chanting of 'chiefs' in the 'gathering house,' because of striking similarities and differences. Lullabies and 'tuneful weeping' share with 'gathering house' chanting a structure in terms of melodic lines, marked musically as well as grammatically, and a set of relatively fixed basic themes which are elaborated and developed in order to be appropriate to particular situations. On the other hand, 'gathering house' chanting is performed by men, lullabies and 'tuneful weeping' by women; 'gathering house' chanting is public, lullabies and 'tuneful weeping' private; 'gathering house' chanting involves a special esoteric language with a focus on metaphor, lullabies and 'tuneful weeping' are in colloquial Kuna with no metaphors; and 'gathering house' chanting presents a moral which is then interpreted as part of the total speech event, while in lullabies and 'tuneful weeping' there is no moral and no interpretation.[24]

## Fun with Speech

There are many Kuna forms of speech whose purpose is playful. I present here a selection which reflects a cross section of ages, sexes, and contexts. Various play languages, derived from colloquial Kuna, are used by adolescents and sometimes understood if not used by adults. Here are some examples of these pig Latin–like linguistic varieties. *Sorsik sunmakke* (talking backward) takes the first syllable of a word and moves it to the end of the word: *osi* (pineapple) > *sio*, *ope* (to bathe) > *peo*, *ipya* (eye) > *yaip*, and *uwaya* (ear) > *wayau*.

Another play language is formed by inserting, after the initial consonant-vowel sequence of each syllable, the sequence *pp* plus the vowel of the syllable: *merki* (North American) > *mepperkippi*, *pia* (where) > *pippiappa*, *ua* (fish) > *uppuappa*, and *perkwaple* (all) > *pepperkwappapleppe*.

Still another play language involves the prefixation of *chi-* before every syllable. Furthermore, each syllable in the original word receives primary stress in the play language form: *ina* (medicine) > *chiíchiná*, *ai* (friend) > *chiáchií*, and *macheret* (man) > *chimáchi-chéchirét*.

Kuna play languages are not used for secrecy or concealment or to set off one group from another, as is the case in many societies. Rather, these languages are spoken by friends in either work or recreational contexts. They are relatively easy to derive from a colloquial language understood by everyone. Their primary function seems to be the pure pleasure derived from manipulating language—they are a form of linguistic play for play's sake. Observers usually find them humorous and respond to them with laughter. At the same time, this form of children's speech play is in keeping with the more general Kuna focus on speech play and verbal artistry, which are highly valued in persons of all ages.

With regard to adults, this play and creativity include expressively altering Kuna sounds, introducing non-Kuna sounds, making use of foreign words, altering the names of people and things, developing metaphors, and inserting relevant anecdotes and personal experiences. Although adults do not use the play languages and usually claim not to understand them, they generally consider them acceptable behavior for children and are amused by them; they seem to recognize them as a children's form of linguistic play. Some traditional ritual leaders are against the use of play languages, however, especially if they think that obscene words are being concealed in them. At the interisland ritual 'gathering' held in Sasartii-Mulatuppu in June 1970, a visiting official from an extremely traditional village complained publicly about one of the play languages and claimed that it was obscene. Since then I have at times heard parents stop their children from using the play languages, reminding them that village officials had declared them obscene. The traditional leaders might have been struck by a similarity between play languages and the 'secret,' the short charmlike utterance which is used to control objects, animals, and human beings and which is considered to be both powerful and dangerous. The language of 'secrets' is considered taboo because it deals with sexual origins. But 'secrets' are not comprehensible to anyone who has not learned them because they involve a code—usually containing nonsense syllables or words from languages other than Kuna (see chapter 4).[25]

'Play names' are short play forms which are a source of much amusement. Known mainly by adult males, 'play names' are used to label various objects, generally animals, and are based on physical characteristics. Examples are *sortukkin nakue* (hangs by tail—a monkey), *kwapin arat* (blue-green tongue—a tarpon), *kaya pirreket* (wide mouth—a tarpon), *naras asu* (orange nose—a curassow) and *us nono* (agouti's head—an avocado) (see also table 4). 'Play names' can be used by themselves, as a humorous focal point, in conversations whose sole purpose is recreation and amusement. They can be used in 'stories' about animals, in order to talk about the characters in the 'story' and embellish the humorous aspects of the performance. And they can be used as part of a riddling game, which seems to be on the wane in recent years, in which one individual mentions a 'play name' and challenges a partner to name the animal.

A: *pete kapur ipya kwat* [you, the one with hot pepper eyes].
B: *suka* [crab].

Humans, too, often receive playful nicknames. These are frequently based on animals, which the Kuna view as similar to humans in many ways and domains. The human nicknames pick up on a perceived comical, physical, or personality similarity between an animal and a particular human. Some Mulatuppu nicknames are *sikkwi seret* (old bird), for a former village secretary—all of whom are often called *sikkwi* (bird)—who likes to sit around and talk a lot without really having much to say; *ia korki* (uncle pelican), for a young man who looks like a pelican; and *kelu* (jack, a Caribbean fish), for an albino businessman who like the *kelu* is fatty, slippery, and white and has a voracious appetite. A nickname from Niatuppu, a village in the western sector of San Blas, is *moli* (tapir), for a man who has the reputation of being a banana thief. Foreigners are also given nicknames: *kilu pippi* (little uncle), *asu suit* (long nose), *sippor* (the white one), and *sika pula* (the big beard), which is also used, because of the picture on the box, to label Smith Brothers cough drops.

'Stories' are a mainly humorous genre, known and performed by traditional leaders in a community, especially 'chiefs.' They are at times performed at home, for the amusement of children. But the main context for their performance is in the 'gathering house' to an audience of men, either before or after an evening's chanting, at an evening 'gathering' where there is no chanting, or on days when—because of important visitors, or interdictions on work due to earthquakes or eclipses, or particular holidays—many men congregate in the 'gathering house.' Typically, the teller recounts the 'story' to another person who responds with short utterances or comments, while the audience listens, laughs, and occasionally comments as well.

'Stories' deal with humorous exploits of humans and animals. Both trickery and pratfalls are common; play and humor are highlighted.[26] The narrator alternates fast and slow, loud and soft, and high-pitched and low-pitched speech; rhetorically and expressively interchanges short and long pauses between lines; rapidly repeats certain words; incorporates onomatopoetic sounds and conversational details; and relates the narrative in passing to familiar humorous incidents that occurred in the community—all in order to enhance his performance.

In animal 'stories,' the characters have human traits which relate them to the most everyday concerns of the audience—they converse, they have human habits and desires, and they possess Kuna kin and use Kuna kin terms with all their affective connotations. Some examples of 'stories' are *us kwento* (the agouti story), *kanir kwento* (the chicken story), *yarmoro kwento* (the tortoise story), and *kaa kwento* (the story of the hot pepper). Here is the first episode of 'the agouti story' as told by Chief Muristo Pérez to his 'spokesman,' Armando, before a group of men in the Mulatuppu 'gathering house' one holiday morning. The quoted portions are slightly faster in pace and higher in pitch.

Well listen Armando.
So let's listen to a bit of a story now.
A story.
It's the agouti story.

So, Agouti, Jaguar the two of them, they were about to compete with each other.

Jaguar, Agouti the two of them Agouti, Agouti is a trickster, ah.

Jaguar likes to catch him.

When he got there he discovered him, ah.

So he saw Agouti sitting-up-straight. [The final phrase is stretched out.]

Uncle saw him Jaguar did.

He started chasing after him.

When he started chasing after him, over there say, it's true.

So Agouti was sitting eating.

So 'I'm eating *ikwa* fruit,' he says.

On top of a hill, seated.

Seated on top of a hill, eating, there to uncle Agouti says to uncle.

'Now, you will eat too say,' he says.

'He was chasing him, ah, he was going to eat,' he says, 'he was going to eat his head.'

[Armando interjects: Really his head was going to be caught, I think.]

Nope, 'what are you eating it's true I will eat some too,' he says.

It's true.

'How did you split it open, ah?' he says.

'How did you split it open?'

No 'I split it open with my balls see say.

With my balls I split it open see listen.'

'You watch,' he says.

He got a rock a rock a rock he got.

Agouti ooopened up his balls he opened up his balls he placed them against the side of the hill. [The last phrase is uttered very quickly.]

TAK [loud noise] the *ikwa* fruit TAK AK [louder noise].

[Armando interjects: Wow what pain!]

'You see,' he says.

It's true.

Ah, Jaguar is astounded, ah.

'Here you'll do it like that too,' he says to him.

Well then he got a rock for him too.

But the other one really placed it on top of his balls, ah.

Did you understand?

This Agouti he tricked him for the fun of it.

Really he smashed against the stone the stone he didn't do it on his balls.

But Jaguar was going to place it right on his balls.

Then he diiid it, TAK.

So he smashed him in the banana. [Muristo here alludes to a humorous incident that had occurred in the village, causing everyone to laugh uproariously.]

It's true.

Well, so, he diiid and he finished off his balls.

Big Boy Agouti knocked him out, he-sure-made-him-jump. [The final phrase is stretched out and higher in pitch.]

Ah.

Poor Jaguar.

He passed out, he was out cold. [The final verb phrase is higher in pitch.]

Agouti took off again started running again.

Running running running run [the verbs are uttered rapidly, in a reduplicated fashion] l-a-u-g-h-i-n-g [stretched out] along down the path, ah.[27]

'Play *ikarkana*,' another humorous genre, are fixed, memorized texts which are chanted. Most of the performers of 'play *ikarkana*' are men, but some women have learned them and perform them as well. Their purpose is recreational, and they are performed primarily in two contexts: in a Kuna house, late at night, the performer lies in a hammock and chants while the other family members lie in adjacent hammocks and listen; in the '*inna* house' during the festivities associated with girls' puberty rites, the performers provide pleasure for both themselves and their audience, human and spirit.[28]

# 7. From Everyday to Ritual: Configurations and Intersections

In previous chapters I have approached Kuna language and speech from various intersecting perspectives—in terms of the sociolinguistic resources in use in the community, including an analysis of the grammatical and lexical properties of Kuna linguistic varieties and styles; in terms of roles in Kuna society, especially the place of language and speech in their definition and practice; in terms of an extensive and intensive description of the three realms of ritual speaking and chanting, paying attention to both the forms of discourse, the verbal texts which are so important in Kuna ritual life, and the contexts of their performance; and in terms of an exploration of everyday speech and communication. It is now possible and useful to bring together these different perspectives, to show how the many and often detailed descriptions and analyses unite in an organized way. The overview which I offer here highlights the patterns, themes, and processes that constitute what is special and unique about Kuna language and speech.

One of the major aims of this chapter is to show the relationships among the three distinct realms of Kuna ritual speech as well as between ritual speech and everyday speech. The boundary between Kuna ritual and everyday speech is not always sharp, as the theoretical literature on this subject generally tends to argue.[1] In addition to the clear constellations and focuses of ritual and everyday speech that have been identified and described in this study, there are also aspects of the relationship between ritual and everyday speech that are best accounted for in terms of continua, with overlaps of various kinds.

One such continuum is grammatical (see chapter 2). Thus, in phonology, there is less and less vowel deletion and consonantal assimilation as one moves from everyday and colloquial speech to more ritual, especially chanted, speech. In morphology the number of nominal and verbal suffixes used is greater in ritual than in everyday and colloquial speech, and certain suffixes in particular occur with greater frequency. The more ritual the speech, the more fixed is the syntactic structure and the more pervasive is the syntactic and semantic parallelism. And a poetic line structure, while a potential and emergent feature of everyday speech, is more formally marked along several dimensions in ritual speech.

Another continuum involves the tightness of the social organization of speech.[2] Ritual speech is characterized by stricter rules of cooccurrence among the components of speaking—setting, participants, goals, act and event sequences, norms of interaction, genres—than is everyday speech, where the rules are much looser.

In this chapter I will focus on two other kinds of relationships between everyday and ritual speech. There is, on the one hand, a set of patterns which cut across the various Kuna contexts for and ways of speaking, configurations which provide an overarching unity to the quite heterogeneous diversity of Kuna verbal life. On the other hand, there is a complex of intersections and interpenetrations which link the various domains of speaking. An exploration of both reveals the dynamic, creative nature of the Kuna theory and practice of speaking.

## Patterns of Speaking
### Talk and Silence

By now it should be obvious that the most striking Kuna pattern of speaking is talk itself, its omnipresence and its central function in all aspects of social and cultural life. The Kuna believe that talk is natural and appropriate in almost all situations, that it is the logical way to get things done. And, as much as they love to talk and feel it necessary to talk, they respect and appreciate listening to others— they have as endless a tolerance for and enjoyment of listening to others as they do for continuing to talk themselves. Speech is a reflection of, indeed the primary manifestation of, an individual's personality and character, including especially abilities, strengths, and weaknesses. Quiet people who do not talk much are considered strange and even weird. Speaking is at the center of work and relaxation, seriousness and play, learning and teaching. The Kuna talk, joke, and argue from early in the morning till late at night. They have a keen sense of their own culture and their own selves as being on display, and nowhere is this more apparent than in their language and speech. People talk about what they are doing as they do it, loudly, clearly, and extensively. As one Kuna woman put it to me quite explicitly and quite vociferously, 'This is not Panama, this is not America. Panama is a quiet place. America is a quiet place. This is Kunaland. Kunaland is a talking place, a laughing place, a noisy place.'

There are very few occasions on which speech is improper or taboo, and then the absence of talk is striking and significant. For precisely this reason, an examination of these occasions is most instructive. A notable everyday avoidance of talk occurs during eating and drinking. Both are typically carried out integrally and completely, without interference from or integration with other activities. Talk occurs before and after but for the most part not during. The leisurely banquet and the dinner party have no Kuna equivalents. Another noteworthy everyday absence of talk is the greeting pattern which involves or at least begins with a marked avoidance of direct communication between two individuals, although there is mutually acknowledged copresence (see chapter 6).

In ritual life, talk and noise are proscribed during certain curing ceremonies, especially when very serious matters are involved, such as snakebites or epidemics. In the case of snakebite, one method of curing involves the entire village in that everyone is supposed to keep quiet during the day, talking only when necessary and then very softly. At night, people should be even more quiet, whispering when they have to talk and going to sleep early in order to avoid talk. Radios are not permitted, outboard motors are silenced, and even rubber-thonged sandals are not allowed because of the flapping noise they make as people walk. The more serious the disease or problem, the more dangerous the evil spirits, and the more susceptible the community to attack, the more silence is required. An example is illustrative.

During an interisland ritual 'gathering' held in Mulatuppu in 1970, at which 'chiefs' from various islands were chanting in the morning and in the evening, an inhabitant of the community who had been sick died. As a result of this death, evil spirits were present in the village. Therefore, although the sessions continued, 'chiefs' no longer chanted. Instead, each stood up and spoke when his turn came. Then one night, still during this event, an inhabitant of the village was bitten by a snake while he was hunting in the mainland jungle, hoping to provide fresh game for the visiting dignitaries. He was brought back to the village by his companions and the curing process began. Since now even more evil spirits were on the loose, not only was chanting prohibited but even loud speaking was forbidden. The 'gathering' was called off in midstream and the visitors returned to their respective villages. In Mulatuppu, during the daytime, people went about their ordinary activities, but they were expected to do so as quietly as possible. No motorboats or radios were allowed. At night rules became stricter. People had to stay in their homes and talk in a whisper or not at all; they were encouraged to and actually did go to sleep very early. Men's 'gatherings' were held every evening in a whisper. The audience was silent, and speakers who stood in the center spoke in barely audible voices. This transition from talk to silence proceeded by stages—gradually chanting went to talking, loud went to soft, nonessential noises were eliminated (see chapter 4).

When evil spirits abound, certain places, times, and people are felt to be especially sensitive to attack and are therefore kept even more quiet. The possibility of attack is greater at night than in the day, greater in the mainland jungle than in the island village, and greater outside in the streets than in the confines of one's home. And women and children are more susceptible than men.

During the 'mass-curing ritual' aimed at eliminating and preventing epidemics and other widespread evils, silence plays a major role. While the 'mass curer' directs the ritual and performs his *ikar*, no one is permitted to talk at all. Outside of the official ritual but during the eight days of its occurrence, the noises of motors, radios, sandals, and loud chanting and talking are all prohibited.

In other curing events, the avoidance of noise does not play the same role as it does in the 'mass-curing ritual.' People typically converse and even joke in the immediate vicinity of most curing events. However, there is always the possibility that the *ikar* performer, the patient's family, or both will be bothered; and they can request others inside or near the patient's house to be quiet.

In the 'gathering house,' during the chanting of 'chiefs,' the audience is expected to be quiet. 'Policemen,' either seated or walking around, cry out *kapitamarye, nue ittomarye* (don't sleep, listen well). The emphasis is more on paying attention and listening than on being absolutely silent; whispered conversations are common. 'Chiefs' from other villages tend to attract a larger, more attentive audience, and 'policemen' are more active then in enforcing silence.

To understand the full significance of Kuna silence, it is necessary to contrast it with the normal, natural, all-is-well state of affairs, which involves not just plenty of talk but carefully controlled and organized talk as well as associated communicative behavior. This normal state of affairs is turned upside down to the extreme in two totally different contexts. On the one hand, there is the letting go during the puberty rites and festivities (see chapter 5), with their uncontrolled yelling, arguing, and fighting. On the other hand, there is the silence that is required when evil spirits are causing sickness, death, misbehavior, and misfortune. When things are not in their natural state, talk and noise, which are some of if not the most characteristic features of normalcy and which always have a potential power in and of themselves, must be carefully controlled. It is not that talk is abandoned—rather, it is both focused and reduced. Talk is focused in the very special mass exorcism carried out in the presence of the entire community in the 'gathering house,' the spirits thus hearing nothing but the ritual specialist's communication with them. And talk is greatly reduced in both quantity and quality during the eight-day ritual, after which things return to normal.[3]

Silence and quiet are thus most rare among the Kuna and contrast sharply with the usual omnipresence of talk and noise—no one would accuse the Kuna of being silent Indians.[4] In this regard they seem to be quite different from certain groups of North American Indians. Ronald Scollon and Suzanne Scollon posit a bush consciousness as characteristic of Athapaskan and Algonquian communities of arctic and subarctic North America.[5] One primary feature of this bush consciousness is nonintervention, of which silent communication is an important instance. Another is an individualistic and nonnormative approach to language and speech. Nonintervention is reflected in learning and teaching and in conflict with the non-Indian, Anglo world. Kuna communicative patterns contrast sharply with this bush consciousness as defined by the Scollons. In fact, reports of language and speech among such groups as the Shavante, Mehinaku, Trio, and Waiwai suggest the existence of an alternative South American tropical forest consciousness, which the Kuna clearly share. This tropical forest consciousness contrasts almost point for point with the bush consciousness—the Kuna are intervening rather than nonintervening, voluble rather than silent. It is precisely because it occurs against the backdrop of the usual volubility of their life that Kuna silence is so marked, almost awesome.

Related to the talk-silence pattern is the interplay of public and private uses of language. There is plenty of public talk among the Kuna, most strikingly in the three ritual traditions. 'Gatherings' especially are defined as public events in that many issues and problems that arise during the day concerning particular individuals or groups are settled publicly at night during the 'gathering.' But there are also matters which are considered appropriate for private discussion. Typical of these are matters between two individuals, for example, financial arrangements. These are carried out in a quite secret manner, out of earshot of anyone else. While there is an attempt to keep financial matters private, however, they can lead to disagreements between individuals or groups and thus often become public matters, resulting in 'gathering house' discussion.

Various types of visits between individuals are also carried out in private. A member of the community who intends to leave the village, in order to work or study, for example, must ask official permission of the first 'chief.' This is often done in the latter's house, although it may also be done more publicly in the 'gathering house.' Individuals also visit the 'chief' at home in order to raise matters with him that will be brought up later in public in the 'gathering house.' Visits to the house of a 'seer' or a 'medicinal specialist' to discuss the disease of a family member are private affairs as well. Ritual specialists converse with both colleagues and students either alone together in the jungle or in the privacy of their own homes, in the afternoon and evening. They speak *arpakke*, a term which signifies secret, both in the sense of a socially private matter and in the sense of a secretive variety of the Kuna language. It is especially matters having to do with the control of spirits that require secrecy, in the form of isolation from others or in the form of an esoteric, ritual language. Finally, visits among family members and friends, in order to greet, converse, report, and gossip, occur in the confines of their own homes. Even though other members of the family living in the house can listen and neighbors can sometimes hear through the bamboo walls, this talk is defined as private and personal rather than public.

### *Speech Play and Verbal Art*

Speech play is the conscious or unconscious manipulation of linguistic elements, forms, and processes, resulting in a focus on language itself; it relates to humor in that it is one of the principal ways of producing comical effects. But speech play can have quite serious ends as well, most notably rhetorical and poetic. For the Kuna, speech play, rhetoric, and verbal art are typically inseparable.

The Kuna sociolinguistic system provides a great potential for play in its diversity of linguistic varieties and styles as well as grammatical and lexical choices; there are many linguistic forms which can be manipulated for rhetorical and stylistic purposes. It is especially with regard to vocabulary that the Kuna themselves are most aware of the possibilities for speech play inherent in their sociolinguistic system—they literally delight in the rich diversity of lexical means at their disposal. And this lexical proliferation borders on and blends into metaphor and verbal symbolism, where speech play reigns supreme. Other aspects of language which are manipulated in

Kuna speech play are phonology (especially the presence or absence of a final vowel in many morphemes), morphosyntactics (the existence of a rich set of prefixes, suffixes, phrases, and sentence patterns distinguishing different styles), and textual structure (particularly various patterns of parallelism and other forms of repetition).

The Kuna are continually and consciously aware of the aesthetic properties of language, most strikingly in ritual speech but in everyday speech as well. Appreciation of verbal artistry is inseparable from any consideration of language use. Thus while the Kuna ethnography of speaking can be approached in terms of certain sociocultural functions of speech—social control, political maneuvering, curing, magic, puberty ritual—these functions are inextricably tied to the aesthetic function, to the pleasingly artistic properties of language. It is by means of verbally artistic language that these other functions are effectively achieved. In addition, the aesthetic and play functions of language are semiindependent from the referential or purely informational functions, working in the service of the latter while maintaining a potential for freedom of expression. An excellent example is provided by a 'chief' from the village of Niatuppu who, after chanting at great length about the different positions of a parakeet on a cotton thread (which symbolizes a person in a hammock, which in turn symbolizes being a village leader), was asked if every different position described had a symbolic interpretation, for example, types of 'chiefs' or types of leadership roles or tasks. He responded no, that he had become carried away with the inherent beauty of the detailed imagery of his description of the parakeet.[6]

Three aspects of the poetic organization of Kuna language and speech which I have highlighted in this study are line and verse structure, parallelism and repetition, and figurative language. These poetic devices are not particular to the Kuna but are found in the verbal art of many other societies as well. Dennis Tedlock analyzes the structure of pauses in performance in order to delineate lines in the narratives of the Zuni Indians of New Mexico.[7] Dell Hymes points out the importance of line and verse structure in the narratives of the Chinookan peoples of Oregon and Washington, analyzing in detail the linguistic elements which demarcate these as well as larger poetic units.[8] He suggests that the Chinookan narrative structure is representative of a Northwest Coast areal pattern. Kuna lines are marked by both intonational patterns, including pauses and, in some ritual genres, a melodic shape and a formalized turn-taking system. There is also a set of affixes, words, and phrases used in every genre and style of speech, serving both to formally mark line structure and to distinguish the genres and styles themselves (see chapter 2). It is difficult to compare the Chinookan and Kuna patterns with the poetic organizational principles at work in the discourse of other societies, since these have rarely been systematically studied. However, current research in American Indian languages and literatures strongly suggests that line and verse structures, marked both by sets of linguistic elements and by various features of the structure of performance, are widespread and important in North and South America.

James Fox, influenced by the work of Roman Jakobson, suggests that parallelism is an extremely common feature of ritual speech throughout the world.[9] Kuna ritual speech is rich in parallelism of many kinds—semantic, syntactic, morphological, and lexical— often resulting in overlapping, parallelistic mosaics. In addition to the various forms of parallelism, there is a marked tendency toward and appreciation of repetition involving all levels of discourse, including whole verbal acts and events, resulting in a pattern I have called retelling (see below).

Enjoyment of repetition may be a widespread American Indian discourse pattern. Among the Chipewyan of western Canada, for example, "repetition is relished. A single story may be told two or three times in succession by either the same or different narrators, with or without changes."[10] Stanley Newman and Ann Gayton say of the Yokuts of California that "although we may regard variety as an absolute virtue of style and repetition as a universal sin, it is obvious that Yokuts cannot be driven in this direction. The broad area of reference covered by Yokuts words gives them a wide range of application, and their literal significance holds them austerely within their proper boundaries of reference. It would be flying in the face of these forces in Yokuts to seek variety by ringing delicate changes upon a recurring notion. When a notion is to be repeated, there is no need to avoid verbal repetition. A passage such as, 'And he walked home. And his friend also walked home. And the people walked home,' however monotonous and slovenly it may appear to English sensibilities, is stylistically appropriate in Yokuts."[11] For the Kuna as well, repetition is one of the principal processes involved in the structuring of discourse and in the creation of the particular quality of their verbal life.

Figurative language is a feature of all Kuna ritual speech, but it is especially characteristic of 'gathering house' speaking and chanting, being one of the primary defining and organizing principles (see chapter 3). Some scholars have pointed to an absence of figurative language in American Indian discourse, especially in North America. Again Newman and Gayton: "Nor are the broad concepts of

Yokuts words sharpened by special figurative uses. A stubborn literalness of reference invades the entire language. The shifts and extensions of meaning that add pungency and vigor to English play no part in Yokuts style . . . The language does not permit its words to cut metaphorical capers."[12] On the other hand, cases of highly developed figurative language and speech have been reported, as in Gary Gossen's study of the semantic multivalence of highland Mayan Chamula proverbs.[13] This very brief comparative excursion is intended to suggest the value of areal studies of the use of figurative language, as well as lineal organization, parallelism and repetition, and other poetic principles and processes at work in the indigenous languages and literatures of North and South America.

## Fixed Speech and Flexible Speech

A distinction between fixed, memorized speech and flexible speech permits a convenient grouping of the three Kuna ritual genres of speaking. Fixed speech characterizes curing and magical rituals and girls' puberty rites; flexible speech characterizes 'gathering house' discourse. Curing and puberty are the most traditional and conservative areas of Kuna ritual life, and it is with regard to these areas that we can most appropriately speak in terms of texts—fixed, unchanging verbal forms. Specialists in curing, the 'ikar knowers,' and in puberty rites, the kanturkana, perform long ikarkana which they have memorized through years of study.

Although the Kuna consider the ikarkana for both curing and puberty rites to be fixed texts and although both sets are learned by means of line-by-line memorization, in actuality they involve different degrees of fixity. Curing ikarkana allow for the inclusion or exclusion of relevant and appropriate sections, depending on such matters as the severity of the illness, the age and sex of the patient, and the presumed origin of the evil spirit.[14] Within each section alterations should not occur. However, slight variations of an essentially nonreferential nature are tolerated, involving very superficial aspects of the phonology and morphology of noun and verb suffixation. The text of puberty rites ikarkana, by contrast, is even more fixed—not the slightest variation in phonology or morphology is permitted.

The degree to which Kuna puberty rites ikarkana are fixed in form is reflected in a personal research experience. In 1970 I made a tape recording of the Mulatuppu kantule, Ernesto Linares, teaching a puberty rites ikar to two students. Between 1970 and 1978 I never discussed this ikar with him. In March of 1979, nine years after the original recording, I brought a transcription I had made of the ikar to him in order to translate it into ordinary colloquial Kuna, from which it differs considerably. Since Kantule Linares does not read or write, he asked me to read him the text. I did so line by line, and he translated each line into colloquial Kuna. Typically, I barely began a line and he finished it, never missing a morpheme or even a phoneme from my transcription. In a few cases where I misread a tiny detail of my own writing, he corrected me. Puberty rites *ikarkana*, then, but not curing *ikarkana*, can be compared to the fixed "compulsive word" characteristic of the ways used in Navajo curing rituals.[15]

The distinguishing feature of 'gathering house' discourse is adaptive and creative flexibility in language use. While certain myths, legends, and themes are conventionally performed in the 'gathering house,' these are not mechanically reproduced as are the curing and puberty rites *ikarkana*. Rather, they are drawn on—as are personal experiences, travels, and dreams—adapted, and often manipulated in order to be incorporated into a topic of immediate concern. Since the 'gathering house' is essentially a political place where individuals maneuver for personal and group advantages, the flexibility and adaptability of 'gathering house' discourse serve this end.

In addition to being the setting for the ritual chanting of 'chiefs,' the 'gathering house' is also the place where a variety of Kuna social, political, legal, and economic matters are publicly carried out through verbal discourse. Advice is given, thefts are discussed and adjudicated, personal experiences are narrated. In these activities there is an even greater focus on flexibility and especially creative manipulation of speech than in the chanting of 'chiefs.' While traditional themes might be alluded to, the old serves the new. Any myth, legend, or metaphor which speakers refer to is secondary to and placed in the service of current issues.

It is interesting that both the fixed puberty rites texts and the relatively fixed curing and magical texts on the one hand and 'gathering house' discourse on the other make use of formulaic expressions similar to those which have been described as the distinguishing feature of the Slavic *guslar* (singer of tales).[16] The Slavic formulas enable the singer to compose his tale anew in each performance. The Kuna formulaic expressions contribute to the performance of a memorized text in certain genres and ways of speaking and to the flexibility and individual creativity of other genres and ways of speaking.

The fixed-flexible distinction is relevant to everyday speech as well. There are everyday verbal genres, such as riddles, which are fixed; they must always be performed with the same words. Other verbal genres, such as lullabies and the 'tuneful weeping' for the dying and deceased, are flexible in that a basic form is adapted and manipulated in order to fit particular situations.

The distinction between fixed and flexible speech is not an absolute dichotomy. Rather, it involves a continuum with the most ritual of discourse being the most immutable and with other areas of ritual life, especially the political and legal, allowing more flexibility. To complete the continuum, we move along in the flexibility direction to spontaneity, this end of the continuum having to do with the most fluid of everyday discourse, most typically with informal conversation. It is not the case that spontaneous speech has no rules or regularity; it most certainly does. But it lacks certain of the features characteristic of both the fixed and the flexible speech of more ritual discourse. It is in colloquial Kuna. It tends not to occur in named, formally recognized genres. It tends to be relatively free with regard to time and place of occurrence. And the possibilities of topic are much more open. The social interactional regulation of spontaneous talk is less overtly formalized than in more ritual discourse, leading to a greater impression of freedom in turn taking and interruption.

Maurice Bloch and Judith Irvine have proposed sets of general and universal features to distinguish formal and ritual speech from informal and everyday speech.[17] An important aspect of both Bloch's and Irvine's formulations, which are based on cross-cultural surveys, is the relative fixity of speech and the associated freedom of choice for individual speakers. My investigation of Kuna speech contributes to this important issue in several ways. The relationship between ritual speech and everyday speech and the relative fixity of speech constitute two separate dimensions which, although connected, are not isomorphic to one another. I have viewed each one in terms of a continuum rather than a categorical and binary opposition. The existence of this fixed-flexible continuum is not particular to the Kuna; more likely, in a general sense, it is a universal which has relevance in all societies. Where societies can be expected to differ is in the way in which this continuum groups and characterizes various speech events and the genres of speaking within them.[18] It is clearly not the case, in spite of the arguments of both Albert Lord and Jack Goody, that there are no pure memorization and no fixed texts in nonliterate, oral societies.[19] The Navajo ways and the Kuna puberty rites *ikarkana* demonstrate the contrary. Nor is memorization the rule in the literature of such societies, as an earlier generation of scholars believed. Both the Slavic singer of tales and the Kuna 'gathering house' speakers and chanters attest to this. Rather, the oral discourse of nonliterate societies provides a rich diversity of possibilities with regard to the relative fixity or flexibility of speech, as well as with regard to other dimensions.

### Dialogue and Conversation

The Kuna label for a two- or three-participant dialogue or conversation, in which one individual reports and the other listens and responds, sometimes with and sometimes without an audience, is *apsoket*. This pattern underlies many Kuna forms and occasions of speaking. All ritual, especially chanted ritual speech, is structured in the form of a dialogue, with an addresser on the one hand and an addressee and sometimes responder on the other. 'Gathering house' chanting involves two 'chiefs,' side by side in adjacent hammocks— one chants line by line; the other responds after each verse with a chanted *teki* (indeed). This ritualized dialogue is performed in front of an audience of Kuna men and women (see chapter 3). In *arkan kae*, the ritual greeting between two 'chiefs,' this same communicative structure is alternated, each 'chief' taking a turn chanting statements and questions in a series of lines and verses while the other responds.

In curing and magical rituals, there are two participants. The addresser is the '*ikar* knower,' the specialist who performs the memorized text of the *ikar*. The addressees are the 'stick dolls' and the spirits of the various animals, plants, and objects to be controlled through his performance. The addressees do not speak during the performance—they are listening and understanding members of the dialogue (see chapter 4). 'Stick dolls' and spirits converse with each other also, sometimes as a result of having heard an *ikar*, and conversations among spirits are often narrated in the text of an *ikar*. For example, in 'the way of the rattlesnake,' used for protection against snakebite, the rattlesnake tells his wife:

'For you I will go and get food; for you I will kill an animal.'

And she responds:

'You are going hunting for me,' she says.
'I will prepare your beverage for you.'[20]

Less ritual than the chanting of 'chiefs' and the curing and magical *ikarkana*, but still relatively formal, are the various spoken 'gathering house' events—reports, personal narratives, 'stories,' and disputes. These too are typically structured in the form of dialogues between two individuals. The addresser is the teller, reporter, or arguer, who stands to speak and usually moves forward toward the center of the 'gathering house,' remaining at the outer edge of the inner circle of 'chiefs' and 'spokesmen.' The addressee is a 'gathering house' official, either the first 'chief' of the village or another 'chief,' a 'spokesman,' or some other leader who has been directing the discussion at that moment. The others present in the 'gathering house' constitute the audience for this conversation.

The typical 'gathering house' communicative structure thus consists of three participants: addresser, addressee-responder, and audience. This formalized structure funnels tempers and conflicts through the village leadership. The focus is on controlled eloquence and rhetoric rather than on any direct expression of anger toward another person; the purpose is deference not to the authority or the power of village political leaders but, rather, to communicative demeanor and compromise. The Kuna, who know full well that their world is full of jealousy, anger, and mistrust, want to see themselves publicly as a cooperative and harmonious society—their three-participant conversational structure provides the means to channel public speaking into a harmonious form.

Everyday conversations, also called *apsoket*,[21] do not have as rigidly formalized a structure as ritual *ikarkana* or formal 'gathering house' events, but the two- or three-participant structure is quite common. Two individuals who have not seen one another for some time or who have important personal business to carry out with each other do so in a two-person conversation, often within the house of one of them and often seated or lying in adjacent hammocks. And typically one person talks, line by line, while the other responds with *teki* (thus, indeed), the sound *aa* or *mm*, or a grunt. After a series of such lines and responses, they switch speaker and responder roles. This two-participant structure lies midway between highly ritualized 'gathering house' and curing and magical chanting, on the one hand, and more spontaneous and informal verbal interactions, on the other. In the latter as well, the two- or three-participant structure often emerges. That is, informal talk among a group of people is frequently organized such that two individuals within the group carry on a conversation which the others, more as audience than as direct addressees, attend to and comment on. Narration, of personal experiences or news, typically occurs according to this pattern.

The two- or three-participant structure emerges most clearly in everyday conversation in certain role relationships and situations. Close friends who see one another regularly every day often converse in the same place, either alone or with others present. Two men in a special relationship, for example, such as father and son, father-in-law and son-in-law, or teacher and student, use the two- or

three-participant structure for their conversations. Similarly, within
a home, a host and a guest converse in this form. The guest, who
often has some experience or news to report, first sits and is offered a
beverage. When the guest finishes drinking, she or he converses with
the head of the household, a friend or relative, and others listen and
comment. But it is clear that the central, primary conversants are
the guest and the head of the household and that any others present
are mainly an audience. The same conversational structure is used
among members of a single household, husband and wife, father and
son, mother and daughter, brother and brother, when one of the pair
has something to report. The more significant the news or the more
potentially conflictual the report, the more likely it is that the two-
or three-participant structure will be used, channeling speech, as in
'gathering house' discourse, into a form in which demeanor is carefully and harmoniously controlled.

On the basis of the various examples investigated here, it is possible to develop a typology of Kuna two- and three-participant dialogic
conversations. First, two officially recognized participants with an
official audience are involved both in 'gathering house' chanting,
where two 'chiefs' serve as addresser and addressee with an official
audience, and in the 'mass-curing ritual,' where the human addresser and his spirit addressees have an official audience. Second,
two officially recognized participants with a possible unofficial, non-
participating audience are involved in the 'gathering house' *arkan
kae*, the ritual greeting between two 'chiefs' who alternate as addresser and addressee; in curing, magical, and puberty *ikarkana*,
with their human addressers and spirit addressees; and in private
conversations between two individuals. Third, two unofficially recognized participants with an unofficial, possibly participating audience are involved in ordinary 'gathering house' discussions and in
ordinary conversations.

Ritualized dialogues, sometimes bordering on verbal dueling or
competitions, have been reported for a number of South American
Indian groups. Among the Araucanians of Argentina and Chile, certain categories of men must carry on a *koyaqtun* (extremely formalized conversation) before proceeding to other business. Participants in this *koyaqtun* are persons between whom tension might
possibly arise, such as father-in-law and son-in-law or native and
stranger. The *koyaqtun* consists of a series of questions and answers
between two participants, each of whom tries to outdo the other in
compliments and comments.[22] In conversations among the Indians
of the northwest Amazon, each participant repeats part of what a
predecessor says, thus indicating understanding, assent or dissent,

and respect. Respect is measured by the degree to which a participant's utterances are repeated; this repetition diminishes as the conversation becomes less formal.[23] Among the Brazilian Kaingang,[24]
there is a speech event called *wainyekladn* during which two individuals sit opposite each other and shout myths at each other, syllable by syllable. One man shouts a syllable, the second repeats it, and
so on. The participants are two friends; the purpose of the event is to
draw them together.[25]

If ritualized dialogue is a South American areal pattern, then one
clear focal point of the pattern is a region north of the Amazon. The
Carib-speaking Trio, who live on either side of the Brazil-Surinam
frontier, have both competitive and noncompetitive ritualized conversations. The noncompetitive form is a staccato conversation
punctuated by the continual response, 'That's it.' These conversations are used to tell others what one is going to do or what one
has done, when it involves something out of the ordinary or when
the participants have not seen each other for some time. In the competitive, highly formalized dialogue, two men on stools sit facing
slightly away from each other in the middle of the square. The participants take turns talking in short rhyming sentences, the listener
responding with a low murmuring grunt at the end of each sentence.
Turns last about ten minutes, and the entire conversation can last
up to twenty-four hours. The language is esoteric and archaic; the
verbal duel is won by the man who can go on arguing the longest.
Trio competitive ritual dialogue is used between strangers or between kin and acquaintances whose relationship has temporarily
lapsed. It has three purposes—to receive visitors or announce one's
arrival in a village, to trade, and to obtain a wife.[26]

In the *oho* (yes saying) ceremony of the Cariban Waiwai, who inhabit the borderland of Guyana and Brazil, two individuals sit on
low stools opposite each other. Each participant chants short and
fast sentences, while the other responds *oho*. In the first stage of the
ceremony, the opener flatters his opponent and speaks disparagingly
about himself. Then the opponent starts his phase of the chanting.
Opener and opponent chant alternately for a considerable time. The
ceremony continues until one participant runs out of words and arguments, rises, and leaves, thus signifying that he has lost his case.
The event generally lasts one or two hours, although an interchange
of twenty-six hours has been reported. The *oho* ceremony is used in
obtaining a wife, in trade, in individual contracts and communal
work, in invitations to a feast by a village leader, in refuting a magical blowing which might cause death, and in death rituals.[27]

The ritualized dialogue of tropical forest South America seems to occur especially on occasions when there is a potential for tension in an interaction, either because of the relationship between the participants or because of the timing of the event—the dialogue relieves tension by focusing it on an elaborate, verbally playful, and artistic form. In similar situations, many North American Indian groups use silence as a communicative device.[28] Although silence is rare among the Kuna, it is used communicatively in ways which bear certain resemblances to the North American pattern (see above).

### *'Counsel'*

The primary purpose of Kuna public 'gatherings' is social control, performed verbally in the form of 'counsel' either to the community at large or to groups or individuals within it. All persons about to embark on a new role or activity receive a public 'counsel' from 'chiefs' and other 'gathering' officials. The 'counsel' for a new 'chief' or other village official is most dramatic. The new 'chief' or 'spokesman' has been chosen in advance, but on this occasion, seated in the 'gathering house,' he pretends not to know anything about it. Suddenly the 'policemen' of the village grab the individual and his wife and lead them to the center of the 'gathering house.' Pretending to be blind, they listen as the head 'chief' of the 'gathering' speaks or chants a 'counsel' to them which provides them with new sight and encourages them to perform their new roles well.

In other public 'gatherings,' students are counseled before school begins and couples are counseled as part of their marriage ceremony. 'Counsels' in the 'gathering house' are also used to remind various individuals of the way to behave in roles they already fill. 'Chiefs' periodically counsel women, curing specialists, or midwives, stressing that they should perform their duties properly. And all 'gathering' chanting, whether about history, myth, personal experience, or metaphor, is ultimately 'counsel' in that it exemplifies, symbolizes, and reminds the audience of proper modes of Kuna behavior.

*Uanaet*, like *apsoket*, is the name for a variety of speech events which cut across ritual and everyday life; exploration and explanation of the various instances of 'counsel' and their relationship elucidate the function of this pattern in Kuna communication. In addition to serving as public advice to a particular individual, social group, or entire community, the 'counsels' are also an important form of punishment in disputes brought before the public 'gatherings.' Once the case has been decided, after thorough discussion, long 'counsels' are performed by 'chiefs' and other 'gathering' leaders, either as an accompaniment to other punishments, such as fines, or as the sole punishment. In addition to focusing on a particular wrongdoing, these 'counsels' stress the importance of proper moral behavior more generally and are rhetorically and poetically developed. And, since they are public, they are aimed as much at the 'gathering house' audience as at the person directly accused of wrongdoing.

The *ikar* performed by a ritual curer consists of 'counsel' from the specialist to the spirit about how to achieve the action desired by the performer. These *ikarkana* are often punctuated with lines stating explicitly that the specialist is counseling the spirit. The spirits, in turn, often counsel other spirits on how to behave, as a result of having been counseled by the performing specialist. The various *ikarkana* used to give life to medicine and render it effective are called 'medicine counsel.' In both 'counsels' directed to spirits and those of the 'gathering house,' social control, rhetoric, and verbal art are intimately linked.

In everyday speech, 'counsel' is common as well. A child's father counsels her or him at the beginning of the school year; if the child attends school in a village away from home, her or his temporary guardian gives advice periodically on proper behavior and always gives advice in the case of wrongdoing. Similarly, before young men leave for work in Panama City or the Canal Zone, they are counseled by their fathers. It is important to note that physical violence is avoided among the Kuna; there are very strong sanctions against it. Parents do not spank their children. Physical fighting is very rare and always becomes the subject of an evening discussion in the 'gathering house,' in which the protagonists are severely reprimanded and fined.

Given the avoidance of physical means of social control, 'counsel' plays a very important role in the regulation of behavior in everyday as well as ritual life. It is particularly interesting that both the verbal advice given in advance of an activity and the verbal punishment levied after wrongdoing are grouped together as 'counsel.' This combination is a reflection of the Kuna belief in the potential of all beings, human and spirit, for mischievous, immoral, or even evil behavior—the 'counsels' are constantly needed, not just after a misdeed has been committed but before it might occur and so that it does not occur. 'Counsels' also often occur in the context of ritualized dialogues; both channel conflicts into a carefully controlled, often verbally artistic form.[29]

### Reporting and Retelling

Another Kuna pattern of speaking which cuts across everyday and ritual domains involves the interplay and intersection among *soke* (telling) and *parsoke* (retelling, reformulating). A typology of Kuna tellings, reportings, and retellings reveals the dimensions of their structure and function, textually, contextually, strategically, social interactionally, and ethnographically. Kuna speakers tend to present facts, opinions, or arguments not as their own but as retellings and reformulations of what others or even they themselves have previously said. Discourse of all kinds is heavily embedded with speech that has previously occurred, typically in the form of first-person direct quotation. In fact, Kuna grammar does not readily make a clear distinction between direct and indirect quotations. The great majority of all quotation is direct—speakers are constantly uttering words that are not their own. And direct quotations are often embedded within direct quotations. The following typical example is from a speech given in the Mulatuppu 'gathering house' by a curing specialist on his return from a period of study in a distant village, a speech that I have quoted from before. Explanations and necessary identifications of speakers appear in brackets.

'Well friend I know that *ikar* see say.
Well some people say see, "it belongs to the Choco [a neighboring Indian group]."
But it does not belong to the Choco' he [the teacher] says.
'A long time ago thus when the seers [Kuna leaders and prophets] started to come down [to earth].
When the great seers came down.
Thus Ipelele [one of the foremost early 'seers'].
Corporally entered a stronghold, a place called Kalu Mattu see say.
Now there in the mountain he showed the letter [giving him permission to enter] see say.
"Well they took the letter away from me," he [Ipelele] says.
"Well the letter was read," he says see say, "[it said], 'come to my place to learn medicine.
Come on Sunday.'
Well the people who found the letter did not want to go.
A Choco entered that place see say.
The Choco remained fifteen days see say.
Below the earth.
Well the Choco was asked [about his experience, when he returned] see say.
'Now I [the Choco] entered that place.
Now therefore when I entered it was dark see say.
As if my eyes were covered.
Well when I entered further it was all right see say.
The people there see say.

Live like people here see say.
The snake is policeman see say.
And the spider.
Is spokesman see say.
The spider then got me a boy see say.
He took me to the chief,' he says.
'Well when they had taken me to the chief, the chief says to me see
    say.
"What have you come here to do?"
I say see say, "I have brought this letter see."
By order of the letter he taught me see say.
"[The 'chief' says], It is well see said.
God gave me this place see say.
'Before men live here [God is speaking], so that no evil spirits enter.
You will use this medicine.'
God said to me see," he [the 'chief'] says see,' he [the Choco] says."'[30]

The extreme point of quotation within quotation is reached toward the end of this passage, when the speaker is quoting his teacher,
who is quoting Ipelele, who is quoting a Choco Indian, who is quoting a 'chief' of the spirit world, who is quoting God. It is important
to point out two significant features of this example, the first having to do with the structure of the telling of narrative, the second
having to do with the grammatical marking of embedded tellings.
With regard to the telling of narrative, there is a single story line.
There is not a story within a story, as is found in some narrative traditions or structures—what is embedded are not stories but tellers.[31]
This is what I have tried to represent by making use of the clearly
insufficient western writing device of single and double quotation
marks.[32]

This leads to the question of the grammatical marking of embedded tellings. While Kuna grammar provides a rich potential in metacommunicative words, phrases, and affixes, there is not a necessary
and unique formal, overt marking for every embedding. Nor do intonational or other stylistic changes mark more than a single level of
embedding, and often they do not go even this shallow distance.
Thus, in spite of a general rule that the last character introduced into
a narrative is most likely to be the next speaker quoted, it becomes
very difficult at each moment of the narration (for analysts as well as
for native members of the community) to decode exactly who is
speaking. Competent listening and understanding involve following
the story line, recognizing the process of the embedding of direct
quotation, and following this to a certain degree.

While quoted, embedded speech is frequently found in colloquial

Kuna, the more formal the discourse, the greater the potential for embedding within embedding—the placing of words in the mouths of others being one of the major Kuna rhetorical strategies. It is possible to adopt a certain point of view or argue for a particular position as though it does not belong to oneself but is simply a report of what someone else has said, in a 'gathering house' speech, in a personal conversation, or in a dream. An individual's own behavior can be cleverly extolled and compared with that of others which is criticized, all as part of a retelling. In the following citation, a 'chief' is reporting on a chant of a 'chief' from another village that he heard when attending an interisland ritual 'gathering.' The quoted 'chief' is in turn reporting the words of a deceased 'chief,' who came to him in a dream. The chanting 'chief' is labeled cc; the 'responding chief,' RC.

cc: "When I was planting I would plant right up to the limit of my neighbors say see.
That is how I was."
RC: Indeed.
cc: "I would enter into the land of my neighbors.
That is how I was on earth say."
RC: Indeed.
cc: "I used to be very active in planting coconuts say see."
RC: Indeed.
cc: "I would take my neighbors' coconuts say hear.
That is how I was say see."
RC: Indeed.
cc: "People who take their neighbors' coconuts are bad say see."
RC: Indeed.[33]

The 'chief' who performed this chant was at the time one of the youngest and most recently named of the many 'chiefs' of Sasartii-Mulatuppu. For this reason, his behavior was particularly on public display and open to judgment and criticism. At the interisland ritual 'gathering' he had just attended, one of the 'spokesmen' who was there with him was critical of the behavior of the political leaders of his own village, Mulatuppu. On his return home, this 'spokesman' was publicly criticized in the 'gathering house' for what he had said. Through the process of embedding direct quotations within direct quotations, the 'chief,' through the mouths of others, was able to indirectly criticize the behavior of other village leaders, thus praising his own by implied contrast. Since the Kuna continually insist on viewing themselves as a harmonious, egalitarian society, the process of deeply embedding criticism of others in the form of quotations within quotations functions, like ritualized dialogue and 'counsel,' to avoid face-to-face confrontation between individuals. This rhetorical strategy is a most appropriate and useful form of social control in Kuna society.

One's own actions can be explained and justified by being presented as retellings of what someone else has said. Here is a 'medicinal specialist' informing his village in the 'gathering house' how much he will charge for his services, for example, providing plants which will keep snakes off farms. By punctuating every line in which he announces his prices with *soke* (he says), the specialist insists on the fact that the prices were determined by his teacher rather than by himself.

'When the farm belongs to a single friend [individual],' he says, 'if a
    single individual wants to plant,' he says.
'You charge him one dollar,' he says.
'Such a farm does not belong to the town,' he says.
'It belongs rather to a single person you don't hear say.'
He said to me.
'As for persons from other islands,' he says.
'Those are charged two dollars see say.
Because other towns might want this also,' he says.[34]

Retellings blend into interpretations, for in resaying what someone else has said or even what you yourself have said on another occasion there is always an implied interpretation. This is so even in seemingly word-for-word repetitions, since their meaning always depends on the context in which they are uttered and the way in which they are delivered. Furthermore, retellings are often purposeful interpretations—words are given a new slant, a new meaning, appropriate to the new context. This is most apparent when the first telling involved language that requires interpretation, either because of its ritual, esoteric style or because of its use of metaphoric or other allusive devices.

Reformulations are most overtly marked in 'gathering house' chanting and speaking, in which they constitute distinct formal units within speech events. A 'chief' while chanting may develop a metaphor, describe a personal experience or a dream, or tell a bit of tribal history. He may or may not explain and interpret what he is chanting, as part of his performance. But it is the explicit and defined role of his 'spokesman,' after the 'chief' has finished, to reformulate the words in more colloquial Kuna. It is important to stress that the use of esoteric and allusive language by the 'chief' in his chant is the official reason for the retelling. In reality, many members of the audience often understand a great deal of the chanting of 'chiefs.' But, whether or not the audience understands the chant, its reformulation is a necessary, formal segment of the total event.

The same pattern occurs semiofficially and semiformally every time a 'chief' speaks rather than chants in the 'gathering house,' to argue for a particular political position or mode of behavior or to counsel a particular group of individuals. His speech is typically followed by a reformulation and reinterpretation by one or more 'spokesmen.' The more significant the content, the greater the prestige of the 'chief,' and the more ceremonial the occasion, the more likely it is that there will be more than one retelling, not only by 'spokesmen,' the official interpreters, but by other speakers as well. In April of 1971, for example, the village of Sasartii installed a new 'chief' after removing from office (for misconduct) an old, traditional, knowledgeable individual who had been the first 'chief' for many years. A 'chief' from the nearby village of Tupwala was invited to perform the 'counsel' for the new 'chief.' The visitor's speech was followed by reformulation after reformulation, reinterpretation after reinterpretation, by Mulatuppu and Sasartii 'chiefs,' 'spokesmen,' and other village leaders, the whole event lasting long into the night.

A parallel, almost isomorphic pattern is found in the communications addressed by curing and magical specialists to spirits. In these *ikarkana*, in which the specialist attempts to convince the spirits to do his bidding, there are repeated reformulations by the specialist. In addition, within the *ikar* texts themselves, the spirit addressees retell other spirits what the specialist has told them. Since, according to Kuna belief, descriptions narrated in an *ikar* occur simultaneously in the spirit world, these spirit retellings are considered to be as real as human ones. The social organization of speaking among spirits parallels that among humans; first there is a two-participant dialogic conversation, then the spirit addressees retell and interpret for others the message of the initial speaker.

A mirror image of this pattern occurs when spirits communicate with humans—just as spirits reformulate what humans tell them, humans reformulate the messages they receive from spirits. Spirits communicate with members of the Kuna community about matters of concern to particular individuals or to the community at large. They usually communicate with 'seers,' but they sometimes address other persons as well. The spirits typically appear in dreams, but they occasionally communicate with a person in waking life, for example, in the mainland jungle. After this communication, the Kuna individual reports the message of the spirits, not only in conversations with friends and family but in a public reformulation in a 'gathering house' speech. An interesting variant of this pattern, quite in keeping with the Kuna adaptation to changing times, involves the use of cassette recorders. A 'seer' from the village of Ailikantii who lives in Panama City sometimes has dreams in which spirits communicate with him concerning matters of relevance to his San Blas village. The 'seer' then tapes a speech in which he reformulates and reinterprets the spirit messages and sends the cassette by plane to Ailikantii, where it is played before an audience in the 'gathering house.'

Retelling and reformulation, which are structurally formalized in ritual speech, are common in everyday speech as well. In ordinary conversations in the afternoon, as individuals sit around and chat, one person will talk for a while, reporting his or her activities that day or some news he or she has heard. These reports are frequently explicit retellings of the words of others. The more significant and special the news or personal experience, the more likely it is to be told and retold, to friends and family, in house after house, culminating in the evening in a more formal retelling at the 'gathering house.' Retelling, reformulation, and interpretation can be used strategically in everyday interaction as well, as a way of indirectly criticizing, reprimanding, commanding, or complaining, using the words of another to state one's own feelings and positions. In addition, as people sit around and converse, it is quite common for one person to pick up on what another has just said and repeat it in other words. Such reformulation is not in another language or dialect; nor is it needed because some participants have not understood what has been said; nor are there esoteric or allusive uses of language to explain, as in 'gathering house' speaking and, especially, chanting. Rather, retelling, reformulation, and interpretation are Kuna communicative patterns, utilized whether or not understanding is at issue.

### Reflexivity and Metacommunication

Retellings and especially interpretations are commentaries on speaking itself; their immediate referent is the discourse they reformulate, whether this is their own or someone else's. All Kuna speech tends to include reflexive and metacommunicative commentary. In ritual chanting and speaking especially, there is a penchant for commentary by performers which describes explicitly and in great detail when and where the event is taking place, who is performing and to whom, what actions are occurring, what topic and content are involved, and why all this is being done. This commentary is reflexive in the sense that it points inward and is directed toward the participants in the event and toward the event itself. And it is metacommunicative in that it is a commentary on every aspect of the communicative event at the very moment that it is taking place. In 'gathering house' chanting by 'chiefs' and spoken interpretation by their 'spokesmen,' reflexive and metacommunicative commentary may become so extensive as to predominate, becoming itself the topic of the discourse. Here is the opening of a 'gathering house' chant, in which a 'chief' will perform the myth of Nele Sipu (the White Seer).

cc: Thus.
Today.
We gather.
rc: Indeed.
cc: Thus before the sun sets.
In truth, 'we are going to gather,' they [the 'policemen'] say.
rc: Indeed.
cc: Thus.
The owners of the golden sticks ['policemen'].
Then circled the golden streets.
rc: Indeed.
cc: 'Go to the golden gathering house.'
The owners of the golden sticks then said.
rc: Indeed.
cc: Now the village leaders.
In truth have arrived.
rc: Indeed.
cc: All the chiefs and all the spokesmen.
Really arrived.
rc: Indeed.
cc: All the policemen.
Really arrived.
rc: Indeed.
cc: God left golden benches and we came to sit on them.
rc: Indeed.
cc: Thus in truth cocoa men ['knowers of the way of cocoa,' used in curing] and hot pepper birds ['knowers of the way of the hot pepper,' used in curing] you arrived to me.
rc: Indeed.
cc: All the medicinal specialists and all the *kanturkana* really arrived.
rc: Indeed.
cc: Thus the knowers of the way of the wind [a curing *ikar*] came.
rc: Indeed.

cc: Everyone has entered their golden bench in God's golden listening house.
rc: Indeed.
cc: All the female relatives all the nieces [women] you came to me.
rc: Indeed.
cc: The bird grabbers [midwives] really arrived and so have the hammock makers.
rc: Indeed.
cc: Those who make molas arrived and those who string beads arrived.
rc: Indeed.
cc: Haircutters you arrived to me.
All the haircutters really arrived.
rc: Indeed.
cc: All of you have arrived to sit on your golden benches.
There is a golden list [of people present].
rc: Indeed.

In these lines, the 'chief' has described the basic components of the Kuna 'gathering house' event. First the 'policemen' announce the event in the streets of the village; then the village leaders take their places on benches that are especially for them; then the women, including ritual specialists, take their places. After this lengthy reflexive description, the 'chief' begins his chanting of the myth and then announces this myth too, reflexively, with a preface.

cc: Thus.
In truth let us listen.
In truth call.
rc: Indeed.
cc: Let us listen to the story of a seer.
Friend say.
rc: Indeed.[35]

Curing and magical ikarkana are also highly reflexive. The spirits addressed are explicitly informed about what is going on while the ikar is being performed and why it is being performed.

The specialist is starting to call you.
The specialist is calling you.
To the sixth level underground the specialist is calling you.
'Your soul he knows,' he says; 'your foundation he knows,' he says.[36]

This passage precisely labels the components of the communicative event of which it is a part: the addresser is the specialist; the addressee is you, the spirit; the setting, the sixth level underground; the communicative channel, calling; and the topic, the knowledge of the spirit's soul and foundation. And all this reflexive commentary is embedded within a metacommunicative verb, 'he says.'

In each of the Kuna ritual varieties and styles as well as in everyday, colloquial speech, there is an elaborate set of affixes, words, and phrases whose precise function is reflexive and metacommunicative. These provide metacommunicative frames[37] which orient the referential and informational content within them; they focus attention on the addresser, the addressee, and the audience in relation to the discourse. Since these linguistic devices are often derived from words meaning say, hear, see, and true, they contribute to the sense that Kuna speech is one or more steps (really one or more mouths) removed from the actual speaker and that what one is listening to at a given moment is always a retelling, a rehearing, a reviewing, or a reinterpretation of something said before. Here are some representative examples. The metacommunicative elements are underlined in the Kuna portion. The first examples are from the chanting of 'chiefs.'

*oparye* (to say, signify, utter):
*sakla nakaki nele sipukwa nekatakkalite oparye.*
In ancient times the White Seer visited utter.

*sunna* (indeed, in truth):
*al inso sunna nek par ittomarsunna nase kole.*
Then in truth let us listen, in truth call.

*soke* (to say):
*al insoki nek ulupalite pilli pakkekine sokkuye.*
Then from the fourth level below is said.

*ittoe* (to hear):
*aya kapmapar oipoar ittoleye.*
Friend, when I awoke, is heard.

*takke* (to see):
*al inso nele sipukwati purpa pal ittote naka sokte taklemarye.*
Then let us listen to the story of the White Seer say, is seen.

These devices can and often do occur in various combinations.

*poniti ippulet sokku tok apesuli takleye oparanto.*
Dangerous sickness say, I don't want here, is seen utter.
*soke l ittole ipitikuetakleparye.*
Say, is heard, thus it is, is seen.
*teki ante pannakutmar sokeittole sunna naki nasitetaklemarye.*
Then we left, say, is heard, in truth, we continued on, is seen.

The interpretations of 'spokesmen' include even more metacommunicative devices than the chants of 'chiefs,' since 'spokesmen' re-tell, reformulate, and interpret the chants. Here are some examples.

*takkenye* (to see):
*pe wis palittosimar takkenye.*
We listened to you a little see.

*takleku* (it seems):
*emite taklekuti pela nase kottemarpali.*
Now it seems all are called.

*owisoe* (to inform):
*sakla anmar owiso takken.*
The chief informs us see.

These devices can also occur in combinations.

*takkensoke* (see say):
*pela takleku ittoet neyse nonimar takkensoke.*
Everyone it seems came to the listening house see say.

*pittosursoke* (you don't hear say):
*enuk piekar pittosurso pittosursokene.*
In order to call his name you don't hear say, you don't hear say.

It is quite common in the speeches of 'spokesmen' for certain lines to consist almost entirely of metacommunicative and reflexive elements, with practically no referential or informational content.

*inso taklekutina emit taklekuti 'panse upononimarye,' sakla an-mar sok takkenye.*
Then it seems now it seems 'you entered,' the chief says to us see.

*pela taklekuti nuk nikkatpi pittosursoke sok takken.*
Everyone it seems who has a name, you don't hear say say see.

Here are some examples from the formal 'gathering house' speech-making style, used, in this case, in the performance of 'the agouti story.'

*ittosa* (heard?):
*nue sichunnat. aa. ittosa?*
He put it well in place, in truth. Ah. Heard?

*napir soke* (it is true say):
*achu nek wiskuarparku napir soke.*
When the jaguar regained consciousness, it is true say.

*-sunto* (in truth):
*parkaletapparsunto.*
He was caught again in truth.

I turn now to curing and magical *ikarkana,* where a distinct set of metacommunicative devices is used.

*uanae* (to counsel):
*apisuati Machi Oloaktikunappi uanaeye.*
The specialist is counseling Machi Oloaktikunappi [the spirit name of the snake].

*penekue* (to contend):
*apisuati Machi Oloaktikunappiti na tar penekuiniye.*
The specialist is contending with Machi Oloaktikunappi.

*soke* (to say):
*'apisuati pe purpati wisikusarpa' kana tar sokekwichiye.*
'The specialist knows your soul,' the specialist says.

Here are examples from 'the way of the *kantule.*'

*sunna* (in truth):
*yainua sunna yakkiriteye.*
The girl in truth is quiet.

*takleke* (to be seen):
*nukki kia takleke.*
There is the mouth-rinsing water it is seen.

And, finally, here are examples from everyday, colloquial speech.

*soke* (to say):
*walapakke soke.*
There were four say.

*ittoe* (to hear):
*ankat mullusuli ittosa.*
Mine is long, heard.

*takke* (to see):
*macheret soke 'ankat suli' taysa.*
The husband says, 'it's not mine,' saw.

*-sunto* (in truth):
*hospitarse kep natsunto.*
Then he went to the hospital in truth.

While in some ways similar to the English phrases "you know" and "you see," which serve as floor holders and fillers in conversations in the United States, the set of metacommunicative and reflexive elements in Kuna is much more developed and has a wider and more complicated range of functions. From a grammatical point of view, these elements are often evidential markers, which serve to validate, qualify, or indicate the source of the information provided

in an utterance.[38] Evidential markers are found as a grammatical cat-
egory in various languages around the world; they are relatively
common in the indigenous languages of the Americas.[39] These metacommunicative affixes, words, and phrases, which are characteristic
of all varieties and styles of Kuna, often mark the beginnings and
endings of phrases, sentences, lines, and verses. They are thus an important aspect of the poetic structure of all Kuna chanting and speak
ing. The use of metacommunicative elements in the poetic structure
of North American Indian literature has been noted by various scholars and is quite possibly a North American Indian areal pattern.[40] Social interactionally, these metacommunicative frames, which are related to the retelling pattern described above, are distancing devices—they set apart the information expressed in an utterance and
connect it to another speaker or event or surround it with commentary about it.[41] And, since there is a unique set of these elements in
each variety and style of Kuna, they are also sociolinguistic indica-
tors, one of the primary distinguishing markers of the different varieties and styles of speaking and chanting.

Because of the extensive and formalized use of these reflexive and
metacommunicative elements in Kuna language and speech, it might
be imagined that their referential meanings, such as say, hear, see,
and truth, have lost their original significance and become purely ar-
bitrary and mechanical for speakers. However, when these elements
are placed in the context of an overall Kuna ethnography of speaking, there is no doubt of the Kuna concern for explicitness with regard to the fact that every instance of discourse is being spoken,
heard, understood, and authenticated.

## Intersections and Interpenetrations of Ways of Speaking

The various patterns of speaking that I have just described constitute one type of relationship which links the various everyday and
ritual ways of speaking. A different type of relationship is the subject
of this section—interactions, intersections, overlaps, and especially
interpenetrations of ways of speaking. Some intersections and interpenetrations have been noted in passing; now I bring them together
in order to highlight their significance.

The sharpness of the differentiation among the three ritual traditions and of their separation from everyday verbal life cannot be
overstressed: the four domains do not blend together or in any way
become confused. It is against the backdrop of this sharp differentiation that the significance of intersections and interpenetrations
must be viewed. Nor do the intersections and interpenetrations occur in systematic patterns. Rather, they must be isolated here and

there, as occasional junctures of otherwise separate domains. The meeting place is sometimes in setting, sometimes in participant or speaking role, sometimes in referential content, sometimes in a discourse form or genre. Given the way I have introduced them, the intersections and interpenetrations might seem to be marginal to the broad sweep of a Kuna ethnography and an ethnography of speaking, unimportant little misfits in an otherwise coherent scheme. But, when explored in some detail, they provide quite interesting insights into the nature of Kuna verbal life.

Kuna intersections and interpenetrations of ways of speaking can be grouped into several general categories—the interpenetration of the everyday into the ritual and the ritual into the everyday, the interpenetration of ritual domains and contexts between and among each other, and the extensive range of contexts for the performance of ritual chants.

### The Everyday within the Ritual

It has been an assumption of research in both symbolic anthropology and the ethnography of speaking that the more ritual and ceremonial a context, the more esoteric and allusive the language and speech used, although there has been no systematic cross-cultural study of this relationship. The investigation of Kuna verbal life confirms this general rule in one sense but contradicts it in another. The set of *ikarkana* which is used in curing, magic, and girls' puberty rites involves linguistic varieties which, especially with regard to vocabulary, are quite distinct from colloquial Kuna and are unintelligible to the noninitiate. On the other hand, much of the actual referential content of these *ikarkana* is not esoteric or symbolic at all. Rather, it consists of detailed description, in the most everyday, banal sense, of the participants and actions involved in the event. The participants might be human actors who behave in the text precisely as the Kuna behave in everyday, real life. Here is an excerpt from the extremely ritual and secretive puberty rites *ikar*, 'the way of the *kantule*,' which describes what happens on the morning of the ritual.

The cock begins to crow.
All the cocks are crowing.
They are crowing all around the house.
The noise is heard all around the island.
All the cocks are making noise.
The women prepare the morning beverage.
The women get out of their hammocks and prepare the morning
   beverage.[42]

Or the participants might be spirit actors (good or evil, plant or animal or object) whose textual behavior reflects the Kuna conception of human behavior, since according to the Kuna the human and the spirit worlds are mirror images of one another. Here is a small portion of 'the way of the rattlesnake.' The rattlesnake's wife is preparing a beverage for her husband to take on a hunting trip, just as Kuna women do for their husbands every day.

Puna Inakunipyaisop [the spirit name of Rattlesnake's wife] responds
    [to Rattlesnake].
'You are going hunting for me,' she says.
'I will prepare your beverage for you.'
The wife says.
She lights the fire.
She turns the firewood.
In the fireplace the fire begins.
The fire burns brightly.
On top of the fire she places a pot.
Inside the pot she places the fruit.
She lowers the liquid [to the fire].
The liquid begins to boil.[43]

The examples I have presented here illustrate two conventional representations, literary topoi, by means of which everyday experience is transformed into narrative in ritual *ikarkana*. These step-by-step descriptions of daily activities as well as conversations which state reflexively exactly what is occurring at the same moment are not abracadabra—they are anything but.

This use of everyday descriptions and conversations in curing, magical, and puberty rites *ikarkana* can be accounted for by considering the Kuna theory of magical control through language, according to which a detailed and exact description of an object, including representations of its spirit language in conversational form and its daily round of activities, demonstrates to it (really to its spirit) that the performer of the *ikar* has intimate knowledge of it and can control it. The subsequent narration of actions and events, addressed to the spirit world, causes their simultaneous occurrence in the mirror-image physical world.

One of the central features of Kuna magical power and control—discovered and learned by specialists in great detail and probably known by many individuals in general—is that secret, magical power through words consists of, in referential terms, very ordinary stuff. What makes the words able to control the spirit world is their secrecy; everyday messages are expressed in an esoteric, secret vocabulary. With the exception of the mythlike narratives which form the core of several major curing *ikarkana*—and even within these narratives—curing, puberty, and especially magical *ikarkana* are characterized by this sharp differentiation between a language which is esoteric and secretive in relation to everyday Kuna and a narrative content which describes actors and actions in the most banal and stereotyped way. Even the curing myths consist of events which, far from extraordinary, are of the most commonplace kind. In fact, the happenings described in such great detail in ritual *ikarkana*, if uttered in everyday conversation, would elicit a 'so what?' reaction, although the Kuna expect and are much more tolerant of minute descriptions of ordinary matters in everyday speech than are most North Americans and Europeans.[44]

There is a relationship between the extent to which an event or a context is considered ritual or esoteric per se and the degree of reportability or banality of the content of the discourse used in the event.[45] The more ordinary the event and the more intelligible the language used in it, the greater the necessity that the content be reportable news. Since curing events and puberty rites are the most special and secretive of all Kuna occasions, the memorized *ikarkana* which are central to them are the most esoteric of all Kuna forms of discourse in that their language—in its phonological, morphological, syntactical, and lexical dimensions—is most distant from everyday Kuna and is the least intelligible of all the ritual varieties and styles for nonspecialists. It is precisely these *ikarkana* which contain the most banal, the least reportable narrations.

Another example of the interpenetration of everyday speech into ritual speech is the inclusion of everyday verbal forms within ritual discourse. 'Chiefs,' for example, often insert conversations they have had into their evening chants. Here a 'chief,' reporting on a recent trip, repeats a conversation which he had in colloquial Kuna with people in another community.

The village leaders said to me, 'just a while before you came a group left,' see say hear.
'They have probably gotten as far as the Pitto River,' say.[46]

Another example involves the 'tuneful weeping' performed by women, in colloquial Kuna, for dying and deceased relatives. Here a portion of this 'tuneful weeping' is inserted into 'the way of the bamboo cane,' the magical chant performed by a ritual specialist in order to insure that the soul of a dead person is properly transported to the other world.

'What great suffering.
Who will care for the children in the empty house?' his wife weeps.
His wife [weeps].
'I will dress you as if you were going to the *inna* house [to participate
.  in the puberty rites festivities].
Never will I see you again,' his wife weeps.
'The children will never see you again.'
His wife weeps.[47]

In this text, the language is no longer the colloquial Kuna used in 'tuneful weeping' but, rather, the linguistic variety and style of curing and magical *ikarkana*.

### The Ritual within the Everyday

Kuna ritual speech, in miniature, momentary versions, is incorporated into everyday discourse for two quite different ends—to show off and to parody. Ritual specialists insert small portions of an *ikar* into conversations among themselves or with nonspecialists, as a way of demonstrating their esoteric knowledge outside of its official context. Among specialists this process is an aspect of learning and teaching (see chapter 8) and is also an expected and accepted mode of conversational practice. At the same time, it is one of the ways of reminding nonspecialist members of the community of one's abilities, outside of the perhaps rare occasions on which the *ikarkana* are officially performed.

A very different occurrence of ritual speech in everyday contexts is in the form of parodic, imitative play. Both children and adults, for purely humorous ends, sometimes momentarily imitate a ritual leader or specialist—a 'chief,' 'spokesman,' or '*ikar* knower.' These imitations are very short; they are not full-blown parodies of a verbal genre. At the same time, they are remarkably accurate mimicries of the linguistic style of the original form. These short imitations are not considered improper or taboo; no desacralization is involved. Observers react to them as verbal play and seem to enjoy them. They are an indication of the Kuna ability to make fun of themselves and to mock the verbal traditions which they nonetheless take very seriously. Out of context and in miniature form, these traditions are reframed—and it is this reframing which makes them seem strange and funny at the same time.

Another point of interpenetration of the ritual into the everyday involves the setting of curing and magical rituals. While 'chiefs' and other political leaders have their ritual center and the *kantule* has his, curing specialists perform their *ikarkana* in the house of the patient, typically with other, quite everyday events, including conversation, going on around them. The official explanation for this interpenetration is that the curing specialist is addressing the 'stick doll' representatives of the spirit world, not the humans in the house. Nonetheless, the proximity and almost overlap of settings of ritual and everyday interaction are striking. The 'stick dolls' themselves constitute an instance of the intersection of the ritual and the everyday. They are overt, physical representatives of the spirit world; they are the addressees of magical, esoteric language; but, bunched tightly together in a wooden box, they are also a continual presence in all homes. Functioning almost as good luck charms in ordinary circumstances, the 'stick dolls' become major actors in ritual drama.

## The Interpenetration of Ritual Domains and Contexts

The three distinct Kuna ritual traditions overlap and intersect in various places and in various ways. One intersection occurs between puberty rites and curing and magical events. As described in chapter 5, during the puberty rites the *kantule* performs a long *ikar* in order to insure the success of the ritual. A completely different set of *ikarkana*, in the distinct tradition of curing and magic, is addressed to the spirit of *inna*, the fermented drink which is consumed in large quantities during the festivities. One of these, 'the way of the making of *inna*,' is used during the preparation of the *inna* and serves to make it stronger. Both the *ikar* of the *kantule* and that of the 'inna maker,' performed by different individuals to different spirits in totally different contexts and linguistic varieties, share striking details of narrative content. Both describe the various preparations for the rites and festivities as well as each aspect of the rites and festivities themselves.

From 'the way of the making of *inna*':

They go to the river to bathe.
They stand up in the river.
The water makes waves.
The water really makes waves.
The water is splashing.
The water is gushing.
The river sardines leave their smell in their hair.
The hair stands and spreads out on the water.

From 'the way of the *kantule*':

She arrives at the river.
She stands up in the river.
She bathes in the river.

The water makes waves.
The water is splashing up and down on her body.
The hair rises and floats on the water.
The hair smells like fish.

From 'the way of the making of *inna*':
The necklaces of the women are making much noise.
They cannot be distinguished one from the other.

From 'the way of the *kantule*':
The women's coin necklaces make noise.
The women's coin necklaces can be heard far away.[48]

The similarities in narrative content between these two *ikarkana* are especially remarkable in that a strict separation of the two ritual traditions is maintained. The performers are not students of each other; in most cases they are probably unaware of the degree of referential similarity in their respective texts. The intriguing correspondences in the two *ikarkana* can again be explained in terms of the Kuna theory and practice of magic and the nature of narration. Since the *ikarkana* describe events which the performer wants to occur, their narration must be as explicit as possible. In the case of both 'the way of the *kantule*' and 'the way of the making of *inna*,' the events the performer wants to occur are identical—the successful completion of the puberty rites and festivities. This is precisely what is described in the two texts.

Attention to the interpenetration of ritual domains and contexts reveals the central and primary role of the 'gathering house' in Kuna ritual life, in terms of setting and in terms of social organization. The most serious and spectacular of all Kuna curing rituals, the 'mass-curing ritual,' used to ward off epidemics of evil spirits, is usually carried out in the 'gathering house,' as distinct from other curing rituals, which are carried out in the patient's house (see chapter 4). The seriousness and significance of this ritual are such that it transforms the 'gathering house,' on all other occasions the center for political meetings, into the setting for a curing ritual—it replaces the 'gathering house' linguistic variety, social organization, and act and event structure with a completely different constellation.[49]

Another intersection of the 'gathering' and the curing and magical domains, in which the 'gathering' maintains a unifying if not dominant role, involves the reports and complaints of curing and magical specialists, teachers, and students, which take place in the 'gathering house' at evening men's meetings. It might be expected, given the number and status of curing and magical specialists, especially in large villages such as Mulatuppu, that they would have their own meetinghouse and their own system for handling reports, complaints, or problems. But they do not. While specialists sometimes work together, there is no community-wide organization. Curing and magic are very individual matters, often involving a considerable degree of competition between specialists. Misunderstandings and disagreements between teachers and their students are fairly common. It is in the 'gathering house,' in the presence of the men of the community and under the direction of the political leaders, that reports are made public and disputes are aired.

In these reports, teachers announce that a particular student has successfully learned an *ikar* and can now perform and teach on his own. Students describe the learning process in detail, especially when, as is often the case, they have studied in distant villages (see chapter 8). In addition, in 'gathering house' meetings unhappy students can complain about their teachers—for charging them too much, not teaching them enough, or not allowing them to graduate when they have mastered an *ikar*. It is also in the 'gathering house' that the teacher responds with countercharges.

When specialists or would-be specialists travel to distant villages to study, complaints involve the sending of letters back and forth. These letters are usually written and read by intermediaries, typically the village secretary, since most ritual specialists and traditional leaders in this essentially nonliterate society do not read or write. For example, in the spring of 1979, a Mulatuppu man traveled to the village of Morti along the Río Chucunaque in the interior Darién jungle, in order to learn snakebite and related medicine. He brought a hunting rifle to his teacher as payment. After the student returned home, he complained in the Mulatuppu 'gathering house' that the teacher took the rifle but refused to teach him. He requested that the Mulatuppu 'chiefs' ask the teacher to return the rifle. As a result, the first 'chief' of Mulatuppu wrote a letter to the Morti 'chief.' A letter came back from Morti explaining that the specialist had indeed been teaching the man in question, that the medicine was complicated and required a long time to learn, that the rifle was payment for what the student had learned thus far, and that if he wanted it back he would have to pay the teacher forty dollars.

When 'seers' report dreams and experiences in which they receive verbal messages from 'stick dolls' and other spirit representatives, this also takes place in the 'gathering house,' in the form of speeches to an evening audience. These involve translations and interpretations of the messages from the esoteric language of spirits to the 'gathering house' speechmaking style of humans, comprehensible to the audience.

It is an important feature of Kuna social life that, while the three ritual social organizations are clearly distinct, participation in more than one is permitted and actually encouraged, especially since prestige accrues from the accumulation of discrete roles (see chapter 2). The 'gathering' is first among separate equals; it is the actual and symbolic meeting point of all three ritual traditions as well as of the ritual and the everyday. Highly respected 'medicinal specialists,' 'ikar knowers,' and *kanturkana* are invited or decide themselves to sit on the central benches during evening 'gatherings.' They are thus at the literal and symbolic center of the community, along with 'chiefs' and their 'spokesmen.' Furthermore, 'chiefs,' in their 'counsel' and in their right to discuss and solve conflicts, to talk to or about any person or any subject, maintain an authority outside their own tradition which is not matched by that of any other Kuna figure.

### The Range of Contexts for the Performance of Ritual Chants

Ritual *ikarkana*, for curing, magic, and girls' puberty rites, are performed in a range of contexts in addition to those associated with their primary official purposes; they are not reserved only for rare, special moments.[50] These less ritual, more everyday contexts involve teaching, learning, practicing, pleasure (personal and familial), play, public display, and reporting. Performance for learning and practice blends into performance for pleasure, for both the performer and those family members who serve as audience, lying in adjacent hammocks and falling asleep as they listen to words they only partially understand. Neighbors and passersby can also hear the *ikarkana*, and the spirit world also listens to these performances and derives pleasure from them as well.

Curing and magical *ikarkana*, quite commonly performed for pleasure during the festivities associated with girls' puberty rites (see chapter 5), exemplify the fact that these rites and especially their associated activities are rites of reversal in a variety of ways. When the *ikarkana* are performed in their primary context and for their primary function, the spirits are the official addressees and the humans are the unofficial bystanders. When the *ikarkana* are performed during puberty festivities for pleasure, these roles are reversed: the humans are the official addressees, the spirits the unofficial bystanders. In addition, while both humans and spirits are enjoying the verbally artistic properties of these *ikarkana*, they are also being publicly informed of the knowledge and ability of the performer.

The range of contexts, primary and secondary, official and unofficial, for the performance of ritual *ikarkana* can thus be accounted for in terms of the transmission of traditional knowledge, the display of personal ability and knowledge, and the appreciation of verbal art and play on the part of both the human and the spirit worlds. There is no desacralization involved in performing ritual *ikarkana* out of their primary context. On the contrary. It is this constant performance of *ikarkana*, for both spirits and humans, in a variety of settings, in a variety of ways, for a variety of purposes, that demonstrates (to insider or outsider) the vitality and dynamism of Kuna ritual life.

# 8. Continuity and Change

The perspective of most of this study has been synchronic and descriptive. I have presented and analyzed the speaking practices of the San Blas Kuna as they exist today, within a time frame which includes a period of research beginning in 1970. The focus of this last chapter is process, and for this reason it looks to the future as well as to the past. I begin with a centerpiece of Kuna continuity as well as change—the transmission of knowledge through learning and teaching. I conclude the chapter and the book by examining what is probably the most striking aspect of Kuna language, culture, and society, an aspect which will be essential in the critical years to come—the dynamic and delicate interplay between conflict and harmony, tradition and adaptation.

## Learning and Teaching

Kuna learning and teaching of both verbal and nonverbal skills are intimately involved in the actual practice of these skills. Children and adults, women and men, learn everyday activities through a combination of observation, participation, and verbal explanation. From an early age, children accompany their parents and participate in such individual or group tasks as farming, fishing, mola making, cooking, and washing clothes. There is a great deal of talk, which includes but is not limited to discussion of the task. The Kuna stress that everything has a name—objects, stages of growth and development, and processes. Learning names is an important aspect of the learning of an activity, increasingly so in ritual matters.

Language learning, like the learning of other everyday activities, is considered natural and normal; that is, no special theories or training are needed. Children just learn to talk through active participation in speech events, as speakers, listeners, and audience. There is much talking to children, and children are listened to with interest and respect. Girls learn such women's speech genres as lullabies and 'tuneful weeping' by listening to their grandmothers, mothers, aunts, cousins, and older sisters and then, at a very early age, trying them out themselves in actual contexts. Adults enjoy observing this learning process. Both boys and girls similarly learn the 'gathering house' speechmaking style through observation and participation. It is remarkable how young children, suddenly accused of a misdeed—stealing, fighting, or bothering someone—are able to defend themselves with a long eloquent speech before an audience in the 'gathering house.'

Kuna schools are integrated into the Panamanian educational system. The majority of teachers are Kuna, however, and there is a popular bilingual education program.[1] While Kuna methods of learning and teaching are not explicitly and consciously employed in the classroom, the facts that the schools are located in Kuna villages, the Kuna language is often used, and most teachers and students are Kuna allow for a maximum local overlay on the Panamanian curriculum. At the same time, the Panamanian school system introduces a potential source of conflict and competition in relation to the traditional Kuna methods of learning and teaching, including a significant social organization, the Panama-trained schoolteachers and administrators.

The learning and teaching of ritual knowledge are directly and intimately related to the structure of the event in which this knowledge is publicly performed, especially to the act of performance. Thus the primary setting for the learning of 'gathering house' tradition is the 'gathering house' itself, which is open to any man who wants to enter, sit, listen, and learn, from the afternoon on. It is of course especially in the evenings when the 'chiefs' chant and the 'spokesmen' interpret these chants that Kuna tradition is publicly available to women, men, and children. Men who have a special interest in learning 'gathering house' tradition—particularly those who have become 'chiefs,' 'spokesmen,' and 'policemen'—also learn through traveling, in an official capacity, to other villages, where they spend most of their time in the 'gathering house' conversing with their hosts, traditional specialists themselves, and of course performing and listening to their hosts perform. 'Gathering house' specialists also learn a great deal in informal and private or semi-public conversations, in the 'gathering house' or in individual homes, while traveling or working together. These specialists are well known to each other, seek each other out, and spend much time together, talking and learning from each other.

When the members of a community, especially its political leaders, feel that an individual is qualified for a 'gathering house' role and that he is interested in and committed to 'gathering house' ritual and tradition, they select him for the role. The choice is not a big surprise to the members of the community, since, given the great amount of traditional knowledge that is required, coupled with a necessary willingness to constantly display this knowledge in the form of public performances, the number of potential new candidates at any given moment is relatively small. The new 'chief,' 'spokesman,' or 'policeman' is inaugurated during an interisland ritual 'gathering' attended by 'gathering house' leaders from many villages (see chapters 3 and 7). He continues to study 'gathering house' tradition, combining this study with active participation in 'gathering house' business and ritual. He often associates himself with a well-known leader in his role, perhaps from his own village but more typically from another one, and spends time studying with him, visiting him in his house and conversing with him at length. If the teacher is from another village, the student stays with him in his house, often for several days, and helps him with various types of work. He also attends evening 'gatherings' and performs as well, chanting if a 'chief,' speaking if a 'spokesman.'

'Medicinal specialists,' '*ikar* knowers,' and *kanturkana* learn their professions through years of study with well-known, respected specialists from their own and especially from other, often distant villages. The student lives with the teacher and helps him with various activities, from farming to gathering medicine. As they work together, they talk about various types of medicine, how and where to find them, and what their function is. An important aspect of the acquisition of curing techniques is the learning of the names of the different medicines and the diseases or problems they are used for.

The teaching of magical *ikarkana* involves a focus on memorization of a fixed text, which must be learned completely and exactly. An '*ikar* knower' or a *kantule* knows his text perfectly and can repeat it identically when performing it in the context of its magical function or when teaching it to others. In teaching sessions, the specialist performs a section of the *ikar* and the student repeats it, the teacher correcting him when he makes a mistake or cannot think of the next line. *Ikar* learning involves considerable effort—long *ikarkana*, such as 'the way of the mass curer' or 'the way of the *kantule*,' require many years of study. Learning is made particularly difficult by the fact that the verbal text must first be perfectly memorized before the teacher explains the meanings of the words and the symbolism. The students of the 'mass curer' and the *kantule* have official roles in the rituals themselves, including performing *ikarkana* along with the teacher. In this way, the students gain recognition for

their efforts, learn their texts through actual practice, and are social-
ized into their ritual role.

Another way in which an *ikar* can be learned is in dreams, in
which case the teacher is either a representative of the spirit world
who knows the *ikar* or a deceased person who knew the *ikar* when
she or he was alive. The *ikar* is learned in a series of dreamed sessions. It is especially 'seers,' who have supernatural mental ability,
who can learn *ikarkana* in dreams. But others can study this way
too. Sometimes, individuals who desire to learn *ikarkana* in dreams
take special medicine. While the medicine might work, it can also
produce undesirable effects; in particular, it can result in the person's unwittingly causing sickness and even death to others. Individuals who have learned *ikarkana* in dreams are accepted as specialists by the community in varying degrees. Their ability is verified
through public performance, and they also acquire students. At the
same time, they are open to criticism from specialists who have
learned their *ikarkana* from live teachers through hard, tedious
work and some form of payment. Such individuals are prone to voice
skepticism about others who claim to have learned by another, less
overt, and obviously less verifiable process.

When a teacher decides that his student has learned enough to be
considered and officially recognized as a 'medicinal specialist,' '*ikar*
knower,' or *kantule*, he makes a speech in a men's evening 'gathering,' announcing the graduation of the student and detailing what he
has learned. If the student traveled to study with a teacher in another village, he will return with a letter written by his teacher or for
his teacher, if, as is usually the case, the teacher is not literate. This
letter, which announces the graduation of the student, is read in the
'gathering house.' The returning student himself gives a speech describing his accomplishments (see also chapter 3). He details his
travels, his relationship with his teacher, the medicines and *ikarkana* he learned, and how he learned them.

These 'gathering house' speeches, by both teachers and students,
serve as occasions on which specialists can remind the members
of their village of their own accomplishments and abilities. The
speeches validate their prestige, just as performing, practicing, and
teaching do; while ostensibly graduation ceremonies, they provide
an occasion for a specialist to brag about himself, to explain how valuable an individual he is to the community. An interesting example
is the case of Olowitinappi, the 'medicinal specialist' and '*ikar*
knower' who received a scholarship to study snakebite medicine and
curing. In his speech on his return, Olowitinappi informs his community that they clearly got their money's worth, since he already

knew quite a bit of snakebite medicine before going. This enabled him to learn quickly and, of course, made him all the more valuable to the community, since he could combine his different sources of knowledge and expertise.

The medicine then that I studied there, as I told you, I had already
    studied a little before.
And I had also used it.
Since I had also used it, how could I not learn it?
But at times it has different names.
'We don't have this one in my village,' I would shout to him [the
    teacher].
'This one we don't have see.'
But when he showed it to me in the jungle, I saw that we have the
    same.
For this reason it was easy for me.

In addition to describing the teaching and learning process, the speech specifies the ways in which Olowitinappi should behave in his community, especially how much he should charge for administering and teaching what he has learned. In this way, he cannot be accused of overcharging. His prices are not really his own; they are what he was told to charge by his own teacher. And he must follow these instructions to the word, just as he must follow the *ikar* that he learned to the word. The description of the pricing policy is detailed and precise. It deals with how much to charge for using medicine to keep snakes from entering farms, distinguishing between communal farms belonging to Olowitinappi's village (to be administered free of charge), farms belonging to private individuals, and farms belonging to persons from other villages. It explains, always in the form of direct quotation of the teacher, how much to charge patients.

'Thus sometimes, perhaps a young person, perhaps a young woman,
    perhaps an old woman will come to you to bathe [as protection
    against snakebites],' he says.
'Two dollars you will charge them,' he says.
'It's cheap see say.
Two dollars for bathing see say.'

The speech explains that Olowitinappi must obtain a student-assistant and that the student must repay him in certain ways.

'Therefore then when you have a student you will teach him the
    same.'

He says to me.

'And the student that you get, he will help you only [will not pay
money] see say.

When you have something that is a little hard see say.

When you clear a banana farm,' he says.

'Or a coconut farm,' he says.

'Whatever thing you have to do,' he says.

'Everything see say.

As for people from other islands [villages],' he says.

'The money that you spent [here].

The money you will spend, they will give you see say.

Therefore friend do not raise the price see say.

There are people then who raise the price very high see say.

As if their teacher had told them to do so see.'

The friend [teacher] counseled me.

The speech also provides an opportunity to boast about one's abilities and knowledge beyond the particular medicine or *ikar* that has
just been learned. While in the interior village, Olowitinappi took
advantage of his situation by learning medicine other than snakebite
medicine, especially childbirth medicine. Since childbirth medicine
is extremely important to the Kuna, knowledge of it is a source of
great prestige. Olowitinappi then, in the context of his narration, is
able to publicly announce that he has expertise in this area as well.

'If you want to learn another *ikar*, if you want to study another time
see say.

I also know that one having to do with women see say.

Like the other one I also have it all ordered see say.

I have twenty-four parts about childbirth see say.'

Thus it was all written in his [the teacher's] notebook and he showed
me everything you see say.

'These are for this birth, these are for this birth, these are for this
birth see say.'[2]

A most effective way to demonstrate that you have indeed mastered an *ikar* or a verbal 'secret' is to cite portions of it in your
speech at the 'gathering house.' Olowitinappi does this most cleverly by quoting or citing his teacher performing the *ikar* in question.
In this way, he shows not only that he has learned the *ikar* but, furthermore, that he has learned it directly from the mouth of the renowned teacher. The quoted *ikar* is represented here by double quotation marks within the single quotation marks which represent the
teacher speaking.[3]

'During childbirth, thus women sometimes faint see say.
The devil at times gets them.
For them I speak [the *ikar*] see say.
"Now I prepared the farm," see say.
"During six days I prepared it," see say.
"Now I planted the medicine," see,' he [the teacher] says to me.[4]

## Tradition, Change, Conflict, and Adaptation

On the edge of the modern, industrial, constantly changing world, less than one hour away from Panama City by air, the Kuna seem most fragile from the outside. Viewed from within, they maintain a delicate yet dynamic balance between old and new, traditional and modern. They have managed to keep their ritual life thriving while making adaptations which prevent stagnation. Adaptation is built into 'gathering house' discourse, for example, with its focus on flexibility. But, even in the more conservative area of curing, changes are possible when necessary. Spirits ever alive to new situations appear in the dreams of 'seers' and other curing and magical specialists and offer new *ikarkana*, new slants on old problems, or new solutions to previously unknown ailments.

Adaptive flexibility is also at the core of the sensitive interplay between official conceptions of patterns of speaking and what happens unofficially, in reality. In official terms, the Kuna sociolinguistic system consists of different languages, dialects, and styles, including some unintelligible to the noninitiate, manifested in the performance of ritual speeches and chants that take years of study to learn. According to the official version, 'gathering house' chanting is not understood by the audience—hence the interpretation by a 'spokesman.' And curing and puberty rites *ikarkana* are said not to be understood by the nonspecialist; they are addressed to spirits and only spirits understand them. In reality and unofficially, there is a great range of understanding of traditional and ritual discourse, depending to a great degree on personal experiences and interests.

Men and women who attend 'gatherings' night after night, year after year, are able to understand the chanting language of the 'chiefs' to a great extent, especially the language of those 'chiefs' who do not make extensive use of esoteric symbolism in idiosyncratic ways. This is even truer of men, such as 'policemen,' who have a manifest interest in the 'gathering' tradition and who try to learn as much as they can in order to become 'spokesmen' and 'chiefs.' The language of curing and magical *ikarkana* and of the puberty rites *ikar* is much more different from ordinary Kuna than is 'gathering' chanting. Yet here, too, nonspecialists possess a range of understanding. Members of households, especially women, who spend most time at home, have heard curing *ikarkana* over and over again as their grandfathers, fathers, brothers, or sons learned and practiced them or as they were performed for sick individuals in their families.[5] Specialists in curing *ikarkana* can often understand much of an *ikar* they do not themselves perform, because of similarities in the language of all curing *ikarkana*. In addition, since such individuals are interested in learning as much as they can about curing they will therefore pay attention to other *ikar* performances, even though officially these are addressed to spirits and there is no human audience.

As a result of this interplay between official and unofficial knowledge, the actual relationship between knowers and understanders of tradition tends to lie along a continuum rather than be a dichotomy between specialists and nonspecialists, as the official version would have it. This makes it possible for ritual language and tradition to be both secretive and nonsecretive, esoteric and nonesoteric, at the same time. Specialists gain prestige for their knowledge and performance, but nonspecialists are not totally frozen out.[6] Performances can be appreciated by many individuals to varying degrees, and participation in ritual events is encouraged. Kuna ritual leaders constantly profess a desire to transmit their knowledge to individuals eager to learn. They complain that nowadays people are no longer interested. The learning of ritual knowledge is open to everyone— anyone who is willing has the right to study and eventually to become a specialist.[7] As a result, most people have at least a little understanding of ritual matters.

Often the most striking instances of innovation turn out on careful investigation to involve the most basic reinforcements of tradition. For example, in recent years, fathers in some villages have found it overly burdensome to provide the great amounts of food necessary for their daughters' puberty festivities. To solve their problem, a cooperative work force on the island-village of Achutuppu will cater and host the whole affair. Nothing could seem more non-Kuna than the catering of a banquet. Yet no event is more traditional for the Kuna than girls' puberty rites. And Achutuppu has the reputation for being one of the most traditional villages in San Blas. By providing their own *kantule* and directing all aspects of the puberty festivities, Achutuppu insures strict maintenance of this important tradition.

Panama City is one of the world's distribution centers for electronic equipment. As a result, growing numbers of Kuna, especially those who work in the Canal Zone or in Panama City, own small radios and cassette recorders. The recorders are used to send messages back and forth between Panama City and San Blas—the compact cassettes are carried by travelers on the daily flights across the cordillera.[8] These spoken letters are in the form and style of the reports that are exchanged in face-to-face conversations by friends and family members or in the 'gathering house.' The cassette recorders thus reinforce rather than eliminate a traditional way of speaking.

The use of foreign languages, especially Spanish and English, provides another interesting example. Because of increasing contacts with outsiders, more and more Kuna can speak Spanish and English. They are respected for this linguistic ability, just as are traditional leaders for their ability to manipulate ritual varieties and styles of Kuna. And some ritual leaders speak Spanish and/or English as well. This is not viewed as being in conflict with their knowledge of traditional Kuna. On the contrary, it furthers their prestige. The example of a highly respected 'chief' from the Cartii region of San Blas is most instructive in this regard.

This 'chief,' in his forties, is relatively young for a celebrated leader, though he is one of a number of young 'chiefs' who have recently gained prominence and authority in San Blas. Before becoming a 'chief,' he worked for several years in the Canal Zone and, being gifted at learning languages, acquired a quite respectable command of both Spanish and English (in addition to being one of the zone's finest baseball players). In keeping with the Cartii region's traditions, as 'chief' he has learned to chant the myths of such legendary Kuna heroes as Ipeorkun and Nele Sipu. His chants are quite long, lasting several hours, and require the best of 'spokesmen' to interpret. Experience in working in the Canal Zone has not led him to reject his own culture. He is one of the staunchest supporters of the strict adherence to Kuna tradition—he is against cement houses, against 'gathering house' chants having to do with recent history or personal dreams, and against increased contact with non-Kuna. His Panamanian experiences and his knowledge of Spanish and English are an aspect of his repertoire, resources which he can draw on to demonstrate his knowledge and expertise and further his prestige. But his learning of Spanish and English should clearly not be viewed as signs of changing times when even 'chiefs' learn these languages. Rather, these linguistic resources are exploited just as are the ritual varieties of Kuna, personal experiences, and the many Kuna legends, myths, and stories—in order to have a stock of knowledge to draw on for public performance.

The Kuna ability to adapt should not be confused with acculturation.[9] It is a constant, traditional feature of Kuna social and cultural life to transform the new into the old, incorporating rather than re-

jecting. The molas of women are a visual version of this incorporation. New themes—mousetraps, coat hangers, baseball games, and
lunar modules—are integrated into the design scheme along with
traditional elements of local ecology. These do not detract from the
beauty or significance of molas but, rather, enrich their thematic
possibilities.[10] It is precisely this creative adaptation to change that
has enabled the Kuna to maintain their traditional verbal life.

It seems useful to compare the Kuna process of dynamic adaptation and incorporation with what Evon Vogt has called encapsulation in discussing the Zinacanteco Maya, defining encapsulation as
"the conceptual and structural incorporation of new elements into
existing patterns of social and ritual behavior."[11] According to Gary
Gossen, encapsulation is characteristic of much of Mayan Indian life
in the highlands of Chiapas. Gossen also suggests the relevance of
this concept for the study of the Navajo.[12] The concept of encapsulation may prove to be useful for the cross-cultural comparison and
classification of societies and processes with regard to speaking, especially with regard to the interplay of tradition, change, and adaptation in language and speech.

While the Kuna pride themselves on being egalitarian and publicly
espouse their goal of being a cooperative and harmonious society,
there are clearly sources of competition, conflict, and tension. Some
of these can be viewed in terms of social organization, in particular
social organization in relation to language and speech. Sources and
instances of social conflict involving language and speech have been
discussed throughout this study, especially in chapter 2. It is useful
to review the major ones here. The sharp differentiation between
men's and women's speaking roles results in men being in positions
of public leadership and restricts women to secondary positions,
mainly involving preparations for ritual matters but not control of
them. Although women can potentially become leaders, they very
rarely do.[13] An investigation of genres and ways of speaking in terms
of men and women reveals that men are involved in speech that is
traditional, ritual, symbolic, esoteric, and public, such as the chanting of 'chiefs' and the performance of curing and magical *ikarkana*,
while women, in their lullabies and 'tuneful weeping,' deal with
matters which are, from the Kuna point of view, more personal, private, and superficial—even though child care and mourning for the
dead are clearly basic concerns of Kuna social and cultural life. The
primary form of women's artistic and communicative expression is
not ritual speaking and chanting but, rather, the decorative and visual mola.[14]

Another source of social tension occurs between ritual and political leaders on the one hand and the community at large on the other. A closely related but not identical distinction is that between older and younger members of the community. While younger individuals, especially men, can and do become involved in ritual life in various ways, there are those who feel that too much power and control are in the hands (really mouths) of older leaders and specialists and that verbal life focuses too much attention on them. Ritual leaders themselves, whether representatives of the same or of different traditions, are also in potential conflict with one another, not so much for actual power as for prestige within the community. Finally, the relationship between humans and spirits is a constant potential source of conflict. Spirits, like humans, can be helpful and cooperative, but they have the potential to cause harm and thus, also like humans, must be continually counseled and controlled.

Kuna speaking practices and processes are not insensitive to these sources of social conflict. Quite the contrary. Women's speaking 'gatherings' and women's participation in men's 'gatherings,' albeit occasional, involve women in public verbal affairs. And there is no doubt that women are on an equal verbal footing with men in more private domains, such as the household. The great number and variety of ritual roles and the openness of access to them encourage younger men to become involved in significant ways in ritual life. The carefully worked out complementarity of ritual roles reduces the possibility of direct competition and confrontation. And the existence of many magical *ikarkana* and associated specialists enables humans to keep the spirit world under their control. The potential for conflict and tension in each of these social domains remains, however, and is an important aspect of the dynamics of Kuna verbal life.

In addition to the various possibilities for conflict inherent in the Kuna social organization, a second major source of conflict is change. While a finely tuned balance among tradition, adaptation, and change is a central and basic characteristic of Kuna verbal life, ever increasing influence from Panama, particularly the introduction of the Panamanian school system into San Blas and large-scale migration of Kuna to Panama City and other parts of Panama, poses considerable pressure.

Finally, there are interpersonal conflicts, tensions, and jealousies caused by a variety of factors, ranging from economic concerns to familial disagreements, including but not limited to marital relations. While 'chiefs' in their 'gathering' chants and speeches daily implore their communities not to be stingy, jealous, or angry, these negative personal traits are real and must be dealt with. The various patterned ways of speaking described in chapter 7, in particular ritualized dialogue, 'counsel,' and retelling, provide an organized means of handling problems through language and speech; they channel both personal and social conflicts into carefully controlled talk, in which the focus is on harmonious, artistic, and elaborate discourse and in which decorum replaces the open expression of disagreement. It has been noted that egalitarian societies in many parts of the world have a tendency to express conflict in the form of indirect speech.[15] Metaphor and other forms of symbolic language have attracted considerable attention in this regard. Metaphor is important in Kuna discourse, particularly in the 'gathering house,' where language is creatively manipulated in order to fit particular situations which often involve conflict. However, metaphor is but one aspect of a dynamic complex of communicative devices which organize and channel much of Kuna social and cultural life, including cooperation as well as conflict, into elaborate and often artistic speech.

I have portrayed Kuna verbal life as involving a delicate yet dynamic balance between old and new, tradition and adaptation, harmony and conflict. Against the backdrop of the Caribbean Sea and the Darién jungle, the Kuna maintain economic and social independence and dedicate a great deal of time and energy to verbally elaborate, playful, and artistic discourse, finely integrated with all aspects of daily and ritual life. The Kuna are most fortunate among nonliterate and especially American Indian societies, most of whom have fared much worse in the modern, industrial world. If they continue to control their land and continue to control the direction of their social, economic, and cultural life, their seemingly idyllic situation should remain intact.

# Guide to Pronunciation

The following symbols are used to represent Kuna terms.

Vowels

| | |
|---|---|
| *i,* | high front open |
| *e,* | middle front open |
| *a,* | low front open |
| *u,* | high back rounded |
| *o,* | middle back rounded |

Consonants

| | |
|---|---|
| *p,* | voiced bilabial stop |
| *pp,* | voiceless bilabial stop |
| *t,* | voiced dental stop |
| *tt,* | voiceless dental stop |
| *k,* | voiced velar stop |
| *kk,* | voiceless velar stop |
| *kw,* | voiced labiovelar stop |
| *kkw,* | voiceless labiovelar stop |
| *s,* | voiceless dental spirant |
| *ch,* | voiceless palatal affricate |
| *m,* | voiced bilabial nasal |
| *n,* | voiced dental nasal |
| *l,* | voiced lateral |
| *r,* | voiced flap |
| *w,* | voiced bilabial semivowel |
| *y,* | voiced palatal semivowel |

# Notes

**Preface**

1. Hymes (1974). It is an interesting coincidence that the Kuna also use the term *ikar* (literally way; plural: *ikarkana*) to refer to forms of discourse and patterns of speaking.

## 1. For a Kuna Ethnography of Speaking

1. In the 1920s, 1930s, and 1940s a group of Swedes from the Göteborgs Etnografiska Museum surveyed Kuna language and culture. (In the published literature dealing with the Kuna, one finds the spellings Cuna and Kuna. In this book, following current Kuna practice, I use Kuna.) Their publications are based on a few short field trips, work with a Kuna informant in Sweden during 1931, and texts mailed to Sweden by literate informants. They published extensive Kuna textual material, in addition to their survey reports. See Holmer (1947, 1951, 1952), Nordenskiöld (1938), and Wassén (1938, 1949). Kramer (1970) is based on published and unpublished materials collected by the Swedish group. Stout (1947b) focuses on aspects of Kuna acculturation. The Panamanian anthropologist Reina Torres de Araúz has studied aspects of Kuna social organization and ecology. See Torres de Araúz (1980) and Torres de Ianello (1957, 1958). In recent years, in-depth ethnographic research has been carried out by Macpherson Chapin (ethnomedicine), Richard Costello (economics), Regina Holloman (social organization), James Howe (social and political organization), Alexander Moore (tribal organization), and Frances Stier (ecology). Most relevant to this study are Chapin (1983) and Howe (in press).

2. In recent years, many Kuna have begun to refer to San Blas as Kuna Yala, which means literally Kuna Mountain and, more generally, Kuna World.

3. However, the Kuna of Caimán Nuevo, in Colombia, live in houses located at a considerable distance from one another.

4. The Kuna criticize the nearby Choco for not living in permanent villages. In fact, the Choco are not nomadic but move their hamlets every few years.

5. This is not to deny certain disadvantages as well, including overcrowding and lack of sufficient resources.

6. See Basso (1972, 1979), Gossen (1974), Irvine (1974), Keenan (1974), Kochman (1972), and Sherzer (1970b).

7. Nor are talking and chanting intermingled with such other behavior as walking, jumping, running, dancing, playing musical instruments, wearing costumes, using masks and body ornamentation, taking drugs, and going into trances, as in the rituals of many South American tropical forest groups. The only exception to this generalization is the *kantule*, who moves about and blows on a flute as part of his ritual performance (see chapter 5). And only in girls' puberty rites are games and dances part of Kuna ritual behavior. But, even in this ritual, speaking is for the most part quite separate and self-contained.

8. See the references in note 1 and also Stout (1947a).

9. Hymes (1977, 1981) has shown that it is possible to reinterpret such texts according to grammatical principles of poetic performance.

10. See Finnegan (1967), Lord (1960), Scheub (1977), and Tedlock (1978).

11. See Labov (1972).

12. Gossen (1974).

13. Chapin (1983) and Howe (in press), dealing with medicine and curing and with politics respectively, have each recognized the central role of language and speech in their analyses.

14. See especially Hymes (1962, 1964).

15. See Bauman and Sherzer (1974), Bloch (1975), Bright (1966), Gumperz and Hymes (1964, 1972), Kochman (1972), and Sanches and Blount (1975).

16. In addition to the collections cited in note 15, see Basso (1979), Bricker (1973), Calame-Griaule (1965), Clastres (1974), Feld (1982), Foster (1974), Gossen (1974), Gregor (1977), Haviland (1977), Salmond (1975), Scollon and Scollon (1979), and Witherspoon (1977), each of which deals with an aspect or aspects of the relationship among language, culture, and society in a particular group.

17. Redfield (1955) provides a useful overview of the various approaches that anthropologists have employed in order to characterize small communities as wholes. He discusses at length viewing communities in terms of ecological system, social structure, human career, personality type, world view, and history. Significantly, he does not mention language and speech, except to note the Sapir-Whorf hypothesis in connection with world view. And yet, as I will show, speaking is an extremely productive way to explore the holistic nature of a community, especially that of the Kuna.

18. See Sherzer and Darnell (1972), written at a more programmatic stage of the ethnography of speaking.

19. See Cole and Morgan (1975), Givón (1979), Goody (1978), Grimes (1975), Gumperz (1977), Halliday and Hasan (1976), Labov and Fanshel (1977), Longacre (1976, 1977), Sadock (1974), Searle (1969), and Tannen (1981).

20. See especially Geertz (1973), Sapir and Crocker (1977), and Turner (1967). Hymes (1968) is written in the framework of an essential unity linking the ethnography of speaking and the ethnography of symbolic

forms in general. Basso (1979) synthesizes and integrates the approaches of symbolic anthropology and the ethnography of speaking.

21. For cognitive anthropology in general, see Casson (1981) and Tyler (1969). For ethnosemantic analyses of the domain of speech, see Abrahams and Bauman (1971), Gossen (1972), and Stross (1974).

22. Finnegan (1977) is an excellent survey of the field of oral literature. Goody (1977) and Lord (1960) are concerned with the nature of the structure and the structuring of nonliterate, oral discourse. In this regard, see also Stolz and Shannon (1976).

23. See Fox (1977) for a comparative study of parallelism.

24. See Hymes (1977, 1981) and Tedlock (1978).

25. Especially Lévi-Strauss (1964, 1966, 1968, 1971).

26. See Berger and Luckman (1966), Goffman (1971, 1974, 1981), and Sudnow (1972).

27. Recently and movingly expressed by Clastres (1974).

28. See Blount (1975) and Irvine (1974), who analyze cases in which both discourse and sociological patterns have emergent rather than predetermined structures.

29. The best discussion of this is Goffman (1974).

## 2. Language and Speech in Kuna Society

1. Kuna terms are in 'everyday Kuna' unless otherwise specified.

2. Kuna is usually classified as a Chibchan or macro-Chibchan language. While there is some evidence for these genetic categories, much more documented research is needed on the genetic and areal affiliations of Kuna.

3. Tzeltal Mayan, which has been described by Stross (1974), uses the word *k'op*, meaning language or speech, in a much more productive way, including not only social roles and genres but physical characteristics, personality, physical arrangement of a group, gestures accompanying speech, manner of delivery, and the truth value of the message, among many others.

4. In the last several years, some parents have given their children traditional names, choosing the name of a renowned deceased ancestor.

5. As a typically Kuna playful joke, my wife, Dina, and I were each given a 'true name,' Olopikintili and Olopili respectively. The Kuna never tire of asking us our names and of listening to us say them, which inevitably makes everyone laugh. We in turn enjoy Kuna names which are derived from well-known North Americans, such as Dempsey, Bing Crosby, and Kennedy.

6. The coining of new words out of native vocabulary has been noted in other American Indian languages. Basso (1967) offers an extended discussion of an interesting Apache example, involving an entire semantic field.

7. See Sherzer (1977).

8. See Howe (1977) for an excellent analysis of 'gathering house' metaphors.

9. The native view is probably historically accurate. The generally more

conservative dialects of the Darién jungle seem to make sparser use of phonological deletion processes than do San Blas speakers (Priscilla Baptista and Ruth Wallin, personal communication).

10. In the formulation of the phonological analysis presented here, another, seemingly more linguistically economical solution was rejected, precisely because it failed to account for the social and cultural realities of Kuna language use. See Sherzer (1975).

11. Compare with Hymes (1977).

12. Compare with Tedlock (1978).

13. Compare with Burns (1980), who describes the role of dialogic structure in the performance of Yucatec Mayan narratives. The Kuna pattern is probably more related to the South American tropical forest ritual dialogic pattern (see chapter 7). The Mayan pattern described by Burns seems to represent an interesting intermediate areal pattern between North and South America in the social interactional structure of narration.

14. Portion of a discussion in the Mulatuppu 'gathering house,' April 16, 1971.

15. Portion of a conversation in Mulatuppu, seated outside o's house, July 17, 1977.

16. Portion of 'the story of the hot pepper,' as told by Chief Mastayans in the Mulatuppu 'gathering house' on February 18, 1971. The complete text of this narration, in both Kuna and Spanish translation, is included in Howe, Sherzer, and Chapin (1980). For an analysis of this 'story' see Sherzer (1979).

17. Portion of a speech by Olowitinappi of Mulatuppu, reporting on his trip to learn snakebite medicine, delivered in the Mulatuppu 'gathering house' on June 16, 1970. Other portions of this speech are cited in chapters 3, 7, and 8. The full speech, in original Kuna and with a Spanish translation, is included in Howe, Sherzer, and Chapin (1980).

18. Portion of a speech by Benilda García in the Mulatuppu 'gathering house' on March 1, 1979.

19. Portion of Spokesman José Cristiano's interpretation of a chant by a Mulatuppu 'chief' on February 21, 1971.

20. Following Hymes (1977).

21. The main difference between *soke* and *oparye* is that *soke* is used in 'everyday Kuna' as well as in 'chief language,' while *oparye* is used only in 'chief language.' In order to translate this distinction into English, I have used 'say' for *soke* and 'utter' for the more esoteric *oparye*.

22. Portion of a chant performed by Chief Mastaletat of Mulatuppu on February 20, 1971.

23. See Sherzer and Wicks (1982).

24. 'The way of the hat' was known and performed by Olowitinappi of Mulatuppu.

25. 'The way of the haircutter' was known and performed by Kantule Ernesto Linares of Mulatuppu.

26. This refers to the activity which most women engage in while attending the 'gathering house' performance.

27. The term *posero* is a confusing one in that it is also sometimes used to translate *arkar* into Spanish.

28. According to Chapin (1983), there is considerable subjectivity in determining whether or not a newborn child is marked as a 'seer.' In any case, a 'seer' must practice his or her special communicative abilities in order to be recognized as an active representative of this role.

29. I am indebted to Henry Selby for pointing out that this complementarity of roles is often considered to be typical of developed societies, à la Durkheim, and that what is interesting about Kuna social organization is that in addition to the complementarity there are also a generalized, accumulative prestige and authority.

30. See Sherzer and Sherzer (1976).

31. There is not, for example, the complaining social singing of the Mapuche of Argentina and Chile (see Titiev 1949).

## 3. The 'Gathering House': Public and Political 'Gatherings'

1. Each verse typically consists of two lines; there are also one-line and three-line verses (see chapter 2). I borrow the terms line and verse from Hymes (1977), which discusses the poetic organization of North American Indian discourse.

2. In the examples presented here, I have translated *teki* as 'indeed,' which captures the combination of surprise and ratification involved.

3. Opening portion of a chant performed by Chief Muristo Pérez of Mulatuppu on June 29, 1970.

4. This is part of a larger issue, namely, the difficulties involved in determining a typology of Kuna forms of discourse in general and of Kuna *ikarkana*. Gossen (1972, 1974) offers a typology of Chamula verbal traditions and argues that this typology is shared by most Chamulas. Yet it is interesting that quite different organizations are proposed by Bricker (1973) and Stross (1974) for nearby and quite closely related groups. Kuna *ikarkana* can be classified in many different ways, depending on the criterion used—such as purpose (sociopolitical control, curing, magic, play); performers ('chief,' 'spokesman,' '*ikar* knower'); linguistic variety ('everyday Kuna,' 'stick doll language'); manner of delivery (chanted, spoken, or shouted); whether a text is fixed or manipulated. These various criteria and the typologies and classifications of *ikarkana* they provide are discussed throughout this book.

5. See Chapin (1970).

6. Portion of a chant performed in Mulatuppu by the visiting Chief Olowitinappi, from the Cartii region of San Blas, on April 9, 1970.

7. Portion of a chant performed by Chief Mastaletat of Mulatuppu on February 20, 1971.

8. Portion of a chant performed by Chief Pinikti of Sasartii on April 2, 1970.

9. Portion of a chant performed by Chief Muristo Pérez of Mulatuppu on June 29, 1970.

10. I am grateful to Dennis Tedlock for pointing out to me that the 'spokesman' is in part an editor. It is interesting to note the existence of editors in oral, nonliterate societies.

11. The quotation marks indicate the degree of quotation within quotation. The Mulatuppu 'chief,' Muristo, is reporting what Juan Sittu chanted (single quotes). Juan Sittu is reporting what Nele War Tummat chanted (double quotes). And Nele War Tummat is reporting what 'stick dolls' told him in a dream (single quotes). Later on in this chant there is still another degree of quotation: two spirits converse with one another, which in turn one of them reports to Nele War Tummat, and so on.

12. Portion of a chant performed by Chief Muristo Pérez of Mulatuppu on June 29, 1970.

13. The famous Chief Nele Kantule of Ustuppu is reported to have incorporated 'stories' into an evening chant if he felt that people were not paying attention and were dozing off. The purpose of the humorous 'story' was to wake them up and get them to pay attention again.

14. For a fuller discussion of 'the story of the hot pepper,' see Sherzer (1979).

15. Verses are set apart by means of extra spaces between lines; see the discussion of the presentation of Kuna discourse in chapter 2.

16. Portion of Mulatuppu Spokesman Armando's interpretation of the chant of a visiting 'chief' on April 9, 1970.

17. Two interpretations typically follow the chant of a single 'chief' during interisland ritual 'gatherings.'

18. 'Chiefs' visit all over San Blas, as well as to and from villages in the interior Darién jungle. At the same time, neighboring villages often have special visiting relationships, and visitors from nearby villages are the most frequent.

19. Portion of *arkan kae* performed by a visiting Niatuppu 'chief' in the Mulatuppu 'gathering house' on July 5, 1970.

20. See the discussion of metaphorical, figurative language in chapter 2 and in Howe (1977).

21. Portion of a 'counsel' for a new 'chief,' performed by Chief Muristo Pérez of Mulatuppu on April 24, 1971, in the Sasartii 'gathering house.'

22. During the interisland ritual 'gathering' held in Mulatuppu at the end of June 1981, new Mulatuppu 'chiefs,' 'spokesmen,' and 'policemen' were installed. On the opening night, the first 'chief' of the 'gathering' chanted metaphorically about the installation of new political leaders, describing the trees and house poles that symbolically represent 'chiefs' and 'spokesmen.' He chanted that the actual installation and inauguration would occur the following evening. That next evening, the 'chief' performed a long spoken 'counsel' for the new officials; then the chanting proceeded long into the night.

23. Portion of a speech by Olowitinappi of Mulatuppu, reporting on his trip to learn snakebite medicine, delivered in the Mulatuppu 'gathering

house' on June 16, 1970. Other portions of this speech are cited in chapters 2, 7, and 8.

24. Portion of a speech by Arango López of Mulatuppu, April 16, 1971.

25. See Clastres (1974), Huxley (1957), and Maybury-Lewis (1967). The Arawakan Mehinaku can be added to the groups Clastres cites; see Gregor (1977).

26. See Leeds (1962).

27. See Sherzer (1970b).

28. Brenneis (1980) reviews this literature. See also Bloch (1975), which deals with political oratory in various societies around the world.

## 4. Curing and Magic: Counseling the Spirits

1. For a fuller analysis of the 'mass-curing ritual,' see Howe (1976).

2. These objects acquired their potential medicinal value as a result of a previous 'counsel,' the one they received from God at the world's beginning. I am indebted to James Howe for calling this to my attention.

3. If the performer even thinks about women while chanting, he will attract women instead of animals.

4. There is some terminological overlap here. The 'souls' are at times also referred to as 'secrets.'

5. Portion of 'the way of the basil,' performed by Pranki Pilos of Mulatuppu.

6. Portion of 'the way of the wasp,' performed by Pranki Pilos of Mulatuppu.

7. Portion of 'the way of the snake,' performed by Pranki Pilos of Mulatuppu.

8. Portion of 'the way of the hot pepper,' performed by Nipakkinya of Mulatuppu.

9. The use of the term stanza, like line and verse, for Kuna poetic-discourse units is adapted from Hymes (1977), which discusses Chinookan narrative structure.

10. Portion of 'the way of the basil,' performed by Pranki Pilos of Mulatuppu.

11. Portion of 'the way of the basil,' performed by Olowitinappi of Mulatuppu.

12. Portion of 'the way of the rattlesnake,' performed by Olowitinappi of Mulatuppu.

13. Portion of 'the way of the bamboo cane,' performed by Manuel Campos of Mulatuppu.

14. Portion of 'the way of the making of *inna*,' performed by Mastaletat of Mulatuppu.

15. Portion of 'the way of the balsa wood,' performed by Pranki Pilos of Mulatuppu.

16. From 'the way of the snake,' performed by Pranki Pilos of Mulatuppu.

17. From 'the way of the wasp,' performed by Pranki Pilos of Mulatuppu.

18. I include identical repetition as a type of parallelism here—although other students of parallelism might not—because of its role in the overall parallelistic patterning and structuring of Kuna magical *ikarkana*.

19. Here and elsewhere in this section, certain lines are indented in order to illustrate the parallelistic patterns. The blank spaces left by the indentations should *not* be interpreted to signify silences or other units of performance or structure.

20. From 'the way of the basil,' performed by Pranki Pilos of Mulatuppu.

21. From 'the way of the snake,' performed by Pranki Pilos of Mulatuppu.

22. Portion of 'the way of the cross,' performed by Mastayans of Mulatuppu.

23. Portion of 'the way of the cooling off,' performed by Pranki Pilos of Mulatuppu.

24. See Jakobson (1960), in which poetry is defined as the projection of paradigmatic axes onto syntagmatic axes.

25. I am grateful to Dennis Tedlock for pointing out this interesting issue. On preliterate oral memorization systems, see Goody (1977) and Yates (1966).

26. Portion of 'the way of the basil,' performed by Pranki Pilos of Mulatuppu.

27. Chapin (1983) argues convincingly that the descriptions contained in the *ikarkana* are to be taken both literally (as actually occurring in the spirit world) and figuratively (as metaphors for the real, physical world).

28. See Howe (1977), Rosaldo (1975), and Tambiah (1968).

29. Kuna magical *ikarkana* are thus performative in the sense of Austin (1965), in that they not only describe actions or events but, through their correct (memorized) narration, actually cause them to occur. 'Gathering house' discourse, by contrast, is exhortative rather than performative.

30. See Malinowski (1935).

31. See Chapin (1976) and Lévi-Strauss (1949).

32. Smith, a respected Mulatuppu '*ikar* knower,' knows two versions of 'the way of birth,' used to alleviate difficult childbirths. One version is longer than the other; Smith considers this longer version to be more powerful and effective. He learned the two versions from two different teachers in two different villages. The longer version cost him more money to learn.

33. These *ikarkana* are in fact new, but according to Kuna doctrine they are old. They have existed in the spirit world but were locally unknown. I am indebted to James Howe for pointing this out.

### 5. Puberty Rites and Festivities

1. For further discussion of the intersections and interpenetrations of the curing and magical tradition and the puberty tradition, see chapter 7.

2. Portion of 'the way of the making of *inna*,' performed by Mastaletat of Mulatuppu.

3. There is much variation in the details of the puberty rites from village to village and region to region. The girl is not everywhere buried in the sand.

4. This *ikar* is also called 'the way of the flute.'

5. Portion of 'the way of the *kantule*,' *iet ikar* (the way of the haircutter), performed by Kantule Ernesto Linares of Mulatuppu.

6.  Ibid.
7.  The drinking of alcoholic beverages by children is prohibited at all times, including during puberty rites and festivities.
8.  Portion of 'the snake's flowers,' performed by Manuel Campos of Mulatuppu.
9.  Several 'play *ikarkana*' are included in Holmer (1952), Nordenskiöld (1938), and Wassén (1938), although they are not labeled as such. Nor is their place in the repertoire of Kuna genres of speaking and chanting described.
10. Portion of 'the way of the sea turtle,' performed by Tilowilikinya of Mulatuppu.
11. See, among others, particularly with regard to American Indians, Goldman (1963) and Norbeck and Farrer (1979).
12. It is no wonder that the village of Mulatuppu once expelled a group of Mormon missionaries from the island for trying to stop the inhabitants from holding puberty rites and festivities.
13. My description is based on observations in Sasartii-Mulatuppu. There are many regional variations in the practice of these events.
14. 'The way of *saptur*' is a type of 'medicine counsel.' See chapter 4.
15. See Prestán Simón (1975).
16. Even when one village has a full set of specialists, those of neighboring islands may be asked to participate.

## 6. Everyday Speech: From Morning to Night, from Birth to Death

1.  This research has increasingly involved an intersection of philosophical, linguistic, sociological, and anthropological perspectives. See, for example, Goffman (1974, 1981), Gumperz (1977), Labov and Fanshel (1977), Lakoff (1972), Sacks, Schegloff, and Jefferson (1974), and Searle (1976). Gregor (1977) uses a dramaturgical model to investigate daily life in a Brazilian Indian community. His analysis does not focus on language and speech, however.
2.  The aim is both to contextualize in the sense (Gumperz 1977) of relating linguistic forms to sociocultural meanings and interpretations and to provide a thick description (Geertz 1973) which integrates linguistic forms with sociocultural contexts and concepts.
3.  There is no work singing, either individual or group.
4.  Since the construction of aqueducts, in Mulatuppu and several other villages, carrying fresh water from mainland sources to islands, women go to the mainland much less frequently. Clothes are washed at home. As a result, most women are at home during the day, talking as they cook, make molas, and wash clothes.
5.  Increasingly, newspapers are flown in to the San Blas airstrips. They are read by literate individuals, and this news becomes still another source for talk. On several of the islands nearest to Panama City, one or two individuals own television sets. And some people have radios, which are used mainly for listening to music.
6.  This is not permitted in every village or at all times. In smaller and espe-

cially more traditional villages, greater control is exercised to maintain maximum attendance at 'gatherings.' And in all villages, as the 'gathering' becomes more ritualized because of the presence of visiting 'chiefs' from other villages, there is greater pressure to attend.

7. See Goffman (1971).

8. See Basso (1972).

9. I am indebted to Judith Irvine for pointing out the role of mutually acknowledged copresence in slowing down and stretching out the greeting process.

10. This formulation is similar to Goffman's discussion (1971: 83–84), which draws for its examples on U.S. society, in which previous absence leads to greetings that are more elaborate verbally than relatively perfunctory everyday greetings.

11. Contrast Sacks, Schegloff, and Jefferson (1974) for middle-class North American whites with Reisman (1974) for Caribbean blacks.

12. Portion of a conversation in Mulatuppu, seated outside o's house, July 17, 1977. The original Kuna version of this same conversation is presented and discussed in chapter 2.

13. For the role of the concept of reportable topics in narrative, see Labov (1972).

14. Portion of a discussion in the Mulatuppu 'gathering house,' April 16, 1971. The original Kuna version of this same conversation is presented and discussed in chapter 2.

15. In the terms proposed by Brown and Levinson (1978), the Kuna might then seem to be a "positive-politeness" culture. But Brown and Levinson's dichotomies and dimensions, although quite suggestive, are inadequate to come to terms with the rich complexities of Kuna speech.

16. What is described here as a very indirect command is a communicative move akin to what Schegloff and Sacks (1973) call opening up closings.

17. For an excellent discussion of the literature on commands and requests, focused on North American English, see Ervin-Tripp (1976).

18. In the sense of Ekman and Friesen (1969).

19. In the examples, plg will be written as an abbreviation for the pointed lip gesture.

20. For a more complete discussion and analysis of the pointed lip gesture, see Sherzer (1973). This Kuna gesture shares features of both form and meaning with similar pointing facial gestures that have been reported throughout the Americas, including the North American Southwest, Guatemala, and parts of South America. Questions of typological and areal comparison, including the possibility of diffusion, remain to be explored.

21. McCosker (1974) offers an analysis of Kuna lullabies. See also Lopez and Joly (1981).

22. Lullaby performed by Donilda García of Mulatuppu.

23. 'Tuneful weeping' performed by Donilda García of Mulatuppu.

24. For a discussion of lullabies and 'tuneful weeping' in relation to other genres of singing and chanting as well as differences in men's and wom-

en's speaking roles, see Lopez and Joly (1981) and Howe and Hirschfeld (1981).

25. For a more complete discussion of Kuna play languages, see Sherzer (1970a, 1976b).
26. As pointed out in chapter 3, 'stories' can also be chanted by 'chiefs,' in which case their moral is highlighted.
27. Episode of 'the agouti story,' performed by Chief Muristo Pérez of Mulatuppu.
28. See chapter 5 for further discussion of 'play ikarkana' and an example.

## 7. From Everyday to Ritual: Configurations and Intersections

1. See Bloch (1975) and Irvine (1979).
2. The concept of tightness-looseness is from Goffman (1963: 199–200).
3. It is interesting to note that severe restrictions against talk and noise go along with strict prohibitions against sexual relations during the same period.
4. In Panama City, in non-Kuna contexts, especially in the company of urban Panamanians, the Kuna tend to be extremely quiet, seeming almost timid. The contrast with communicative behavior in San Blas, or with groups of Kuna among themselves in Panama City, is most striking. This contrast is one source of misunderstanding between urban Panamanians and the Kuna.
5. See Scollon and Scollon (1979). Rushforth (1980) offers a critique.
6. I owe this example to James Howe. See Howe, Sherzer, and Chapin (1980: 13, 49, 60).
7. See Tedlock (1978).
8. See Hymes (1977, 1981). Bright (1979) utilizes the perspectives of both Tedlock and Hymes in an analysis of a Karok myth.
9. See Fox (1977).
10. Scollon and Scollon (1979: 34).
11. Newman and Gayton (1964: 374–375). Dennis Tedlock (personal communication) feels that the issue here is not so much Yokuts or Kuna-English but, rather, oral-written. In my opinion, both orality and American Indian-ness are involved. The issue is a significant one that requires much more empirical, cross-cultural research.
12. Newman and Gayton (1964: 374).
13. Gossen (1973). There is a great interest on the part of anthropologists in symbolism in tropical forest South America. The approach to symbolism, however, tends to be in terms of relatively abstract concepts rather than concrete uses of language in context.
14. According to Chapin (1983), the longer curing ikarkana are the more power they have, length being created by the addition of more sections.
15. See Reichard (1944).
16. Notice that metrical factors are crucial to the Parry-Lord definition of the formula (see Lord 1960). This is not so for Kuna formulaic expressions, which are also akin to what literary scholars call topoi (see Curtius 1953). See Stolz and Shannon (1976) for discussions of the applica-

bility of the concept of the formula to various oral literatures around the world.

17. See Bloch (1975) and Irvine (1979).

18. See Finnegan (1977: 52–87).

19. See Lord (1960) and Goody (1977).

20. Portion of 'the way of the rattlesnake,' performed by Olowitinappi of Mulatuppu.

21. The word *apsoket* is also used to translate the notion read, as in *karta apsoke* (read a book). Here the dialogue seems to be between book and reader.

22. See Titiev (1951).

23. See Sorensen (1972).

24. The group that Henry (1964) labeled the Kaingang is probably better classified as the Shokleng (Greg Urban, personal communication).

25. See Henry (1964).

26. See Rivière (1971). Rivière also discusses the areal distribution of ritualized dialogue.

27. See Fock (1963). Fock was the first person to identify ritualized dialogue as an areal pattern.

28. For North American Indian silence, see Basso (1972), Darnell (1979), Philips (1972), and Scollon and Scollon (1979).

29. For further discussion of 'counsels,' see Howe (in press).

30. Portion of a speech by Olowitinappi of Mulatuppu, reporting on his trip to learn snakebite medicine, delivered in the Mulatuppu 'gathering house' on June 16, 1970. Other portions of this speech are cited in chapters 2, 3, and 8.

31. A comparison with *The Arabian Nights' Entertainments* and Plato's *Symposium* is interesting. In these literary classics, the embedding of both stories within stories and tellers within tellers is a distinctive characteristic. It is an interesting question whether this process is a feature more of oral than of written literature. John Barth's modern short story, "Menelaiad" (1968), uses tellers within tellers and tellings within tellings to refashion a classic story.

32. The embedding of direct quotation within direct quotation, especially the process of moving in and out of such embeddings, renders translations of Kuna texts difficult to follow. This is one of the problems with the Kuna texts collected and translated by Swedish anthropologists and linguists in the Etnologiska Studier Series.

33. Portion of a chant performed by Chief Dionisio of Mulatuppu on March 12, 1979.

34. Portion of a speech by Olowitinappi of Mulatuppu, June 16, 1970.

35. Portion of a chant performed in Mulatuppu by the visiting Chief Olowitinappi on April 9, 1970. A portion of this chant and of its interpretation by the 'spokesman' appears in chapter 3.

36. Portion of 'the way of the rattlesnake,' performed by Olowitinappi of Mulatuppu.

37. In the sense of Bateson (1972) and Goffman (1974).

38. See Jakobson (1957).
39. See Sherzer (1976a).
40. See Hymes (1977), Silverstein (manuscript), and Tedlock (in press).
41. See Goffman (1974).
42. Portion of 'the way of the *kantule*,' performed by Kantule Ernesto Linares of Mulatuppu.
43. Portion of 'the way of the rattlesnake,' performed by Olowitinappi of Mulatuppu.
44. A comparison with the conversation which opens Eugène Ionesco's absurdist classic *The Bald Soprano* is not outlandish.
45. For the concept of reportability in discourse, see Labov (1972).
46. Portion of a chant performed by Chief Muristo Pérez of Mulatuppu on June 29, 1970.
47. Portion of 'the way of the bamboo cane,' performed by Manuel Campos of Mulatuppu.
48. 'The way of the making of *inna*' was performed by Mastaletat of Mulatuppu. 'The way of the *kantule*' was performed by Kantule Ernesto Linares of Mulatuppu.
49. James Howe (personal communication) feels that, as a crisis ritual, the 'mass-curing ritual' mobilizes elements from all the ritual traditions. See also Howe (1976).
50. A cross-cultural comparison seems appropriate. Many observers of Bali have been struck by the constant involvement and incorporation of the ritual in the everyday. For example, flower arrangements to the gods are found everywhere. At the same time, certain temples are deserted apart from their one-day-a-year festival, when they are a flourish of activity.

## 8. Continuity and Change

1. In 1981 funding cutbacks restricted the bilingual program, much to the dismay of members of the community.
2. Portion of a speech by Olowitinappi of Mulatuppu, reporting on his trip to learn snakebite medicine, delivered in the Mulatuppu 'gathering house' on June 16, 1970. Other portions of this speech are cited in chapters 2, 3, and 7.
3. This system of representation and translation of oral discourse with written single and double quotation marks captures the quotations within quotations of the original but not the ritual, esoteric language of the quoted *ikar*.
4. Portion of a speech by Olowitinappi of Mulatuppu, June 16, 1970.
5. Chapin (1983) discusses the unofficial participation of women in Kuna curing.
6. Judith Irvine has pointed out to me (personal communication) that, since nonspecialists know more than they are officially supposed to, they possess a kind of secret knowledge that nicely parallels and complements the secret knowledge which specialists have.
7. That is, any adult. Since ritual knowledge, especially magical, is related to conception and birth, it is felt not to be appropriate for children. Fur-

thermore, access to official and especially significant leadership roles within the ritual system is in actual practice rather difficult for women and for younger men.

8.  Apartments in Panama City shared by groups of Kuna men from the same village often have two mailboxes, one for incoming and outgoing letters and one for incoming and outgoing cassettes.

9.  See Stout (1947b).

10. See Sherzer and Sherzer (1976) for a discussion of the concept of incorporation in the Kuna mola. Parker and Neal (1977) provide excellent visual illustration.

11. Vogt (1969: 582).

12. Gossen (1979: 127).

13. A Kuna woman, like a Kuna man, can be a 'seer,' which is by definition an ascribed role (see chapter 2), and interpret messages from the spirit world for the human community, thus playing a very significant role in Kuna life. The role of 'seer,' however, is restricted and limited when compared with the more central and continually active roles of political leaders and curing specialists, who are exclusively, or almost exclusively, men.

14. See Howe and Hirschfeld (1981), Lopez and Joly (1981), and Sherzer and Sherzer (1976).

15. This cross-cultural generalization is stated in slightly different ways by Brenneis (1980), Irvine (1979), and Rosaldo (1973).

# References

Abrahams, Roger, and Richard Bauman
   1971 Sense and nonsense in St. Vincent: Speech behavior and decorum in a Caribbean community. *American Anthropologist* 73: 762–772.
Austin, J. C.
   1965 *How to Do Things with Words*. New York: Oxford University Press.
Basso, Keith
   1967 Semantic aspects of linguistic acculturation. *American Anthropologist* 69: 471–477.
   1972 'To give up on words': Silence in western Apache culture. In Pier Paolo Giglioli (ed.), *Language and Social Context*, pp. 67–86. Harmondsworth, Middlesex, Eng.: Penguin Books.
   1979 *Portraits of "The Whiteman": Linguistic Play and Cultural Symbols among the Western Apache*. Cambridge, Eng.: Cambridge University Press.
Bateson, Gregory
   1972 *Steps to an Ecology of Mind*. New York: Ballantine Books.
Bauman, Richard, and Joel Sherzer, eds.
   1974 *Explorations in the Ethnography of Speaking*. Cambridge, Eng.: Cambridge University Press.
Berger, Peter L., and Thomas Luckmann
   1966 *The Social Construction of Reality*. Garden City, N.Y.: Doubleday.
Bloch, Maurice, ed.
   1975 *Political Language and Oratory in Traditional Society*. New York: Academic Press.
Blount, Ben G.
   1975 Agreeing to agree on genealogy: A Luo sociology of knowledge. In Mary Sanches and Ben G. Blount (eds.), *Sociocultural Dimensions of Language Use*, pp. 117–135. New York: Academic Press.
Brenneis, Donald
   1980 Straight talk and sweet talk: Political discourse in a community of equals. *Working Papers in Sociolinguistics* 71.

Bricker, Victoria Reifler

1973  *Ritual Humor in Highland Chiapas*. Austin: University of Texas Press.

Bright, William, ed.

1966  *Sociolinguistics*. The Hague: Mouton.

Bright, William

1979  A Karok myth in "measured verse": The translation of a performance. *Journal of California and Great Basin Anthropology* 1: 117–123.

Brown, Penelope, and Stephen Levinson

1978  Universals in language usage: Politeness phenomena. In Esther N. Goody (ed.), *Questions and Politeness: Strategies in Social Interaction*, pp. 56–289. Cambridge, Eng.: Cambridge University Press.

Burns, Allan F.

1980  Interactive features in Yucatec Mayan narratives. *Language in Society* 9: 307–319.

Calame-Griaule, Geneviève

1965  *Ethnologie et langage: La parole chez les Dogon*. Paris: Gallimard.

Casson, Ronald W., ed.

1981  *Language, Culture, and Cognition: Anthropological Perspectives*. New York: Macmillan.

Chapin, Macpherson

1970  *Pab igala: Historias de la tradición Kuna*. Panama City: Universidad de Panamá.

1976  *Muu ikala*: Cuna birth ceremony. In Philip Young and James Howe (eds.), *Ritual and Symbol in Native Central America*, pp. 57–65. University of Oregon Anthropological Papers 9.

1983  Curing among the San Blas Kuna of Panama. Ph.D. dissertation. University of Arizona.

Clastres, Pierre

1974  *La société contre l'état*. Paris: Minuit.

Cole, Peter, and Jerry L. Morgan, eds.

1975  *Syntax and Semantics*. Vol. 3: *Speech Acts*. New York: Academic Press.

Curtius, Robert Ernst

1953  *European Literature and the Latin Middle Ages*. Princeton: Princeton University Press.

Darnell, Regna

1979  Reflections on Cree interactional etiquette. *Working Papers in Sociolinguistics* 57.

Ekman, Paul, and Wallace V. Friesen

1969  The repertoire of nonverbal behavior: Categories, origins, usage, and coding. *Semiotica* 1: 49–98.

Ervin-Tripp, Susan

1976  Is Sybil there? The structure of some American English directives. *Language in Society* 5: 25–66.

Evans-Pritchard, E. E.
  1937  *Witchcraft, Oracles and Magic among the Azande*. Oxford: Clarendon Press.
Feld, Steven
  1982  *Sound and Sentiment: Birds, Weeping, Poetics, and Song in Kaluli Expression*. Philadelphia: University of Pennsylvania Press.
Finnegan, Ruth
  1967  *Limba Stories and Story-telling*. London: Oxford University Press.
  1977  *Oral Poetry*. Cambridge, Eng.: Cambridge University Press.
Fock, Niels
  1963  *Waiwai: Religion and Society of an Amazonian Tribe*. Copenhagen: National Museum.
Foster, Michael K.
  1974  From the earth to beyond the sky: An ethnographic approach to four Longhouse Iroquois speech events. National Museum of Man Mercury Series. *Canadian Ethnology Service Paper* 20. Ottawa.
Fox, James J.
  1977  Roman Jakobson and the comparative study of parallelism. In Daniel Armstrong and C. H. van Schooneveld (eds.), *Roman Jakobson: Echoes of His Scholarship*, pp. 59–90. Lisse: Peter de Ridder Press.
Geertz, Clifford
  1973  *The Interpretation of Cultures*. New York: Basic Books.
Givón, Talmy, ed.
  1979  *Syntax and Semantics*. Vol. 12: *Discourse and Syntax*. New York: Academic Press.
Goffman, Erving
  1963  *Behavior in Public Places*. New York: Free Press.
  1971  *Relations in Public*. New York: Basic Books.
  1974  *Frame Analysis*. New York: Harper.
  1981  *Forms of Talk*. Philadelphia: University of Pennsylvania Press.
Goldman, Irving
  1963  *The Cubeo: Indians of the Northwest Amazon*. Urbana: University of Illinois Press.
Goody, Esther N., ed.
  1978  *Questions and Politeness: Strategies in Social Interaction*. Cambridge, Eng.: Cambridge University Press.
Goody, Jack
  1977  *The Domestication of the Savage Mind*. Cambridge, Eng.: Cambridge University Press.
Gossen, Gary H.
  1972  Chamula genres of verbal behavior. In Américo Paredes and Richard Bauman (eds.), *Toward New Perspectives in Folklore*, pp. 145–167. Austin: University of Texas Press.
  1973  Chamula Tzotzil proverbs: Neither fish nor fowl. In M. S. Edmonson (ed.), *Meaning in the Mayan Languages*, pp. 205–233. The Hague: Mouton.

1974   *Chamulas in the World of the Sun: Time and Space in a Maya Oral Tradition.* Cambridge, Mass.: Harvard University Press.

1979   Review of Gary Witherspoon, *Language and Art in the Navajo Universe. Language in Society* 8: 120–128.

Gregor, Thomas

1977   *Mehinaku: The Drama of Daily Life in a Brazilian Indian Village.* Chicago: University of Chicago Press.

Grimes, Joseph E.

1975   *The Thread of Discourse.* The Hague: Mouton.

Gumperz, John J.

1977   Sociocultural knowledge in conversational inference. In Muriel Saville-Troike (ed.), *Linguistics and Anthropology: Georgetown University Round Table on Languages and Linguistics 1977,* pp. 191–211. Washington, D.C.: Georgetown University Press.

Gumperz, John J., and Dell Hymes, eds.

1964   *The Ethnography of Communication. American Anthropologist* 66, pt. 2.

1972   *Directions in Sociolinguistics: The Ethnography of Communication.* New York: Holt.

Halliday, M. A. K., and Ruqaiya Hasan

1976   *Cohesion in English.* London: Longman.

Haviland, John Beard

1977   *Gossip, Reputation and Knowledge in Zinacantan.* Chicago: University of Chicago Press.

Henry, Jules

1964   *Jungle People: A Kaingáng Tribe of the Highlands of Brazil.* New York: Vintage.

Holmer, Nils M.

1947   *Critical and Comparative Grammar of the Cuna Language.* Etnologiska Studier Series 14. Göteborg: Göteborgs Etnografiska Museum.

1951   *Cuna Chrestomathy.* Etnologiska Studier Series 18. Göteborg: Göteborgs Etnografiska Museum.

1952   *Ethno = linguistic Cuna Dictionary.* Etnologiska Studier Series 19. Göteborg: Göteborgs Etnografiska Museum.

Howe, James

1976   Smoking out the spirits: A Cuna exorcism. In Philip Young and James Howe (eds.), *Ritual and Symbol in Native Central America,* pp. 67–76. University of Oregon Anthropological Papers 9.

1977   Carrying the village: Cuna political metaphors. In J. David Sapir and J. Christopher Crocker (eds.), *The Social Use of Metaphor,* pp. 132–163. Philadelphia: University of Pennsylvania Press.

in press   *The Kuna Gathering: Contemporary Village Politics in Panama.* Austin: University of Texas Press.

Howe, James, and Lawrence Hirschfeld

1981   The star girls' descent: A myth about men, women, matrilocality, and singing. *Journal of American Folklore* 94: 292–322.

Howe, James, Joel Sherzer, and Macpherson Chapin, eds. and comps.
  1980  *Cantos y oraciones del congreso Cuna.* Panama City: Editorial
        Universitaria Panamá.
Huxley, Francis
  1957  *Affable Savages: An Anthropologist among the Urubu Indians of
        Brazil.* New York: Viking Press.
Hymes, Dell
  1962  The ethnography of speaking. In T. Gladwin and W. C. Sturtevant
        (eds.), *Anthropology and Human Behavior,* pp. 13–53. Washing-
        ton, D.C.: Anthropological Society of Washington.
  1964  Introduction: Toward ethnographies of communication. In John J.
        Gumperz and Dell Hymes (eds.), *The Ethnography of Communica-
        tion,* pp. 1–34. *American Anthropologist* 66, pt. 2.
  1968  Foreword. In James L. Peacock, *Rites of Modernization,* pp. xi–
        xvii. Chicago: University of Chicago Press.
  1974  Ways of speaking. In Richard Bauman and Joel Sherzer (eds.), *Explo-
        rations in the Ethnography of Speaking,* pp. 443–451. Cambridge,
        Eng.: Cambridge University Press.
  1977  Discovering oral performance and measured verse in American In-
        dian narrative. *New Literary History* 8: 431–457.
  1981  *"In Vain I Tried to Tell You": Essays in Native American Ethno-
        poetics.* Philadelphia: University of Pennsylvania Press.
Irvine, Judith T.
  1974  Strategies of status manipulation in the Wolof greeting. In Richard
        Bauman and Joel Sherzer (eds.), *Explorations in the Ethnography of
        Speaking,* pp. 167–191. Cambridge, Eng.: Cambridge University
        Press.
  1979  Formality and informality in communicative events. *American
        Anthropologist* 81: 773–790.
Jakobson, Roman
  1957  *Shifters, Verbal Categories, and the Russian Verb.* Cambridge,
        Mass.: Harvard University, Russian Language Project.
  1960  Closing statement: Linguistics and poetics. In Thomas A. Sebeok
        (ed.), *Style in Language,* pp. 350–377. Cambridge, Mass.: MIT
        Press.
Keenan, Elinor
  1974  Norm-makers, norm-breakers: Uses of speech by men and women
        in a Malagasy community. In Richard Bauman and Joel Sherzer
        (eds.), *Explorations in the Ethnography of Speaking,* pp. 125–143.
        Cambridge, Eng.: Cambridge University Press.
Kochman, Thomas, ed.
  1972  *Rappin' and Stylin' Out: Communication in Urban Black Amer-
        ica.* Urbana: University of Illinois Press.
Kramer, Fritz W.
  1970  *Literature among the Cuna Indians.* Etnologiska Studier Series 30.
        Göteborg: Göteborgs Etnografiska Museum.

Labov, William

1972   *Language in the Inner City: Studies in the Black English Vernacular*. Philadelphia: University of Pennsylvania Press.

Labov, William, and David Fanshel

1977   *Therapeutic Discourse: Psychotherapy as Conversation*. New York: Academic Press.

Lakoff, Robin

1972   Language in context. *Language* 48: 907–927.

Leeds, Anthony

1962   Ecology of Yaruro chieftainship. In *Akten 34th Internationaler Kongress der Amerikanisten*, pp. 597–608.

Lévi-Strauss, Claude

1949   L'efficacité symbolique. *Revue de l'Histoire des Religions* 135: 5–27.

1964, 1966, 1968, 1971   *Mythologiques*. Paris: Plon.

Longacre, Robert E., ed.

1976, 1977   *Discourse Grammar*. Dallas: Summer Institute of Linguistics.

Lopez, Griselda Maria, and Luz Graciela Joly

1981   Singing a lullaby in Kuna: A female verbal art. *Journal of American Folklore* 94: 351–358.

Lord, Albert B.

1960   *The Singer of Tales*. Cambridge, Mass.: Harvard University Press.

Malinowski, Bronislaw

1935   *Coral Gardens and Their Magic*. Vol. 2: *The Language of Magic and Gardening*. London: Allen and Unwin.

Mauss, M., and H. Hubert

1902–1903   Esquisse d'une théorie générale de la magie. *Année Sociologique* 7: 1–146.

Maybury-Lewis, David

1967   *Akwē-Shavante Society*. Oxford: Clarendon Press.

McCosker, Sandra Smith

1974   *The Lullabies of the San Blas Cuna Indians of Panama*. Etnologiska Studier Series 33. Göteborg: Göteborgs Etnografiska Museum.

Newman, Stanley, and Ann Gayton

1964   Yokuts narrative style. In Dell Hymes (ed.), *Language in Culture and Society*, pp. 372–377. New York: Harper and Row.

Norbeck, Edward, and Claire R. Farrer, eds.

1979   *Forms of Play of Native North Americans*. St. Paul: West.

Nordenskiöld, Erland

1938   *An Historical and Ethnological Survey of the Cuna Indians*. Etnologiska Studier Series 10. Göteborg: Göteborgs Etnografiska Museum.

Parker, Ann, and Avon Neal

1977   *Molas: Folk Art of the Cuna Indians*. Barre, Mass.: Barre Publishing.

Philips, Susan U.

1972   Participant structures and communicative competence: Warm Springs children in community and classroom. In Courtney B.

Cazden, Vera P. John, and Dell Hymes (eds.), *Functions of Language in the Classroom*, pp. 370–394. New York: Teachers College Press.

Prestán Simón, Arnulfo

1975 *El uso de la chicha y la sociedad Kuna.* Mexico City: Instituto Indigenista Interamericano.

Redfield, Robert

1955 *The Little Community.* Chicago: University of Chicago Press.

Reichard, Gladys A.

1944 *Prayer: The Compulsive Word.* New York: J. J. Augustin.

Reisman, Karl

1974 Contrapuntal conversations in an Antiguan village. In Richard Bauman and Joel Sherzer (eds.), *Explorations in the Ethnography of Speaking*, pp. 110–124. Cambridge, Eng.: Cambridge University Press.

Rivière, Peter

1971 The political structure of the Trio Indians as manifested in a system of ceremonial dialogue. In T. O. Beidelman (ed.), *The Translation of Culture*, pp. 293–311. London: Tavistock.

Rosaldo, Michelle

1973 I have nothing to hide: The language of Ilongot oratory. *Language in Society* 2: 193–223.

1975 It's all uphill: The creative metaphors of Ilongot magical spells. In Mary Sanches and Ben G. Blount (eds.), *Sociocultural Dimensions of Language Use*, pp. 177–203. New York: Academic Press.

Rushforth, Scott

1980 Review of Ronald Scollon and Suzanne B. K. Scollon, *Linguistic Convergence: An Ethnography of Speaking at Fort Chipewyan, Alberta. Language in Society* 9: 270–273.

Sacks, Harvey, Emanuel Schegloff, and Gail Jefferson

1974 A simplest systematics for the organization of turn-taking for conversation. *Language* 50: 696–735.

Sadock, Jerrold

1974 *Toward a Linguistic Theory of Speech Acts.* New York: Academic Press.

Salmond, Anne

1975 *Hui: A Study of Maori Ceremonial Gatherings.* Wellington: A. H. and A. W. Reed.

Sanches, Mary, and Ben G. Blount, eds.

1975 *Sociocultural Dimensions of Language Use.* New York: Academic Press.

Sapir, J. David, and J. Christopher Crocker, eds.

1977 *The Social Use of Metaphor.* Philadelphia: University of Pennsylvania Press.

Schegloff, Emanuel, and Harvey Sacks

1973 Opening up closings. *Semiotica* 8: 289–327.

Scheub, Harold

1977    Body and image in oral narrative performance. *New Literary History* 8: 345–367.

Scollon, Ronald, and Suzanne B. K. Scollon

1979    *Linguistic Convergence: An Ethnography of Speaking at Fort Chipewyan, Alberta.* New York: Academic Press.

Searle, John R.

1969    *Speech Acts.* Cambridge, Eng.: Cambridge University Press.

1976    The classification of illocutionary acts. *Language in Society* 5: 1–23.

Sebeok, Thomas A.

1953    The structure and content of Cheremis charms. *Anthropos* 48: 369–388.

Sherzer, Dina, and Joel Sherzer

1976    *Mormaknamaloe*: The Cuna *mola*. In Philip Young and James Howe (eds.)., *Ritual and Symbol in Native Central America*, pp. 21–42. University of Oregon Anthropological Papers 9.

Sherzer, Joel

1970a   Talking backwards in Cuna: The sociological reality of phonological descriptions. *Southwestern Journal of Anthropology* 26: 343–353.

1970b   La parole chez les Abipone: Pour une ethnographie de la parole. *L'Homme* 10: 40–76.

1973    Verbal and nonverbal deixis: The pointed lip gesture among the San Blas Cuna. *Language in Society* 2: 117–131.

1975    A problem in Cuna phonology. *Journal of the Linguistic Association of the Southwest* 1: 45–53.

1976a   *An Areal-typological Study of American Indian Languages North of Mexico.* North-Holland Linguistic Series 20. Amsterdam: North-Holland.

1976b   Play languages: Implications for (socio) linguistics. In Barbara Kirshenblatt-Gimblett (ed.), *Speech Play*, pp. 19–36. Philadelphia: University of Pennsylvania Press.

1977    Semantic systems, discourse structures, and the ecology of language. In Ralph W. Fasold and Roger W. Shuy (eds.), *Studies in Language Variation: Semantics, Syntax, Phonology, Pragmatics, Social Situations, Ethnographic Approaches*, pp. 283–293. Washington, D.C.: Georgetown University Press.

1979    Strategies in text and context: Cuna *kaa kwento*. *Journal of American Folklore* 92: 145–163.

Sherzer, Joel, and Regna Darnell

1972    Outline guide for the ethnographic study of speech use. In John J. Gumperz and Dell Hymes (eds.), *Directions in Sociolinguistics: The Ethnography of Communication*, pp. 548–554. New York: Holt.

Sherzer, Joel, and Sammie Ann Wicks

1982    The intersection of music and language in Kuna discourse. *Latin American Music Review* 3: 147–164.

Silverstein, Michael
  manuscript  The culture of language in Chinookan narrative texts; or, on saying that . . . in Chinook.
Sorensen, A. P., Jr.
  1972  Multilingualism in the Northwest Amazon. In J. B. Pride and Janet Holmes (eds.), *Sociolinguistics*, pp. 78–93. Harmondsworth, Middlesex, Eng.: Penguin Books.
Stolz, Benjamin A., and Richard S. Shannon, eds.
  1976  *Oral Literature and the Formula*. Ann Arbor: Center for the Coordination of Ancient and Modern Studies, University of Michigan.
Stout, David B.
  1947a  Ethnolinguistic observations on San Blas Cuna. *International Journal of American Linguistics* 13: 9–13.
  1947b  *San Blas Cuna Acculturation: An Introduction*. Viking Fund Publications in Anthropology 9. New York: Wenner-Gren Foundation for Anthropological Research.
Stross, Brian
  1974  Speaking of speaking. In Richard Bauman and Joel Sherzer (eds.), *Explorations in the Ethnography of Speaking*, pp. 213–239. Cambridge, Eng.: Cambridge University Press.
Sudnow, David, ed.
  1972  *Studies in Social Interaction*. Englewood Cliffs, N.J.: Prentice-Hall.
Tambiah, S. J.
  1968  The magical power of words. *Man* 3: 175–208.
Tannen, Deborah, ed.
  1981  *Analyzing Discourse: Text and Talk*. Washington, D.C.: Georgetown University Press.
Tedlock, Dennis
  1978  *Finding the Center: Narrative Poetry of the Zuni Indians*. Lincoln: University of Nebraska Press.
  in press  Verbal art. In William C. Sturtevant (ed.), *Handbook of North American Indians*, vol. 1, chap. 50. Washington, D.C.: Smithsonian Institution.
Titiev, Mischa
  1949  Social singing among the Mapuche. *Anthropological Papers of the Museum of Anthropology of the University of Michigan* 2.
  1951  *Araucanian Culture in Transition*. Ann Arbor: University of Michigan Press.
Todorov, Tzvetan
  1973  Le discours de la magie. *L'Homme* 13: 38–65.
Torres de Araúz, Reina
  1980  *Panamá indígena*. Panama City: Instituto Nacional de Cultura, Patrimonio Histórico.
Torres de Ianello, Reina
  1957  *La mujer Cuna de Panamá*. Mexico City: Instituto Indigenista Interamericano.

1958  Aspectos culturales de los indios Cunas. *Anuario de estudios americanos* 15: 515–547.

Turner, Victor

1967  *The Forest of Symbols.* Ithaca: Cornell University Press.

Tyler, Stephen A., ed.

1969  *Cognitive Anthropology.* New York: Holt.

Vogt, Evon Z.

1969  *Zinacantan: A Mayan Community in the Highlands of Chiapas.* Cambridge, Mass.: Harvard University Press.

Wassén, Henry S.

1938  *Original Documents from the Cuna Indians of San Blas, Panamá, as Recorded by the Indians Guillermo Haya and Ruben Pérez Kantule.* Etnologiska Studier Series 6. Göteborg: Göteborgs Etnografiska Museum.

1949  *Contributions to Cuna Ethnography.* Etnologiska Studier Series 16. Göteborg: Göteborgs Etnografiska Museum.

Witherspoon, Gary

1977  *Language and Art in the Navajo Universe.* Ann Arbor: University of Michigan Press.

Yates, Frances

1966  *The Art of Memory.* Chicago: University of Chicago Press.